Ways of Aging

Edited by **Jaber F. Gubrium** *and*
James A. Holstein

Blackwell
Publishing

© 2003 by Blackwell Publishers Ltd
a Blackwell Publishing company
except for editorial material and organization © 2003 by Jaber F. Gubrium and
James A. Holstein

350 Main Street, Malden, MA 02148–5018, USA
108 Cowley Road, Oxford OX4 1JF, UK
550 Swanston Street, Carlton South, Melbourne, Victoria 3053, Australia
Kurfürstendamm 57, 10707 Berlin, Germany

The right of Jaber F. Gubrium and James A. Holstein to be identified as the Authors
of the Editorial Material in this Work has been asserted in accordance with the UK
Copyright, Designs, and Patents Act 1988.

First published 2003 by Blackwell Publishers Ltd

Library of Congress Cataloging-in-Publication Data
Library of Congress data has been applied for.

ISBN 0-631-23058-0 (hardback); ISBN 0-631-23059-9 (paperback)

A catalogue record for this title is available from the British Library.
Set in 10/12 pt Plantin
by Kolam Information Services Pvt. Ltd., Pondicherry, India.
Printed and bound in the United Kingdom
by TJ International Ltd., Padstow, Cornwall.

For further information on
Blackwell Publishing, visit our website:
http://www.blackwellpublishing.com

Ways of Aging

Contents

Contributors

About the Editors

Jaber F. Gubrium is Professor of Sociology at the University of Missouri, Columbia. His research focuses on institutions as discursive environments; of particular interest is the narrative organization of personal identity, family, the life course, aging, and adaptations to illness. Gubrium is the editor of the *Journal of Aging Studies*, and the author of several books, including *Living and Dying at Murray Manor*, *Oldtimers and Alzheimer's*, *Out of Control*, and *Speaking of Life*.

James A. Holstein is Professor of Sociology at Marquette University. He has studied diverse people processing and social control settings, including courts, welfare offices, and mental health agencies. Holstein has published numerous books, including *Court-Ordered Insanity*, *Dispute Domains and Welfare Claims*, *Reconsidering Social Constructionism*, and *Social Problems in Everyday Life*. He is the editor of the journal *Social Problems*.

Collaborating for nearly two decades, Gubrium and Holstein have developed their distinctive approach to everyday life in several projects, including *What is Family?*, *Constructing the Life Course*, *The Active Interview*, *The New Language of Qualitative Method*, *The Self We Live By*, *Institutional Selves*, and *Inner Lives and Social Worlds*. Their recent collaboration, the *Handbook of Interview Research*, provides an extensive overview of interview practice and interview knowledge in contemporary society.

About the Authors

Barbara M. Barer is Senior Research Associate in the Division of Medical Anthropology at the University of California, San Francisco, where she specializes in aging issues. Barer's publications include "Men and Women

Aging Differently," "The Secret Shame of the Very Old," and "The Grands and Greats of Very Old Black Grandmothers." She is the co-author of the book *Life Beyond 85 Years*.

Helen K. Black is Senior Research Scientist at the Polisher Research Institute in Philadelphia. Her research focuses on the cultural and spiritual aspects of elders' identity, particularly how those aspects inform the meaning of life experiences such as poverty, suffering, and forgiveness. She is the co-author of *Old Souls: Aged Women, Poverty, and the Experience of God*.

Christopher A. Faircloth has been a Post-Doctoral Research Fellow at the Boston University Gerontology Center and currently is Health Research Scientist at the VA Medical Center in Gainesville, Florida. His research centers on the experiential contours of chronic illness, the body, and qualitative methods. He is the author of numerous articles and is currently editing a book on aging and the body, to be published by AltaMira Press.

Mary Gergen is Professor of Psychology and Women's Studies at Pennsylvania State University, Delaware County. Her major scholarly activities are found at the intersection of social constructionism and feminist theory. Her most recent book is *Feminist Reconstructions in Psychology*. She has edited *Toward a New Psychology of Women*, with Sara N. Davis, and is a co-editor, with Kenneth J. Gergen, of *A Social Constructionist Reader*. She is a founder of The Taos Institute.

Kenneth J. Gergen is the Mustin Professor of Psychology at Swarthmore College. His work centers on social constructionist and relational theory as applied to issues of aging, dialogue, therapy, conflict reduction, and organizational change. His major works include *Realities and Relationships*, *The Saturated Self*, and *An Invitation to Social Construction*. He is a founder of The Taos Institute.

Colleen L. Johnson is Professor of Anthropology at the University of California, San Francisco. Her research focuses on aging, the family, and ethnicity. She is the author of numerous articles and several books, including *Ex Familia: Grandparents, Patents, and Children Adjust to Divorce* and co-author of the book *Life Beyond 85 Years*.

Tanya Koropeckyj-Cox is Assistant Professor of Sociology at the University of Florida and an affiliate of the Institute on Aging and the Center for Women's Studies. Her research combines qualitative and quantitative approaches to examine the implications of life-long childlessness or parenthood for well-being in middle and old age.

Sarah H. Matthews is Professor of Sociology at Cleveland State University. Her research interests focus on various aspects of the social relationships of old people. In addition to two books – *The Social World of Old Women* and *Friendships through the Life Course* – she has published extensively on how old parents' daughters and sons divide responsibility to meet their needs.

Debora A. Paterniti is Adjunct Assistant Professor at the Center for Health Services Research in Primary Care in the Department of Internal Medicine at the University of California, Davis. Her research focuses on illness identity and decision-making in issues of informed consent, quality of life, and aging. She is co-editor, with Kathy Charmaz, of *Health, Illness, and Healing* and the author of a number of articles on doctor – patient communication and decision-making.

Dana Rosenfeld has been an NIMH post-doctoral fellow at the University of Kentucky College of Medicine and currently is Assistant Professor of Sociology at Colorado College. Her research interests include aging and the life course, identity, and gender and sexuality, all of which inform her work on health, medicine, and the body. Rosenfeld's forthcoming book on the identity work of homosexual elders will be published by Temple University Press.

Deborah K. van den Hoonaard is Associate Professor of Gerontology at St. Thomas University in Fredericton, New Brunswick, Canada. Her research interests include widowhood, gender and aging, and qualitative methods. She is currently interviewing widowers about their experiences and has authored *The Widowed Self: The Older Woman's Journey Through Widowhood*.

Joan Weibel-Orlando is Associate Professor of Anthropology at the University of Southern California. For the past 15 years she has worked with, made films on, and written about aging and elderly Native Americans in both urban Los Angeles and their rural ancestral homelands. In addition to over 30 articles and book chapters on the topic, she also has authored the ethnographic monograph, *Indian Country, L.A.*, now in its second printing.

Introduction

Beyond Stereotypes

Jaber F. Gubrium and James A. Holstein

People think of growing older and being old as universal experiences. We all get older; we simply can't avoid aging. Because these experiences seem so familiar and inevitable, we tend to regard aging as something that we all share in common. We're inclined to figure that "old age" is pretty much the same for everyone – except, of course, for the particular details of individual lives and relationships.

Ways of Aging takes a different perspective. While it appreciates those things we share in common, the book highlights the ways in which we might age differently. Diversity is the watchword. Stressing the variety of contemporary aging experiences, *Ways of Aging* considers the distinct and assorted identities that people develop as they grow older under different circumstances. The various social, cultural, and material contexts of everyday life provide the bases for these considerations.

The theme of *Ways of Aging* is that the category "old" and stereotypes of old age belie the varied ways people experience the later years. This contradicts the prevailing view that "old age" is a distinct stage of life, with common characteristics that contrast with those of earlier life stages. Stereotypes of aging make it seem that growing old is a uniform occurrence – a singular way of life. Instead, as the chapters of this book richly illustrate, the experience and meaning of being old are amazingly varied and multifaceted.

Categories and Stereotypes

People categorize things in order to make sense of them. We use categorical labels to help us distinguish between different objects and experiences. As useful as they are, however, categories have a way of making things within them seem more alike than they actually are. Because categories often come in pairs – such as child and adult, men and women, or dependent and independent – differences between categories overshadow differences within them. This is in the nature of categorization; it doesn't necessarily depend on what the categories are about. Regardless of whether the pairs are, say, Republicans and Democrats, or rock 'n' roll and jazz, paired categories tend to divide their respective members into homogeneous collections of polar opposites. We accentuate the common ground among Republicans, for example, while simultaneously emphasizing how different they are from Democrats. Categories underscore similarity and subtle variation can get lost in the shuffle.

Consider how this can happen with the categories of child and adult. People use the term "child" to cover a wide age-range. Understandably, it's applied to youngsters from the earliest years. But it's also used to categorize persons in their 20s – even their 30s – when they aren't gainfully employed, are still in school, or are otherwise dependent on their parents for support. Applying the category across the board conveys common characteristics, even though toddlers are clearly distinct from 20- and 30-year-olds. Regardless of age differences, persons called "children" are taken to share characteristics that, for the most part, don't apply to persons we categorize as adults. By the same token, "adult" is a category whose characteristics we take to be the opposite of children. Characteristics of "children" are uncharacteristic of adults. To be an adult – the opposite of a child – one should be gainfully employed, finished with school, and no longer materially dependent upon one's parents, for example.

Of course, in actual practice, there are many exceptions. Young people often hold paying jobs; teenagers are sometimes able to support themselves. In contrast, some young people "never grow up" and continue, well into their 20s and 30s, to "live at home" with their parents. Yet, notice the effect of categorization when we refer to the former as being "just like adults" or the latter as "childish." Despite the way they contradict empirical fact, categories can sustain exceptions to what they otherwise mean. As counterfactual as categories may be, they nonetheless provide contrasts for understanding the varied, even nonconforming, characteristics of the world we live in.

Stereotypes operate in a similar fashion, except that they exaggerate differences even more. Stereotypes are sets of categories that take differences between categories to extremes. At the same time, they accentuate similarities within categories. For example, to label individuals as men and women is one thing, but to then go on to describe the "typical" male or the "typical" female is stereotypic because it greatly exaggerates differences and overstates similarities. The exaggeration can be so extreme that exceptions to the rule seem impossible. Through stereotypes, every man, in effect, becomes a typical male, and every woman becomes a typical female. The outcome is all black-and-white, with no variations, no shades of gray.

Stereotypes of Aging

Just as men and women are opposing categories with contrasting characteristics, old age and aging have their associated categorical distinctions. Old age, of course, is commonly distinguished from other life stages such as childhood and middle adulthood. We differentiate the process of aging from what we call "development" in childhood. "Growing up" is center stage in early life. Maturation, or "coming of age" and "coming into one's own" are characteristic developmental achievements a bit later in life. Against this background, old age takes on its opposite characteristics. By sheer categorical contrast, old age is a time when growing up and coming of age are over. Things that might be considered developmental achievements are overshadowed by their opposites – growing and being elderly. The emphasis shifts from growth and accomplishment to hanging on to life satisfaction and taking stock of life gone by. If the younger years center on getting ahead and carving out a place for oneself in the world, old age is categorized as a time of contemplation and resignation. The categorical characteristics of old age are construed in opposition to the categorical characteristics of earlier life stages. Older people are decidedly different from children and younger adults – by categorical definition. Our notions of the life course are suffused with such polarities. They are stereotypes of the aging process – empirical exceptions notwithstanding.

As a stereotype, the category "old" takes these differences to extremes. It's as if the aging process unfolds uniformly, without exceptions. The stereotype of "old age" signals any and all characteristics that aren't typical of younger persons. Older persons come to be seen in familiar stereotypic terms – physically declining, psychologically frail, and socially retiring. In contrast to younger persons, who are healthy, old people are sick. If the young have their wits about them, the old are demented, or senile. The list is nearly endless, with stereotypes of old and young starkly contrasting with each other. Getting up in years makes one distinctively old, in diametric opposition to the stereotypic youthful scheme of things. This produces a persistently negative portrait of aging – as a matter of becoming sick, impoverished, cognitively impaired, and, perhaps most salient, socially dysfunctional and disengaged.

An Uphill Battle

It's hard to defy the representational force of categories. They are like eyeglasses and contact lenses. They literally affect how the world appears to us. Put on proverbial "rose-colored glasses" (or contact lenses, if you prefer) and the world comes into view as warm and cheery. Insert gray-colored and uncorrected lenses, and the world is somber and blurry. Stereotypes make matters worse. In one sense they are like lenses we can't remove. We're stuck with them, yet often we don't know that we are. Because we haven't seen the world from any other perspective, we take for granted that the world appears to be exactly as we see it. In another sense, stereotypes are like funhouse mirrors, exaggerating everything about us, distorting things to the extreme. But, like unremovable lenses, if we haven't seen things in any other way, the distortion appears "only natural."

Altering stereotypes is an uphill battle. It's difficult to convince those who hold them to view things differently. It's hard to introduce a more nuanced perspective. Such a view at the very least would entertain exceptions to what stereotypic categories crudely represent. Yet stereotypes persist, captioning experience in overly broad and excessive terms. The resulting representational dilemma regarding categories is a version of the old cliché, "You can't live with them, you can't live without them." We can't do away with categories; they are the way we come to understand the manifold features of our lives and experiences. This-or-that detail is an instance of such-and-such a category of things or actions. It's how we construct meaning. Without categories, we wouldn't know what a particular detail meant to us, where it fit in a scheme of things.

What can we do to make ourselves and others aware of the effects of categories and stereotypes on the way we view the world and its members? In particular, how can we refigure the categories of aging and old age with richer understanding? As a first step, we need to understand how categories and stereotypes take things to extremes. This is not to suggest that we can do away with categorization. As we noted earlier, that's simply impossible. Instead, we must vigilantly monitor how categorization influences our views of experience, ourselves, and each other. Following this, we need to entertain new, more nuanced categories that allow us to understand and appreciate objects and experiences differently, more in keeping with the complexities of everyday life. This moves us beyond stereotypes, limiting categorization's homogenizing tendencies.

Considering Context

Refiguring stereotypes of old age is a point of departure of *Ways of Aging*. While we often categorize older people as sick, dependent, and otherwise resigned to their circumstances, it's not the only interpretive possibility. The authors of the book's various chapters present some fascinating alternatives. Rather than using shop-worn categories to convey what old age is like, the authors open our eyes to varied ways of experiencing aging. The ways of aging they describe incorporate positive sentiments and achievements directly into the characteristics of later life, rather than viewing them as atypical of older people. This casts the later years with much more diversity.

None of the chapters suggests that old age is a bed of roses. But, taken together, they send the strong message that later life is a configuration of experiences that transcends stereotypes. The chapters suggest that we use more contextually sensitive terms of reference as we consider aging and the lives of older people. The authors of these chapters change our interpretive lenses, so to speak, to present alternative perspectives on how aging and old age are constructed. They expand the range of possibilities for appreciating how it feels to grow older. They open our eyes to the variety of things that can matter most and matter least in the context of the aging experience.

The authors do this by considering the aging experience contextually. They give more weight to variable characteristics than to the crude categories that ostensibly organize them. Rather than ask what the later years are like categorically, they present the particulars of later life in relation to contexts such as historical circumstances, cultural backgrounds, and biographical experiences. In the context of history, for example, old age is not simply a conglomeration of common experiences and characteristics that contrast with those of the younger years. Rather, old age takes on particular meanings in relation to the specific historical era in which one came of age or became old. The categories of age – both old and young – come alive as times of life that have characteristics that reflect historical understandings in this instance. They are not simple polar opposites.

Cultural background and biographical experiences are contexts that operate similarly. Race and ethnicity, for example, don't necessarily organize the characteristics of age in the way the polar categories might. In some cultural contexts, for instance, aging is viewed as the final accomplishment of life rather than as a time following one's peak achievements. In others, the triumphs of later life might be characteristically balanced against late-life failures, producing complex configurations of meaning that don't simply contrast with those of the early years. Biographical context adds elements of lifelong experience, instructing us that the later years can only be understood in relation to times of life that came before. Experience isn't left behind when we check into the later years. Instead, it's continually taken up and transformed as the issues of later life come into play.

Persistence, Adaptation, and Change

Ways of Aging is divided into three parts, each of which takes up questions of how context affects the relationship between personal experience and the social world. The chapters of Part I focus on the *persistence* of lifelong meanings and claims to personhood into the later years. The leading concern of these chapters centers on how circumstances of later life relate to configurations of meaning drawn from earlier periods of life. The chapters make it clear that biography influences later life in manifold ways. The category of old hardly does justice to the many ways that the meanings of the later years resonate with experiences earlier in life. The chapters convey the impression that old age is not a distinct developmental stage but instead is a time of diverse meanings tied to persistent, if malleable, features of biography.

In "Narratives of Forgiveness in Old Age," Helen Black discusses the seemingly unshakable belief that old age is stage of life when people right old wrongs and forgive old grievances. Black presents a more complicated picture of a period of life that may still be riven with perceived and remembered injustices and mixed emotions that can't easily be put aside. The following chapter, "Elderhood in Contemporary Lakota Society" by Joan Weibel-Orlando, places personal identity squarely into cultural context. Weibel-Orlando's portrait of a momentous ceremonial event in Charlotte Standing Buffalo Ortiz's later years poignantly illustrates how Charlotte achieves the meaning of her old age. Charlotte combines elements of Lakota culture and a life of meaningful sacrifice to her community to construct a Lakota way of aging. The next chapter, "Claiming Identity in a Nursing Home" by Debora Paterniti, offers virtual outbursts of personhood in the context of a familiar institution. While residents suffer from aches, pains, illness, and disability, they also lay claims to identities that reflect preferred biographies. In portraying who they once were and now are, residents fend off unwanted institutional categories and definitions.

Part II moves the focus from persistence to issues of *adaptation*. Here, the personal and social sides of life are presented as adjustments to one another. These chapters highlight the many ways that older people adapt to their circumstances. The chapters challenge the view that older people are the helpless puppets of situations, a perspective that stereotypically contrasts the stagnation of old age with the activeness of earlier stages of life. So often, public perception homogenizes older people into groups of sick or worn-out individuals gathered together into senior housing or retirement communities, or existing at the margins of family life. The leading theme in this view is that old people passively give in to the problems and isolation of the later years. While there's a grain of truth in this – as there is in most perspectives – it's far from the whole picture. Yes, there's a significant number of older persons residing in what are called "geriatric ghettos," but their lives aren't necessarily dominated by passive resignation. As the chapters of Part II illustrate, older people actively construct their ways of life.

Tanya Koropeckyj-Cox's chapter, "Three Childless Men's Pathways into Old Age," shows how childless men build meaningful lives in old age in the absence of an intergenerational legacy. The lifestyles of these men come alive, but not in terms of domestic deficits or psychological disadvantage. Instead, the men forge complex ways of organizing later life as husbands who are not fathers. In "Constructing Community from Troubles," Christopher Faircloth takes us to a senior public housing complex, which, for all intents and purposes, appears to house the languishing poor. A closer look reveals a vibrant community, whose "troubles talk" produces a distinct way of aging centered on interpersonal complaints. Despite the troubles theme, the community and its way of life are remarkably alive and supple. The last chapter in this section, "Family Lives of Aging Black Americans" by Colleen Johnson and Barbara Barer, presents a surprisingly broad range of domestic arrangements for elderly African Americans. The adaptive strategies of these elderly persons show that they play both stereotypically passive and uncharacteristically active roles in the context of their domestic lives. Their lifestyles defy the stereotypic, one-dimensional view of their place in the black family.

Part III focuses on *change*. In contrast to Part I, which highlighted the persistence of personhood into old age, the chapters of Part III show us various ways in which change affects how older people manage their identities. Each chapter places us in the context of a particular kind of change, illustrating how, in the later years, change can alter and diversify understandings of who individuals figured they were all their lives.

Sarah Matthews's chapter, "Aging and Change in a Religious Community," poignantly describes how, in old age, a group of nuns confronts the issue of who they are as religious women. While this is something that we would expect to be resolved much earlier in life, social change makes it the center of the aging nuns' lives. Changes in the Catholic Church, which decloistered these women, confront the nuns with altered identities, seriously questioning the persistence of earlier understandings of who and what they are. Dana Rosenfeld's chapter, "Identity Careers of Older Gay Men and Lesbians," also considers social change and personal identity. In this case, Rosenfeld focuses on how a changing climate of acceptance of sexual nonconformity affected the identities of aging gay men and lesbians.

Here again, we find that identity can emerge as a significant issue of the later years, altering what it means to come of age and grow old in the context of one's sexuality. Finally, in "Expectations and the Experience of Widowhood," Deborah Kestin van den Hoonaard discusses how widowhood comes to be experienced and understood in light of widows' expectations of significant social relationships. The author shows that expectations, as much as actual social interactions, figure into how older women view themselves in their new roles as widows.

The book concludes with an epilogue by Mary and Kenneth Gergen entitled "Positive Aging." It's a fitting final reminder that, despite their advanced years, older people can, and do, continue to construct their lives in affirmative ways. The Gergens provide an optimistic turn to the story of aging that is too often told in terms of pessimistic categories. "Living well," to paraphrase the Gergens, is the best corrective for pernicious stereotypes. Of course, very real material constraints on everyday life pose ubiquitous and enduring challenges to "living well." Still, as the book's theme suggests, we need to find new and varied ways of meeting these challenges for positive aging to become an attainable goal for everyone.

Taken together, the contributions to *Ways of Aging* offer a compelling lesson in diversity. Their combined portraits and vivid descriptions urge us to go beyond stereotypes of aging. They invite us to look around traditionally narrow depictions of what it means to be old, views which portray older people as if they were all the same. From this perspective, the aging experience is varied, complex, and heartening, far more promising than stereotypes would lead us to believe.

Part I

Persistence

Chapter 1

Narratives of Forgiveness in Old Age

Helen K. Black

A common assumption about the aging experience is that forgiveness of self or others should or must occur toward the end of life. The end of life is the last opportunity to put negative experiences to rest. Forgiveness is a special challenge to the aged because they are viewed as engaged in life review (Butler and Lewis 1982), which presses elders to supply endings for incomplete or problematic chapters in their lives (Koenig 1994). Notions such as finitude (the sense that human life is limited) and the developmental tasks of aging (attaining ego integrity; demonstrating generativity) have been associated with acts of forgiveness in elders. Perceived nearness to death is considered to invite elders to clean the slate on their own or others' misdeeds in order to achieve peace of mind.

Research, however, shows no evidence that older age in itself demands forgiveness of self or others in order to achieve a sense of equanimity, or even that equanimity is a desired state for elders (Black 2001). Rather, an elder's need to resolve wrongs is mediated by his or her personal past, a cohort history, and the cultural, ethnic, racial, and religious traditions to which the elder adheres (Snowden 2001). Most importantly, the concrete incident or event that raises the issue of forgiveness is central to whether an elder forgives or withholds forgiveness (Calhoun 1992).

The immediate circumstances in which a person finds herself in the later years – such as being impoverished, in good or poor health, being alone or being part of a network of supportive others – also influence the choices she makes concerning forgiveness (Black and Rubinstein 2000). Some of the choices may be to "hold a grudge, save face, turn the other cheek, ignore or embrace the wrongdoer" (Enright 1996). These choices are based not only on the elder's belief about what is moral, right, or good, but also on if and how the elder continues to be affected by the perceived wrong, and on whether and in what way the wrongdoer remains in the elder's life. The overall lesson of this research is that the relation between the present conditions of an older person's life and her choice to forgive or withhold forgiveness is not fueled by a simple developmental imperative to forgive, but is drawn through forgiveness's complex social landscape.

The Study

This chapter draws on research conducted with 40 elders, 70 years of age and over, that dealt with the experience of forgiving and being forgiven (Black 1999). Life stories and stories of forgiveness provide the basis for this study. Respondents were recruited in Philadelphia from the Polisher Research Institute's past and present rosters of community dwelling informants, as well as through senior centers, churches, and synagogues. Respondents were first asked to tell the "story of your life." Other inquiries requested them to (1) tell a story of forgiveness; (2) engage in a specific discussion of whether anyone could "never" be forgiven and why; and (3) discuss whether religious beliefs act as a motor for forgiveness, including forgiveness of self by God or forgiveness of God. No pre-set definition of forgiveness was offered. Rather, forgiveness was to be defined and determined by respondents in their narratives. A key premise of the study was that the word "forgiveness" has little meaning separate from the experiences with which it is linked (cf. Gubrium 1993).

All interviews were conducted in respondents' homes, took approximately 2 hours, and were completed in one session. Respondents were offered an honorarium for their time. All told, 20 men and 20 women were interviewed for the project. The average age of the men was 77, the oldest being 88 and the youngest 70. Fourteen of them were Caucasian and 6 were African-American. Their average years of education was 12. Four men defined themselves as upper income, 12 said they were middle income, and 4 defined themselves as lower income. Ten of the men were currently married, 9 were widowed, and one was never-married. The average age of the women was 77, the oldest being 83 and the youngest 72. Thirteen of them were Caucasian and 7 were African-American. Their average years of education was 11. Three women described themselves as upper income, 10 as middle income, 5 as lower income, and 2 said they were poor. Six women were divorced, 8 were currently married, 5 were widowed, and 1 woman never married.

Three case studies are used here to explore how elders' discussion of events or incidents of forgiveness are worked into their life stories, focusing especially on how cultural background, spirituality, the specific events in question, and the social relations surrounding the events figure in forgiveness. Throughout, it is evident that notions of forgiveness relate to an already-fashioned identity that elders continue to refine in later life. The case materials show that elders accommodate stories of forgiveness to the self that they present throughout life and to the themes that knit their life story to the life lived.

The case studies show that narratives of forgiveness do not stand outside the life story. They are embedded in the elder's past, present, and anticipated future, and in the view that the elder holds of herself and the world. The forgiveness story displays patterns of attitudes and behaviors that the elder revealed throughout life. It highlights the same moral tone that the elder uses to judge herself and others as good, bad, right, or wrong, in most life situations. When placed within the context of the entire life story, the story of forgiveness is a thread knotted to the events, perceptions, and hopes of a lifetime.

Mr. Marks

Mr. Marks is a 72-year-old married man who lives with his wife of 51 years in a large home on the outskirts of Philadelphia. Although he recently retired from the food brokerage business, he continues to "buy and sell at home" for longstanding clients. Mr. and Mrs. Marks recently returned from a trip to China that combined business and pleasure. Good health and past success allow them to remain active in retirement. They volunteer at their synagogue and for local social service organizations.

When asked to tell the story of his life, Mr. Marks answered briefly.

> I was born and bred in Philadelphia. Went to school here. My father had been a retailer until 1939. Then he went into food services. First, I worked with my father-in-law in the upholstery business but I couldn't stand it. I worked with him four years, two more than I intended. Then my father said, "I'm getting older. It's time you take over." So I left and went with my father. And I did that for 48 years.

Mr. Marks begins his life story with his father's work history and the loyalty he showed to his father-in-law by joining him in a business he "couldn't stand." His opening comments show the salience of work in his life as well as the belief that work is a legacy both to inherit and bequeath.

After serving in World War II, Mr. Marks attended and graduated from a local college on the GI Bill. He married a girl from the North Philadelphia neighborhood where they both grew up. The couple bought a row house in Northeast Philadelphia and had three sons in quick succession. Although he described raising his children as "hectic," he realizes now that his wife took major responsibility for child rearing and he regrets is that he was "not there more" for his children. However, he believes that because education was stressed in their household, the boys did "very well." The oldest son became a doctor. The middle son works as a biomedical researcher and is considered "a genius in his field." Mr. Marks paused before mentioning his youngest son, Jeb.

Jeb was different from his brothers. Others thought that he had given up on his work [in high school] because he said he could never do what his brothers had done. Ted [the oldest son] sat him down and said, "You have traits that we don't have. You're nicer. You're more compassionate. You do things that we don't do. Don't you quit. You go to college."

This foreshadows further talk of Jeb's "difference." It also shows the family as a strong unit, and that the older brothers are aware and protective of Jeb's sensitivity. Jeb eventually attended a small college in the South where he met and married a classmate. Both graduated the next year and had a son a year later. Jeb's difficulty in finding a job after graduation prompted him to ask his father if he could join the family business. The Marks were delighted that their youngest was "coming home" with a wife and child. Mr. Marks saw Jeb's return to the area as a gift to himself and his own father. With Jeb, the business would span three generations.

> We looked for a house for them and found one a mile away. We got it all painted up and redone before he moved in. And I gave him a good salary; paid all his expenses. Then I gave him 10% of the business and I said, "As we increase the business, you'll get a bigger percentage." He was with me for a couple of years before he got sick. That was in December. A bad cold. Then he felt better. In March, he had pain in his muscles. He finally went to a doctor. The doctor said something's wrong. March 19 they said he had cancer. He only lasted 10 months. [Pause] Ahh, maybe it was better. We had friends who had a daughter with the same cancer and she went through all this radiology – three years of misery. Who knows what's better?

Mr. Marks displays little emotion while talking about his son's illness, but he clips his words, breaks off at mid-sentence, looks away from the interviewer, and glances around the bright kitchen. Perhaps he is remembering the first time he heard word of Jeb's illness, or how often he sat in this kitchen and asked the unanswerable question: Why? After a short silence the following exchange ensues.

Mr. Marks: You know, I don't think I let my mind know it [that Jeb was dying]. My wife did. I kept it out of my mind. I wouldn't believe it.
Interviewer: Were you shocked then, when Jeb died?
Mr. Marks: It still didn't sink in then. It took some time.

Mr. Marks suddenly seems uncomfortable and asks pointedly, "Is this [interview] about forgiveness?" Although he seems to have closed the issue of Jeb's death, it remains open throughout the interview. He remarks that his story of forgiveness concerns someone he "could never forgive" – Jeb's wife, whose name he does not mention in the interview – for what she did after Jeb died.

The ironic thing is he [Jeb] had $800,000 worth of life insurance which we paid for, every penny. And we didn't want it to come to us, but he [Jeb] did. Now she's [Jeb's wife] suing us for it. It's our money. And well, it's just that I can't forgive her because she's getting worse. She lost a lawsuit against us in one court, now she's in a second court. I mean, how much do I have to take from her?

Lawsuits and court dates kindle Mr. Marks' anger. Anxiety about the court's decision keeps stress ever-present, linking what can't be forgiven to pressing matters. As if to drive home the point, he adds that his daughter-in-law's attempt to "get money" is an almost trivial addition to why he cannot forgive her. She is "unforgivable" because she denied him access to her own memories of Jeb, and to Jeb's only child. She does not allow the Marks's to see their grandchild. To be deprived of this relationship robs Mr. Marks of the company of Jeb's offspring, as well as the sense of legacy and generativity that is significant in his life story. He and his wife are forced to catch sight of their grandson, Tim, "on the sly."

She started right away keeping Tim away from us. We never had him overnight. She brought him at 2 o'clock and came back for him at 6. Everything was set. And we could never pick him up or bring him back. This was her control. The last we saw him was in February [4 months earlier]. We knew he was going to be in a school show. So we got tickets and went to the show. But we didn't talk to him personally. We just saw him in the show. He's got a beautiful voice. He did very well. He's in junior high. We were e-mailing, but he stopped returning. [Pause] It eats at me.

Mr. Marks' comment "It eats at me" is heard repeatedly in elders' stories of forgiveness. Added to this expression of being devoured inwardly is often an admission, as in the case of Mr. Marks, that he had a painful ulcer, or like other respondents, that they "had lost weight for no reason." Mr. Marks graphically expresses the physical sign of his inability to forgive. When asked if there was any way to make peace with the situation, he shook his head.

> **Mr. Marks:**   I don't know any way. I don't know any way. She's got a mind that's set and I can't get into that mind to know what she's thinking.
> **Interviewer:**   Can you imagine her coming to you one day and saying, "I'm sorry," or even, "Forgive me?"
> **Mr. Marks:**   No, I can't imagine her doing that.
> **Interviewer:**   If she did, could you forgive her?
> **Mr. Marks:**   That's a hard one. I don't expect it to happen. It's not going to happen. You know, I never hurt anybody, never in my life... [Pause] I don't think I can ever forgive her. No. It's just beyond... See, what makes it unforgivable is well, the loss of your son is one thing, but she compounded it with the loss of a grandchild. So I'm not going to forgive.

Mr. Marks is aware that both cruelty and forgiveness are decisions consciously and willfully made. He perceives his daughter-in-law as having not only the power, but also the motivation, to hurt. The mystery of this motive is part of her wrongdoing – why would she want to hurt him? He cannot forgive his daughter-in-law because he sees her actions as carefully and cruelly planned. Because of the ongoing lawsuits, she remains an active and negative force in his life. Also, he "cannot imagine" her acting differently and, in this way, knows that repentance "will not happen." He foresees no end to his pain.

When asked to relate "other incidents, events, or stories about forgiveness," Mr. Marks described his duties at the close of the Second World War as "interesting."

> **Mr. Marks:**   I was a warden at Nuremberg. The guys we watched, Goering, Hess, and all those bastards. Well, I look back on it, and it was interesting. My friend had been through Burma. He was 19. You know the average age of the soldiers in the Battle of the Bulge was 18.9 years old. We were young kids. I was 18. The responsibility they gave me as an 18-year-old. [Pause] He [commanding officer] handed me the orders and said, "Here's your orders. Go do it."
> **Interviewer:**   At that time, did you realize the import of what you were doing?
> **Mr. Marks:**   No. It didn't rub in on us. I was a guard. And I don't think we really... We knew what we had to do. We knew we couldn't let these guys do anything, you know, kill themselves.

Interviewer: What did you feel?

Mr. Marks: [Long pause] Well, when it was over, I just knew I was going to go home. There was no sense of history that I can remember.

Mr. Marks does not use the word forgiveness in this narrative, nor does he say whom he would or would not forgive. He emphasizes the inexperience of youth as well as its unawareness of the larger context of life-altering events as they occur. He also highlights the expectation that the youth of his era would, without question, fight wars, guard dangerous prisoners, obey orders and, he intimates, ultimately be expected to emerge from such trauma unscathed. Lurking between the story's lines is a surprised and troubled wonder about his lack of conscious thought and feeling while in Nuremberg.

It wasn't 'til the end of the trail that we realized what the hell these guys did. [Pause] You know, there was a prison psychologist there who I just didn't like. But he lived with those guys [the prisoners]. He went into the cells every day and talked with them. And I used to think, I can't think of anything more boring than doing that. But he wrote a book on these guys, and I finally read it just a few years ago. When I look back, I see he was right about the insight of what he said about them. I remember a good many of them. It was just like this guy described them. This book, I skipped a lot of pages. Anything that's too descriptive, I can't take, you know. If they were facts, maybe I can . . . [Silence]

Mr. Marks views the prisoners' genocide, the psychiatrist's insight, and the significance of his role at Nuremberg with the vantage of time. Reading the prison psychologist's biographies fifty years later now reminds him not only of the enormity of *his* duties, but that he initially thought that the psychologist's job was "boring." Perhaps for Marks, to attempt to "get into anyone's mind" seems a thankless and mostly unfulfilling task.

It is interesting that earlier in the interview, Mr. Marks admitted his reluctance and inability to "get into his daughter-in-law's mind." One wonders if this expressed incapacity is more an aversion to "see" or "picture" the cruelty inside someone else. However, agreeing with the psychologist's insight shows that he formed deep and lasting perceptions about the prisoners he guarded. Although he believed that the events of the war "didn't rub in on us," his recollection stirs at the links of death, youth and cruelty that came later in life. Still, Mr. Marks had no trouble returning to the site of these horrors.

Mr. Marks: Three years ago my wife and I were on a trip to Europe and we rented a car and went over to Nuremberg. The House of

Justice. And it was kept exactly the same way. In fact they rebuilt part of it because it had been bombed. It's still a courthouse.

Interviewer: Was it painful to go back?

Mr. Marks: No, not at all. You've got to remember, we were the conquerors. We hung them. The night of the hanging, I had to spend the whole night staying up. I was in charge of quarters in case anybody started trouble. It was quite a night. They had built three gallows. That was the night Goering took the cyanide. You know, it was only ten months of my life, but it was very . . . In fact I have a picture of me with Goering. I was behind him. I remember I wanted to take my gun out and point it at his head.

His last comments are powerful, violent, contradictory, and spark within the interviewer a plethora of questions that Mr. Marks cannot or chooses not to answer. Why does he keep a picture of himself with Goering? Is it to help remember or forget the event? Is the horror of war lessened because he is on the side of the "conqueror"? Did those "ten months" of his life come to define his worldview? Some of the interviewer's questions are answered later, when Mr. Marks describes a movie he watched five years after the war ended.

Mr. Marks: This is a strange thing, but after I was married, I guess I was about 24, and we had the first boy. We went to a movie called the *Pawnbroker* with Rod Steiger. He [Rod Steiger's character] had flash-backs of the concentration camps. When the Nazi prisoners were brought in – the SS, the Gestapo – to testify at their trials, one of my jobs was to show them movies that were taken by our Army Signal Corps when we liberated the camps. These [in the movie] were the same pictures. I used to show them once or twice a month [after liberation] and there was no effect [on me] when I showed them. Five years later, sitting in this movie, I couldn't watch it. It started to hit me. I had to leave.

Interviewer: Why do you think that was?

Mr. Marks: [Pause with a shrug] I got older.

Although he had seen these pictures many times, the scenes of the Holocaust, shown within the movie's plot, surprise and horrify him. He is stunned by the larger-than-life panorama that reveals the mass murder of the young, old, and defenseless. Perhaps he can no longer claim ignorance of humans' ability to hate and hurt innocent others. In the context of the interview as a whole, we are being told that no amount of "understanding" can call up forgiveness for horrific acts such as genocide, the premature death of one's own child, and the unprovoked hostility of his wife.

Interviewer: You have experienced one of the hardest things that a person can endure, the loss of a child. Where, if anywhere, is God in this loss? Is that something you've ever wondered about or needed to forgive Him about?

Mr. Marks: I don't have a feeling on that. My wife does. She feels if there was a god, he wouldn't let that happen. And yet we still go to service and support the synagogue. [Pause] But we don't have that feeling that there's a god there or anywhere. See, I can't picture it. I can't see that somebody can talk to God and have an answer from him.

Contradiction and awareness of contradiction abound in this comment. Mr. Marks sees a discrepancy between going to service and not believing in God. Yet, attending service is a public display and social support of Jewish identity, which, for the Marks's, is something separate from belief in God. For them, a "god" would not have let their son die or have allowed millions of Jews to perish. He cannot "picture" God's existence, and therefore God need not be forgiven because God does not exist. Throughout the interview, Mr. Marks uses phrases such as "I can't see that" and "I can't picture it." Perhaps to imagine the existence of God is similar to "seeing" his daughter-in-law saying, "I'm sorry," or "picturing" a close relationship with his grandson. Imagined "pictures" have never come easily to Mr. Marks. When asked if it was easier to forgive in old age, Mr. Marks considered:

No, I think it gets harder because life gets harder as you get older. So it's really... it's really tougher to forgive. Maybe you remember back things people shouldn't have done, so it's tougher now to forgive. Of course, we as Jews don't want to forgive. [Pause] But I don't have anything to repent for. I don't think I'm a saint. But I just can't picture that I've done something so terrible.

For Mr. Marks, older age does not alter his beliefs about who should be forgiven or why, which for him is mediated by his Jewishness and the historical events that lead him to declare that "we as Jews don't want to forgive." Nor does old age appreciably change his view of himself. If anything, his self and worldview are cemented by the accumulated wrongs he experienced throughout his life. Indeed, Mr. Marks was an active player in the horrific events of a particular historic era – he stood close enough to "aim a bullet" at a Nazi war criminal. He endured severe personal grief – losing a child to illness and a grandson to a "forced" estrangement. In various ways, his description of forgiveness is rooted in these concrete and profound experiences of his life, and in his personal inability to "see" or "picture" a reason or resolution for these realities. His definition of forgiveness reiterates his continuing questions about the horrors and injustices of life: "Let bygones be bygones. But don't forgive. I mean, how can you? You can't obliterate your memories. They're real. How do you forgive?"

Mrs. Hesh

Mrs. Hesh is a 76-year-old Caucasian divorcee who lives in the second floor apartment of the three-story building she owns. Her front door opens onto a large living room. A narrow path, defined by baskets, boxes, old holiday cards, and a cat shuttle and litter pan, leads into a small kitchen. Before things began, she brought a stool for the interviewer to sit next to her at the tiny wood table. She looked around her apartment and waved, "It's cluttered, but it's clean." Newspapers, magazines and foodstuff cover every available surface in the living room and kitchen. Seed packet pictures form a collage on the back of the living room door and on the refrigerator. She pointed to the colored-water filled bottles set on the wide windowsills. "My permanent rainbow," she announced proudly.

Mrs. Hesh begins her life story by relating her parents' ongoing battle over the education of their only child.

> He [father] used to say to my mother, "Why do you send her to school? I quit when I was nine years old. I had to go to work. Why doesn't she?" My mother fought that tooth-and-nail. She was an ignorant peasant woman born in the old country. But she recognized that the best thing I could do was to get a good education. And she encouraged me in a lot of good things. She would steal a few pennies from her household money to send me to dancing school.

Mrs. Hesh describes her father, a hardware store owner, as "nasty and mean. He ridiculed me and ridiculed her [mother]." She says little more about her childhood except that it was painful. She quickly jumps to the next stage of her life, her mid-teen years, when she "quit regular [high] school," enrolled in a vocational school for office practice, and graduated at the top of her class. Her mother suffered a stroke and was hospitalized on the last day of classes.

> She signed herself out of the hospital to come to my graduation. And then she had a second stroke and a third [crying]. I think life was too much for her. In 1940, she died and I was not yet 17 years old. My father didn't want anything to do with me after her death. He disclaimed me as his child. And I look like him.

Mrs. Hesh stayed "temporarily" with an aunt and uncle, until they found a social service agency that rented rooms to single working girls. She was not surprised that her aunt and uncle would not keep her. They disapproved of her self-described characteristics – "I was a smarty, smart beyond my years" – and believed she would be a bad influence their own children. She dismisses any sadness this rejection caused and focuses instead on the uncommon drive she showed as an adolescent.

> I worked at Sears Roebuck in the comptometer [precursor of the calculator] department. We would sit there for 8 hours a day. They'd give us a list of numbers and we'd punch them in and add up columns of figures. Deadly, boring, gut wrenching, disgusting work. The greatest amount of money I earned was $6 a month.

Even "gut wrenching" work could not keep her from the prize of earning enough money to become "independent." When asked if she felt lonely as a 17-year-old living on her own, she shrugged.

> I just knew I had to survive. That was the basic instinct, survival. And I would do whatever it took – that was legitimate – to keep my head above water. I would volunteer to do kitchen duty at the home. Then women in the neighborhood would call the home for babysitters. I'd baby-sit. And at holiday time I got a job at Gimbels, cashiering and wrapping. I lied about my age. You were supposed to be 18.

Mrs. Hesh considered her drive to succeed and high energy to be a legacy of her "hated" father. Although he disclaimed her, he could not erase his own dark looks from her face, nor could he deny how like him she was in talent and motivation.

> My father was a very good businessman. He was very talented. He really could do any kind of work. Also, he was the one who exposed me to dance. Now my mom was a meek little nebbish and he took advantage of her.

Mrs. Hesh saw her father only once again, more than 15 years later, and by chance, on the boardwalk in Atlantic City. Although they "looked at each" other, she is not sure if he recognized her. They did not speak. She reminds herself that it was her mother who "saved pennies" to educate her, and she cries when she thinks of her mother's sacrifices to better her. However, she believes that it was her father who taught her the "finer, more interesting" things about life. In other words, she seems to identify more strongly with her "hated" but "talented" father than with her "nebbish" mother who "got taken advantage of" and succumbed, at an early age, to the hardness of life.

Mrs. Hesh paints a picture of herself in young adulthood as an ambitious, energetic survivor, ever driven to acquire more money. This is her father's legacy, not only the benchmark of security and success, but also of survival. When asked how she saw herself when she was a working teen, she answers thoughtfully.

> I was always aloof with the other girls [at the home]. I was careful. And whatever they told me to do, I did it, and I earned the maximum amount of money I could. And I was never a spendthrift. I made do with what I had. Instead of throwing away socks I would darn them. Instead of taking a dress to a tailor I learned how to do it myself. And I didn't make emotional ties. I was stingy with my money, and I was stingy with my feelings. You had to be careful with both.

Mrs. Hesh recognizes that her frugality was both emotional and monetary. The feelings her childhood evokes are anger and resentment because of her father's abandonment, and pride because of the ambition she believes she inherited from him. However, the memory of her youth elicits sadness despite her drive and perceived success. She cries as she remembers her late adolescence and young adulthood, perhaps weeping for the "emotionally careful" woman she became.

She lived at the home for over three years and "stashed away" as much money as possible. Proficient as a bookkeeper, she had several lucrative job offers after the War broke out. When she was 20 years old, she left the home for a better job in Atlantic City, lived as a boarder with a "nice old lady," and was making "sometimes $75 a week, with overtime." This was in the early 1940s.

> **Mrs. Hesh:**   I bought war bonds. And I liked to work. To me it was productive. It was a means of providing money legitimately, 'cause I could very well have gone the other way. But I was determined I was going to have a home of my own one day with or without a partner.
> **Interviewer:**   Were you interested in marriage and children?
> **Mrs. Hesh:**   I don't know. There were a lot of guys, but mostly they were interested in the sex.

Mrs. Hesh acknowledges that she knew ways to make money legitimately and otherwise. She repeats that there was no parent or guardian to guide her along the right path. However, she decided to pursue her dream without guidance, and with a single-minded focus – to own the home that she never had as a child, as well as the security that she believed a home supplied. Although marriage had little part in her dream, fate intervened. To be close to a better job, she moved to another rooming house in southern New Jersey. A new tenant moved in shortly thereafter whom she describes as "a Latino type." She explains that "good sense" had nothing to do with allowing him to be part of her dream.

> You know, the dark eyes and dark hair and you know, he had the line of – if you'll excuse the expression – bullshit. You could hang clothes on his line, you know. He was charming; he was good-looking. I was 24 and all my girlfriends were getting married. And he was very pleasant to me at that time.

Mrs. Hesh reports that her marriage was good "in the beginning." She gave birth to a son two years after their marriage. Shortly thereafter, her husband's abusiveness, infidelity, and lack of ambition and desire to work led to physical violence. Although her husband "took advantage" of her role as primary breadwinner, she believes that it also added to his resentment toward her.

> I set him up in business [as a barber]. I bought all the equipment, the barber chairs, the mirrors. He liked barbering. He liked people. He was a real, like I said before, bullshit artist. Everybody thought he was the cream of the crop. They got one vowel wrong. He was cream of the crap.

When Mrs. Hesh left her husband after five years of marriage, she also left their three-year-old son with his father. She lists the reasons.

> He had been abusive to me physically. He broke my nose. Besides that he was chasing skirts. One time I walked in on a little scene between him and the baby sitter. So I moved out. And he took the baby with him because I had nobody to help me and he had his mother and his mother worshipped that baby. She just adored him. It was the only alternative I had.

Mrs. Hesh looks at the interviewer closely, trying to gauge whether any judgment lurks within the quiet listening. Although she reiterates that leaving her son was her "only alternative," she realizes she continues to pay a heavy price for making this choice over 45 years ago. When asked whether anyone was unable to forgive her for a real or imagined wrong, she admits that her son never forgave her for leaving him despite her generosity to him in other ways.

> He [son] has a shop in Wildwood, which I financed. I've always been the banker. I think he sort of thought he had it coming to him. I don't

know [crying]. And if he's grateful, he has a very odd way of showing it, because he's disrespectful. My son's a very strong-willed kid. And he knows how to push buttons. Man, can he turn my buttons. I guess what surprises me is how long children keep that anger up. He's 50 years old.

Mrs. Hesh notes the irony in her words and laughs.

I'm always forgiving. There's a certain kind of forgiveness. You know, all this hostility that I had toward my father. It's gone. It's done. It's forgotten. What's the point of hanging onto it? And my ex-husband, he's out of my life. And whatever his problems are, they're his, not mine.

With this comment, Mrs. Hesh captures an important component of forgiveness. She no longer sees her father or ex-husband; they no longer affect her life. Although she does not forget their abuse and abandonment, she believes that she has "moved on." However, when asked if there was any event, incident or person in her life that could not be forgiven, she answered,

Mrs. Hesh: Oh, yes. The one I can't forgive is Joseph, this gentleman friend of mine that I've been going with for 34 years. It was 34 years this past November. I had no interest in seeing anybody else or going with anybody else.
Interviewer: Why can't you forgive him?
Mrs. Hesh: [Adamantly] His laziness. His negligence. His irresponsibility. No ambition.

At this point in the interview Mrs. Hesh breaks down. She cannot speak because of her emotion. Although the interviewer suggests ending the interview or moving on to another topic, Mrs. Hesh shakes her head and continues.

Mrs. Hesh: He got himself into a situation where he's hopeless. He has Alzheimer's disease. I told him three years ago to go to a decent doctor and get himself evaluated. I can't forgive him for not taking care of himself, for not being responsible for himself and for putting me in a position of having to be responsible. I just can't forgive that he was that stupid. I'm full of anger. [Shakes her head and closes her eyes]
Interviewer: Do you know why?
Mrs. Hesh: [Crying] Because I thought in our old age we would have each other. I figured we would have some degree of comfort. But I should have known. He never had any money either. He never saved.

Mrs. Hesh's comments reveal not only her disappointment with Joseph but with herself for not remembering to be emotionally frugal and to trust no one. She has finally learned that Joseph is simply another man in the parade of those who have abused, betrayed, or disappointed her. She is, however, willing to share part of the blame for her disappointment. She "should have known" to be as stingy with her emotions in older age as she was when younger.

Joseph's belongings remain in her hallway, sad mementos of the time they once shared this apartment. They are also a reminder that her dreams of love and companionship are dying. She can no longer bear either to see Joseph or speak with him.

> He has called me a couple of times and I've told him, "Don't bother me any more. I wish you would die. If you would die, you would put yourself out of your agony and you'd put me out of my agony." [Crying]

The despair in Mrs. Hesh's words is painful to hear. Like Mr. Marks and his daughter-in-law, there is an ever-present possibility that Joseph will call and reopen Mrs. Hesh's wounds. Only Joseph's death might presage the beginning of a resolution. As Joseph becomes more cognitively impaired, his capacity to know that she suffers because of him diminishes. This is also unforgivable to her – to suffer and not to have the one who causes it care that he does so.

Unlike Mr. Marks, when Mrs. Hesh was asked whether she had ever done anything that required forgiveness from another, she began to cry again, this time more quietly, and with more sorrow than anger.

> I took my temper out on the cat. This poor little guy, he's having a hard time. He's sick. He poops all over the place. I just got so frustrated with the situation with Joseph. He would call me nine times a day. And there's no conversation. He'd interrupt what I was doing. I'd say, "What do you want?" "I just want to know if you're all right?" I said, "Yes, I'm fine. Now leave me alone." And the cat would poop right in the middle of the living room floor and I'd have to clean it up, or throw up. And I kicked him with my bare foot, not my shoe. And I hollered at him. Then I said, "Please God, forgive me." I shouldn't have done that. [Sobbing]

Her pet is old and sick and becomes a target for her resentment against Joseph. Yet, she strongly identifies with the "poor little guy" and feels a powerful guilt for her unkindness. Her need to tell stories that disclose the positive as well as the negative aspects of her personality is greater than her need to hide from the interviewer a glimpse into the dark corners of her life. Her story greatly moves the interviewer.

Mrs. Hesh's way of forgiving is her way of aging – with great reluctance to let go of the dreams and desires that remain unfulfilled. Yet she remembers, with honesty and self-insight, that she is the one who can both be wronged and do wrong. Although her ability to forgive Joseph collapses along with her hope in him, she acknowledges that she also, in a moment of anger and weakness, betrayed a trust. The meaning of forgiveness for Mrs. Hesh, as it is for others, is linked with the past and the ongoing desires, hopes, and resentments of her life. These, not the last years of life in their own right, serve to articulate whether or not she is ready to forgive.

Miss Mel

Miss Mel, as she prefers to be called, is an 80-year-old African-American woman who lives in her own home in North Philadelphia. She keeps her front door unlocked for regular visitors, such as her nephew, niece, social service workers, and Meals-on-Wheels because she has difficulty walking. Neighbors on each side watched as the interviewer knocked on her door, showing their concern for her.

The interior of Miss Mel's home seems dilapidated because it needs painting and repairs, but it is filled with comfortable furniture, knick-knacks, family portraits drawn by her nephew, and pictures of her family of origin and their children.

When asked to tell the story of her life, Miss Mel replied,

> Most of my life I worked at a hotel. One of the best here in Philadelphia was the Bellevue Stratford. Then I went back to school and got a course in nursing. I did that up until the time of my retirement in 1978.

In her brief opening comments, Miss Mel leaves out all of her early life and most of her life in general. Only through the interviewer's prompts does she answer questions about her childhood and young adulthood. She was born and raised in southern Florida, the seventh child in a "happy home with a very good mother." When asked how she remembered her early years in the South, she said,

> Well, I've had some bad times. They're not forgotten. But they become good memories of how I come this far through a whole lot of stormy, stormy years. Those I will keep to myself because God has given me a peace of mind and there is no need in hashing things over.

The remark is an example of Miss Mel's reluctance to dwell on the unpleasant aspects of her past. It also exemplifies her ability to transform negative situations by her perception of them as instructional or useful. This skill becomes a theme throughout her interview. Bad times become good memories if she has learned something from them, and especially if they have been overcome.

Miss Mel was married twice, both marriages ending in divorce. Of her first marriage, she says simply, "We had two boys." Her first ex-husband resides in Florida and "never sees the boys." When asked if her children live nearby, she answered,

> It was a murder committed. He [the older son] was there. They were supposed to go to a party. When they got there, the boy my son was with started a robbery. My son left before the actual killing. This is what the lawyer has proven. But one of the boys my son was with had been a close friend – or so he thought he was a close friend. He testified against him.

In teasing out what is left unsaid in this dense remark, the interviewer learns that Miss Mel's older son has been in prison for murder since 1972. She does not entertain the possibility that her son is guilty. She believes that the scales of justice were weighed against him as soon as he stepped in the courtroom.

> Justice is not equal. Don't you see the scale of justice? It's always uneven. And see the one that's in prison is dark like I am; it would all be different if he wasn't so black. Because my younger son was a drug addict and now he's studying for the ministry. He could get a job anywhere. He's accepted anywhere. But not the dark one.

In this passage, Miss Mel succinctly describes the paths each of her sons took toward his middle age. She is aware of the cultural realities that make social equality improbable if not impossible for her older son. However, she makes it clear that there is a higher justice in which she places her trust. Indeed, since her younger son's life was transformed from drug addict to ministry student, there is no reason to doubt that God has the same conversion in mind for her older child. In fact, he is scheduled to come before a parole board later this month. Despite feeling that his very "blackness" makes him appear guilty to a jury, she explains that she is concerned but not worried about the outcome of the parole board's decision: "I'm 80 years old now and I've come a long, long way through a lot of trials. I seen a lot. With God – all things, not some – all things are possible. And this is what I depend on."

Miss Mel notes that she is "poor and housebound" and therefore unable to physically "be there and fight" for her son at his hearing. However, because her strength and her wealth are spiritual and she has joyfully shared her largesse with others, she believes she will be rewarded with an affirmative answer to her prayer about her son's release. Indeed, she relates with pride that most people in her neighborhood describe her as the "praying lady." People of all ages call or come to her home to ask her to "pray with them," for reasons ranging from hoping to become pregnant or not to be pregnant, to finding a job.

After discussing some of the infirmities that keep her housebound, Miss Mel showed that she paints her self-rated health with a broad brush. When asked about her "day to day" health, she replied, "Physically it's not good but it's what the Lord allows. Mentally I think from my thinking I'm very alert, very good. Spiritually [points to the ceiling and smiles] the sky."

While this answer may be construed as compartmentalizing different aspects of herself, it may also be that Miss Mel holds an all-encompassing view when she assesses "how she feels." She believes that the spiritual aspect of her life is both the most treasured and the most salutary. Because it is the repository for her talents and her riches, her spirituality becomes the instrument by which she interprets herself and the world.

Miss Mel seemed eager to talk about the subject of the interview – forgiveness. When asked if she ever had reason to forgive someone, she answered,

> My husband was a very handsome man. He was a very good provider. Well, this woman belonged to our church and she kept on and kept on with him until he began a relationship with her. It went on for years and years and years and I left the church. Because I would go [to church] with a heavy heart because I knew she [the other woman] was going to say some smart thing. Anyway, she said she had a child from my husband. It was a pathetic thing with sickle cell anemia. My husband's side of the family never had it, but my husband's friend [gentleman from the same church] had it [sickle cell anemia]. This left us in the clear.

It is not clear whom Miss Mel forgives in this passage. Her comments intertwine the "wrongdoers." Did she forgive her husband, to whom she gave great love and devotion, the other woman, or the baby that *might* have resulted from their affair? Since sickle cell anemia was not passed down from her husband's family, her remarks might be taken to mean that she disbelieved that her husband had an affair. However, when the interviewer posed this possibility, Miss Mel shook her head and replied that she knew all about his infidelities. Indeed, he had been consistently unfaithful throughout their marriage, and it was neither the first nor the last time his philandering made her suffer.

> It was a crying time because all you can do in a situation like that when you don't want to be in trouble is to cry and hope and pray that it will

end. I had to lift myself out of hatred. It was dark and ugly. Revenge is dark and ugly. See, we had an altercation and she [the other woman] had me locked up.

Her comment might suggest that she needed to forgive the other woman for pressing charges against her, although she does not detail the nature of their altercation. Perhaps her husband's infidelity stands out because it was carried on with a church member which made this affair more memorable, painful, and needful of forgiveness. Her remark could also be taken to mean that it was her own unnamed act of revenge for which she needed to forgive herself. Finally, she explains that it *was* she who needed to be lifted out of the "darkness and ugliness" of hatred. When asked how this was accomplished, she answered:

I told Belle [the other woman], "Go ahead. We'll just have my husband together." [Pause] That was a terrible, terrible thing! I was letting myself down to no esteem whatsoever. Because I knew it was wrong for me to share my husband and to take abuse from an outside woman. I was letting her do it to me. I sat there and I said, "Mel, you're a nothing." When you can analyze yourself this way, then you realize that you've got to come up. You cannot stay down below the line of self-respect. I had lost that. "Mel, you're a nothing."

Miss Mel's manner of telling her forgiveness story is powerful because of its meandering, yet deliberate route toward a mysterious and powerful climax. In suggesting to her husband's mistress that they "share him," she realized how "low" she had sunken. She berated herself for becoming a "nothing" in her own view. Interestingly, she does not blame her husband, but targets Belle with the worst of her anger and resentment. When the interviewer mentioned her leniency with her husband, Miss Mel answered adamantly,

A man cannot go any farther than a woman lets him. See, she [Belle] could have stopped it. But some women enjoy conquest and especially with a married man. Yes, I blame the woman. Because it was a weakness on his part. God said, "Man is a dog; he'll do anything."

But the bright side came through, too. Miss Mel explains that her transformation from a "nothing" to regaining self-respect had to go through several stages to be accomplished.

Well, I went back to the church and I became the president of the church club. And I just trusted in God. I appointed Belle as the secretary. It took one year and then I woke up one morning and

> I didn't hate nobody. And I called her and I said, "Belle, how you feeling this morning?' She said, "All right." I said, "I want to tell you something. I don't hate you no more. I love you." She said, "I never did hate you." I said, "Well, I sure hated you."

Miss Mel calls anger a "burden," and connects her resentment with "being down low and heavy." She links forgiveness to acknowledging her hatred and apologizing to the "hated" party even if that person is the perpetrator of a wrong. Ultimately, she connects forgiveness with high self-esteem. In fact, as she encouraged church members to be kind to Belle, she believes she was lifted to a "sacred place" where she could "forgive anybody anything."

> I would look at her [Belle] and I would feel so sorry for her. "Stop being standoffish to her, stop saying those sly things," I would tell them [other church members]. [Pause] See, she was a big woman, and she would sit down sometime and her dress would come way up around here [points to thigh] and I went to her and I pulled it down. She looked at me with the most . . . I don't know what kind of smile it was. [Pause] It was a Mona Lisa smile.

This poignant passage shows the core of forgiveness in Miss Mel's mind – recognizing another human being's frailty, witnessing an incident that would shame her, and quietly giving her back her dignity. For Miss Mel, forgiveness is as all-encompassing as her worldview; it is physical, mental and spiritual.

Miss Mel describes her second husband as a "stranger," and thinks of him "in the past." Ultimately, she divorced him not because of his philandering, nor because she had "sunk down low" due to his infidelities, but because his gambling jeopardized the security of her home.

> I realized that if we had not been divorced he [husband] would try to come back. I had worked so hard for this [home] and my son, too. I was determined nobody was going to get between my children, myself, and my home. It is the only thing I have and it belongs to me as long as I have breath in my body.

Miss Mel's home is a symbol of achievement in the face of adversity. It also represents her older son's "legitimacy" in society. While serving in Vietnam, he sent Miss Mel money each month to buy the home. It is therefore the haven to which she believes her son will return. Indeed, Miss Mel cannot bear imagining that she will never see him again. However, she focuses on how his character has improved during his prison stay. This focus is consistent with her desire to transform negative situations into learning experiences, for herself and others.

See, I look at it this way. Had he been out here, he would be running with the same crowd that I didn't want him to be with. He would have been dead. But he still has a chance to rectify himself into society. And he has learned patience. If you're not patient, you will flare up at somebody saying something to you in the wrong tone of voice. He's well respected in there [prison]. Had he not been in prison, he would not be alive, so I have something to thank God for.

Miss Mel reasons that life in prison is better than death because "life means hope" and "death is not temporary." She underscores her logic by telling a story about a neighbor's son. The thirty-something year old man was killed on a street corner in a drug war. His mother did not learn of his death for days, and is now "crazy with grief." In comparison, Miss Mel sees her son as "safe." Oddly enough, in this context, prison is a blessing.

Miss Mel believes that her capacity to forgive enlarged with age. "Younger peoples" are hampered by "more thoughts, more energy, and more anger" when someone wrongs them. Miss Mel's way of forgiving seems, to the interviewer, as complex and circuitous as her self-described way of aging, and indeed, her way of living. Her way of forgiving is embedded in cultural and racial traditions concerning appropriate behaviors for men and women, and in the belief that a personal spirituality is transformative.

Miss Mel finished the interview by pointedly sharing an aspect of her active, worldly spirituality with the interviewer. She suggested that the interviewer's "work" and "work relationships" are the forums in which the interviewer is tested for "righteousness in the Lord's eyes."

> **Miss Mel:** When you go back to your office, if there is somebody younger than you, or lesser than you, you take this person, you reach back and put them next to you. Reach back every time. And you help them. If you see them getting ahead of you give them a push. Let them go farther ahead. Will you do that?
> **Interviewer:** I will.
> **Miss Mel:** Good [joyfully]! Because I want you to shine.

Conclusion

Elders' stories of forgiveness are soldered to their life stories like links in a chain. They elaborate the self by recalling events or incidents when the act of forgiveness, or not forgiving, was appropriate. Elders' stories show how they resolved past or present wrongs, or why no resolution is or was possible. Acts of forgiveness or statements about their inability to forgive join other links – already in place – of a personal and communal history, and the historical social era in which the elder grew and developed.

Mr. Marks connects an unforgivable experience that "eats at him" – the control and greed of his daughter-in-law – with the historical events of the Holocaust. This is articulated in relation to unforgivable acts of intentional cruelty, and his inability or unwillingness to "get into the mind" of people who perpetrate such acts. Mr. Marks cannot forgive his daughter-in-law because she remains in his life as a stressful reminder of the loss of his son, his grandson, and the "unimaginable" satisfaction that she and others gain from their inhumanity.

Mrs. Hesh is unable to forgive her friend Joseph for not taking care of himself, and therefore for not being able to take care of her. Her sadness takes the shape of mourning, perhaps for the dream that she would finally, in old age, enjoy the companionship of a man who would neither use nor betray her. Her anger with Joseph intensifies as his symptoms worsen and the death of her dream closes in.

Throughout her interview, Miss Mel said, "God don't like ugly," a phrase used often by the sample of African-American women. She connects a lack of forgiveness with a lack of self-esteem, a poor self-view, and ultimately, with internal and external ugliness. For Miss Mel, forgiveness is also linked to spiritual power, both her own and God's. If God is to forgive whatever part she believes she played in her son's misdeeds, she must forgive all who have wronged her. It is through her own and God's forgiveness that her prayer – the release of her son from prison – will come to pass.

The women interviewed more easily discussed the nuances of relationships within their stories of forgiveness. For example, both Mrs. Hesh and Miss Mel spoke easily about their negative relationships with men. Although men's stories of forgiveness were also about relationships, they were often about the nuances of power differentials in a relationship and who should not be forgiven due to an abuse of power. For example, Mr. Marks told the interviewer that he could not forgive his daughter-in-law because of her desire to "control" the situations in which they came together. In fact, the Caucasian men in the sample especially viewed forgiveness as weakness.

A salient feature of elders' stories of forgiveness is that the subject of forgiveness itself is a problematic topic for them (Enright 1996; Fow 1996), perhaps because it presupposes that the respondent did something wrong and needs to be forgiven or a wrong was committed against him or her. These admissions call into question issues of having "bad" relationships with others or being a "good" person, both of which are significant to individuals' esteem and identity (Blazer 1991).

Following from this, another salient aspect of elders' stories of forgiveness is the cognitive route respondents took in telling their tales. Stories of forgiveness were as unpredictable as mystery stories. Like a mystery, the actors were apparent but the actual wrong, the wrongdoer's motive, or the reason why the narrator could not forgive was not always clear to the interviewer, at least until the end of the story.

Taken together, the interview narratives show that there is no one way for elders to forgive, just as there is no way one way for old people to live or to age. Nor, for that matter, is forgiveness an imperative of aging. Rather, a forgiveness is something constructed out of lifelong constellations of meaning. These, in turn, are understood in relation to particular beliefs about what is right or wrong, but also to hopes, to dreams, and to cultural or spiritual legacies.

References

Black, Helen K. 1999. *Forgiveness as Concept and Tool at the End of the Life Span*. Principal Investigator. Research supported by the Nathan Cummings Foundation.

Black, Helen K. 2001. *Entering the Storehouse of the Snow: Elders' Narratives of Suffering*. Unpublished Dissertation. Temple University, Philadelphia, PA.

Black, Helen K. and Rubinstein, Robert L. 2000. *Old Souls: Aged Women, Poverty, and the Experience of God*. NY: Aldine de Gruyter.

Blazer, Dan. 1991. "Spirituality and Aging Well." *Generations*, 15, 1, Winter: 61–5.

Butler, Robert and Lewis, Myrna L. 1982. *Aging and Mental Health*. St. Louis: C. V. Mosby.

Calhoun, C. 1992. "Changing One's Heart." *Ethics, 103*: 76–96.

Enright, R. D. 1996. "Counseling within the Forgiveness Triad: On Forgiving, Receiving Forgiveness and Self-Forgiveness." *Counseling and values*, 40, 2: 107–26.

Fow, N. R. 1996. "The Phenomenology of Forgiveness and Reconciliation." *Journal of Phenomenological Psychology*, 27, 2: 219–33.

Gubrium, Jaber F. 1993. *Speaking of Life: Horizons of Meaning for Nursing Home Residents*. New York: Aldine.

Koenig, H. G. 1994. "Religion and Hope for the Disabled Elder." In J. S. Levin (ed.), *Religion in Aging and Health*. Thousand Oaks, CA: Sage Publications, 159–75.

Snowden, David. 2001. *Aging with Grace*. Boston, MA: Beacon Press.

Chapter 2

Elderhood in Contemporary Lakota Society

Joan Weibel-Orlando

In the spring of 1989 Charlotte Standing Buffalo Ortiz, a Lakota-speaking Oglala Sioux[1] was confronting her own mortality. Her telephone call to me that April would turn out to be one of those long distance, marathon gab and mutual advisement sessions in which we'd engaged every few months since 1980, the year she moved back, after 27 years in Los Angeles, to her family homestead on the Pine Ridge Sioux Reservation in South Dakota.[2]

Charlotte had not felt well for a long while. Diagnosed years earlier as having adult onset, type two, diabetes mellitus, concern about her roller coaster blood sugar levels was not the primary reason for her call. After all, at nearly 71 years of age,[3] she had not yet suffered any of the physical ravages she had seen her less fortunate diabetic Indian brothers and sisters endure. Unlike many of her Lakota community members, diabetes was not her major health threat.[4]

Her doctors at the Indian Health Service (IHS) hospital on Pine Ridge had discovered that her shortness of breath at the least physical exertion, general fatigue, and recurring chest pains could be attributed only partially to her extra weight, her diet, lack of exercise, and the stresses of dealing with – as its matriarch – her family's periodic crises. A battery of cardiologic tests and soft tissue imaging procedures had indicated that Charlotte was in an advanced stage of congenital heart disease.[5] Her heart, after a turbulent, fully expressed life, simply was wearing out. Even the private practice heart specialist in Gordon, Nebraska[6] to whom the physicians at the IHS facility had referred her for a second opinion, confirmed the initial diagnosis. A modified lifestyle could prolong her life, she had been advised. But, all of the western medical physicians concurred, and Charlotte finally (if reluctantly) agreed, it was simply a matter of time.

Mrs. Standing Buffalo had not taken the news fatalistically. As was characteristic of her, she had looked for alternative (Lakota) solutions. She turned to a mainstay of her personal and cultural belief systems. Whether at her Long Beach, California or Pine Ridge Reservation home, she had always practiced what she called her "Indian spirituality." When the need arose, Charlotte would make strings of tobacco ties.[7] With petitions to *Wakan tanka* (the Great Spirit) for help and guidance, she would toss the tobacco ties into the lower branches of a backyard tree as an offering to the spirits – a gift to demonstrate her appreciation of their anticipated intervention on her behave.

When life stresses reached insurmountable proportions, Charlotte sought the counsel of her personal spiritual guide.[8] The seriousness of her heart condition was such a personal crisis. At its diagnosis, Charlotte had begun to consult with her "medicine man" about her illness on a regular basis. He had created a potable for her from a number of local herbs, wild roots, barks and grasses in his personal pharmacopoeia. His "tea" seemed to have helped. Charlotte had exclaimed to me in an earlier phone call:

> Those IHS doctors and the specialist in Gordon couldn't come up with anything to get rid of my chest pains. But Rick's tea really works. I haven't had any chest pains since I started drinking it.

So, when Charlotte confided that "even 'Rick's tea' wasn't working the way it used to," I had an immediate sense of foreboding. No longer looking to the Lakota spirits and their communicants for deliverance, the no nonsense, pragmatic Charlotte took over. Having finally accepted that it was, in fact, "just a matter of time," she also acknowledged the necessity for "putting her life in order" and finishing up the work of her Lakota old age.

Elderhood

Pine Ridge residents use two terms when referring to senior members of their community (Weibel-Orlando 1989). Marla Powers (1986: 180) suggests that "elderlies" is what "the old people [collectively] are commonly called in English." In my experience, however, when Kyle community members refer to people as "elderlies," they are usually talking about seniors with diminished social or political cachet in their communities. "Elderlies" tend to be people who are among the community's oldest and most infirm, devoid of personal resources and dependent upon their families or tribal welfare services for their well-being. Charlotte Standing Buffalo Ortiz was decidedly not an "elderly."

In August, 1988 the Pine Reservation community's annual fair and powwow planning committee had elected Mrs. Standing Buffalo to be its 1989 chairperson.[9] To be asked to accept the responsibility for organizing the town's most important annual ceremonial event is one of the highest honorifics the community council of Kyle, South Dakota bestows upon its members. But Charlotte had earned the honor. Through years of dutiful and voluntary service to the community, she had paid her Lakota social and cultural dues.

Even though a diabetic with a heart condition, in 1989, Mrs. Standing Buffalo was still one of the most engaged, energetic and effective members of her community. She had helped raise four of her grandchildren as well as several foster grandchildren. She had taught students at the Little Wound School in Kyle to read and speak Lakota. She had served as a liaison between the members of Kyle's senior citizens' center and its administrative headquarters in Gordon, South Dakota. With this record of community service, it had been just a matter of time before Charlotte would be asked to take on the responsibility of the Kyle Fair and Powwow chairpersonship. Her Lakota neighbors and kin people clearly recognized her leadership qualities and had already raised her to the community status of "elder" by the time I visited her in 1984.

The central identifying and interrelated qualities of Lakota elderhood are community service, self-esteem, dignity, and sagacity. Charlotte Standing Buffalo embodied all four. Her community service had started within a year of her return to the reservation. A sense of her own competence and self worth had enabled her to complete a Bachelor of Arts degree at Oglala Lakota College in Kyle. That year *The Lakota Times* (the weekly tribal newspaper) lauded her as the oldest person ever to graduate from the college. Her recognized skills in money market management, programs grant writing, and as a Lakota speaker and ceremonial participant convinced her neighbors of her cultural knowledge and sagacity. Mrs. Standing Buffalo clearly epitomized coveted Lakota elderhood. In fact, Charlotte's status passage from mother, grandmother, and ceremonial traditionalist to community elder had begun even before her return to reservation life. As early as 1978 when we first met, she was already recognized by many in the culturally heterogeneous Los Angeles Native American community[10] as one of its "elders."

During the 1978 Los Angeles Indian Center's New Year's Eve powwow, a pre-elder (a Sioux woman in her late 30s and a former student at UCLA) sitting next to me in the bleachers proudly pointed out Mrs. Standing Buffalo. In full dance regalia, Charlotte was leading an honoring dance[11] across the gym floor. "Women elders like Mrs. Standing Buffalo provide role models for the next generation of Native American women in Los Angeles," I was told. "Those of us who take pride in our Native American heritage and want to preserve it try to conduct ourselves the way she does." When asked to elaborate, the young woman offered,

> She speaks her language. She goes to and participates in most of the community powwows. She knows the powwow traditions. She practices the traditional crafts. She tries to pass these traditions on to our younger generations. She's generous. She's kept up her ties to her reservation. She doesn't drink or hang out in the Indian bars.[12] She leads her life with dignity.

Without intentionally having solicited them, I had been given a working definition of and the criteria for Lakota, Siouan and, perhaps, even Native American elderhood.

Hunka Lowanpi – The Making of Relatives

After Charlotte and I had finished catching up on each other's lives since our last long distance conversation, she finally disclosed the principal reason for the call. She wished to use her authority as the de facto Kyle Fair chairperson to include an optional ritual event into the 1989 powwow ceremonies. For some time she had been thinking about sponsoring a *Hunka Lowanpi* ceremony for her family. As this Lakota ceremony is regularly held during the annual Kyle powwow, it was the logical and appropriate time and locus for her to carry out the important and traditional ritual process for her family.

"You know, I haven't been feeling so hot lately. I don't think I have too much longer . . . " her voice dropped off into inaudibility. Recovering, she added, "So, if I'm ever going to do it for my kids, I'd better have the *Hunka* this year." She elaborated:

> The thing of it is, a couple of my grandkids are so young, they won't get anything out of the ceremony. The older grandchildren and even my own kids don't speak much Lakota. And, since the ceremony is mostly in Lakota, they won't be able to make much sense of it without someone translating it for them.
>
> Do you think you could bring one or two of your visual anthropology students[13] out to Kyle during powwow week to film the *Hunka* ceremony and then have them put together a video that explains the ceremony in English? And could you make enough copies of the video so that I can give one to each of the kids who will be given their Indian names during the ceremony? That way, they'll have a permanent

reminder of their *Hunka*, of their Lakota heritage and what I did for them – even when I am not around any more...

Again, her voice trailed off at the thought of her looming mortality.

I could not believe my good fortune. Charlotte's proposal was an anthropologist's dream-come-true. To be asked by an indigenous member of and authority in a community to record an important ritual event was a godsend. It eliminated months of negotiations with community representatives in order to gain permission to visually record a traditional ritual event in which twentieth-century recording devices are often banned. To have the sponsorship and cooperation of the community's ritual organizer was the best of all possible fieldwork contexts. "I'll talk to some of the graduate students tomorrow and see if anyone would be interested in the project," was my immediate, if ingenuously tentative reply. Silently, I vowed that not even a third Wounded Knee incident would keep me from witnessing and recording Charlotte's intended family as well as ethnohistorical event that summer.

Fortunately, I already had research funds at my disposal sufficient to support a field trip of this magnitude to South Dakota.[14] Three students in the Master of Visual Anthropology (MAVA) program not only voiced interest in the project but, already having worked together on earlier filming projects, presented themselves to me as an established film team.[15] Within a week I was able to inform my Lakota friend that, indeed, the *Hunka* ceremony she would sponsor that summer would be recorded for posterity.

Hunka Lowanpi **in ethnohistorical perspective**

Hunka Lowanpi is a well-documented traditional Lakota (Walker 1980: 193–241, 1982: 63, 105) and, in particular, Oglala ritual (Powers, W. 1977: 100–1 and Powers, M. 1986: 94–5). Between 1896 and 1914, a number of Oglala ritualists and elders provided James R. Walker (the Pine Ridge agency physician at the time) with their versions of the origins and purposes of the *Hunka* ceremony and its validating myths (Walker 1982: xiii). A *Hunka* ceremony was recorded by the No Ears, Short Man, and Iron Crow (Oglala) winter counts[16] as having taken place as early as 1805 (Walker 1980: 198, 1982: 131). Afraid of Bear (Walker 1980: 201), however, insisted that the *Hunka* tradition was much older than that. "It was performed by our fathers, by our grandfathers, and by their fathers. It came with our people when they came from the Land of the Pines."[17]

No Flesh provided Walker (1980: 193–8) with the *Hunka* origin myth paraphrased here. Somewhere in the distant past and upon the death of his four grown sons, the head chief of all the Sioux mourned them deeply and sought a vision. *Yomn*, an emissary from the spirit world, told him to travel to a lone tipi and bring back to his people what he found in it.

After traveling for four days, the bereaved chief came upon the afore-mentioned tipi. In it he found a baby boy and a baby girl. He brought them back to his camp and proclaimed to all the people that he took these children for his son and daughter. The people made a great feast. They sang and danced, played games, and gave presents to the chief and his newly constructed family. The chief then called the councilors, the keeper of the mysterious pipe, and the shamans together for a feast. After they had feasted and smoked, he told them that they were called to choose a name for the boy and the girl. They smoked sage, sweet grass, and then they smoked willow bark in the pipe. While they were smoking, a shaman said to the chief, "What was the last word *Yomn* said to you?" "*Hunka*," was the chief's reply. Then the shaman said, "This boy and this girl are *Hunka* (persons, humans, relatives) and you are *Ate* (sponsors, advisers, adoptive parents). So they will be forever. When they are a man and a woman, then we will know what to name them."

The No Flesh narrative then goes on to describe the exemplary kinds of adults the adopted brother and sister became.

> So the people named the boy Bull Bear, because he was a leader of the people, and because he was brave and cunning. They named the girl Good Heart, because she was industrious and generous.

Toward the end of his life, the chief was counseled by a shaman to do something important for his people before he "travel[ed] to the ghost land."

> Make a great feast for your people. Proclaim this to the people. *Yomn* taught you this thing. When one's heart is good towards another, let them be as one family. Let them proclaim this to the people. Let them do so with feasting and presents.

The chief obliged. He, the tribal councilors, the other chiefs, and the shamans agreed "this thing should be for a law forever." Then the chief had the head marshal proclaim to the people,

> As long as they were a people, when anyone wished to do a great favor to another he should choose him as a *Hunka*, or as an *Ate*. And ever since that time this has been the law among the Sioux.

Little Wound provided Walker (1980: 195) with an historical account of the mythic origin of the *Hunka* ceremonial structure as established in 1805.

> My father was a *Mihunka* (adviser/guardian) to all the people... He told me of the year when They Made the Ceremony over Each

Other with the Horses' Tails [established the ritual of the *Hunka Lowanpi*].

In ancient times...anyone could choose another for a *Hunka*. If such a person with a good heart, he would give a feast and make presents. The chiefs and the councilors and the shamans counseled about this and they proclaimed that it was not good....

A shaman sought a vision. His vision was a ghost like a cloud. He followed this ghost and it led him into a great hole in the earth. When they came into this hole...there were many people there. All were feasting and singing and giving presents...They taught the shaman the songs and the ceremony. Then *Tate* (another spirit world emissary) carried him through the air back to his people, and told him that when one chose a *Hunka* (relative) or an *Ate* (sponsor, mentor, parent), then this ceremony and those songs should be done and performed...He did this by waving horses' tails over all the people...Since that time when a person is made a *Hunka*, this is done with this ceremony.

The sociopolitical purposes of the *Hunka Lowanpi* are clear.

The ceremony was performed to make the Indians akin to each other...When Indians became kin in this way, it was like kin by birth...In old times when there were many wars, a *Hunka* was bound to help his *Hunka* kin in every way...(George Sword as told to Walker 1980: 198–9)

With regard to the enculturation purposes of the ceremony, George Sword argued that "the *Hunka* ceremony taught the *Hunka* to be what the Indians thought was good" (Walker 1980: 200). More than seventy years later, Powers (1986: 64–5) stressed that *Hunka* ceremonies were still important ritual elements and cultural learning strategies of Oglala community life.

In the *Hunka* or adoption ceremony, two persons, an unrelated adult and child, publicly expressed a relationship stronger than friendship or family. A *hunka* gave preference to his *hunka* above all others.

Referring to the Walker (1980) and Densmore (1918) ethnographic accounts, Powers (1986: 64–5) also provides an outline of the major ritual elements of the *Hunka* ceremony to which I will refer as I describe the ritual sequence of the *Hunka* Mrs. Standing Buffalo held for her children in 1989.

The contemporary *Hunka Lowanpi*

The charter qualities of the *Hunka* origin myth are obvious. Ethnographic accounts of the past century could have provided Charlotte Standing

Buffalo with the culturally accepted model of the Lakota "making of relatives" ceremony had she needed it. This grandmother, however, needed no scholarly verification of this Lakota ritual process, even though Walker's key informants (1980: 198) asserted that the *Hunka* ceremony had fallen into disuse after the Sioux "came into [the] reservation." Powers (1986: 190) also confirmed that the *Hunka* "had fallen into disuse for almost fifty years." She noted, however, that it "was revived in the early 1970s [a period of intense political activism and cultural restoration among the Sioux] and is still an important ritual even though it has been somewhat modified."

Charlotte Standing Buffalo, born four years after Walker had left his medical post at the Oglala Agency and a personal acquaintance of the Powers, had borne witness to the last sixty years of Lakota social and cultural history. Horn Chips, Charlotte's grandfather, had been one of the most respected medicine men on the reservation. She vividly remembered accompanying him on trips to *Hunka* ceremonies over which he had presided in the 1920s. Charlotte had received her "Indian name" at the *Hunka* given for her when she was still a girl. And, since the 1970s and the re-emergence of the *Hunka* ceremony as a community event, Charlotte had become *hunka ate* to a number of younger members of both her urban and reservation communities. Mrs. Standing Buffalo needed no anthropological references to instruct or validate her performance of tribal ritual. Life as a Lakota woman had taught her how to celebrate a proper *Hunka Lowanpi*.

Preparations for the *Hunka Lowanpi*

> If one was poor, the ceremony did not amount to much. If one was unpopular, the ceremony did not amount to much. If one had much, the ceremony was largely attended and lasted many days. (George Sword as told to Walker 1980: 199–200)

Charlotte's *Hunka Lowanpi* was sure to "amount to much" and be "largely attended." After a lifetime of industry, careful spending, and sage investing, Charlotte and her husband had retired, sold their Long Beach, California home and moved back to Pine Ridge with what they thought would be enough of a "nest-egg" for them to enjoy a "comfortable old age." Most of their Kyle neighbors considered them "well-heeled," even "rich." Considering Charlotte's resources and the number of people for whom she was sponsoring the ceremony, the 1989 *Hunka*, the people of Kyle assumed, was, indeed, going to be a "big deal."

> The preparation for the ceremony is to choose the one to conduct it, to invite the friends, to provide the feast, to provide the presents. He may ask his friends to help him in this. [But], it was the greatest honor to

provide all these things without help. (George Sword as told to Walker 1980: 199–200)

If Charlotte meant to follow the traditional mandates of *Hunka Lowanpi* ceremonial correctness, clearly she would have her hands full for most of its preceding year of preparation.

Any good Oglala could be a *Hunka*. (John Blunt Horn as told to Walker 1980: 204)

* * * *

If a man's heart is good towards a child because he likes the child, or because he likes the father, or the mother, then that man may adopt that child as his own. In old times this was done by initiating the child as a *Hunka*. The man then became like her father [and] . . . would always be like a father to her. A *Hunka* was supposed to live a good life. . . . A man that was a good *Hunka* wanted to do right. (Thunder Bear as told to Walker 1980: 211–12)

The Oglala tribal elders who counseled Walker about the *hunka* relationship and ceremony agreed that the establishment of kin bonds between people unrelated by blood could be initiated by either one of the two people involved upon the sanctioning of the bond by the other. While this was eventually the case in the eight *hunka* relationships established in the public ceremony Charlotte sponsored, she made the initial decisions about who were to be *hunka* and *hunka ate* to each other.

Choosing who were to be made *hunka* and given their Indian names had been easy. Every one of her children and grandchildren who had not been made a *hunka* previously would be bound to his or her *hunka ate* that day. The adoptees included Mrs. Standing Buffalo's second son Dennis (about 40 years of age) from her first marriage to a full blood Lakota and his twelve-year-old Lakota/Navajo son "little Dennis." Her 33-year-old third son, Ralph (from her second marriage to an Anglo man) also was given his Lakota name that day. All four of Lorraine's (the 28-year-old daughter from Charlotte's third marriage to a Mexican-American) children would participate in the ceremony. They included her son Jesse (10) and daughter Naomi (6) from her first marriage as well as her two children, Jonathan and Madison (34 and 23 months respectively), from a second partnership.[18] The eighth *hunka* would be Kelly (12), the full blood Sioux foster granddaughter the family had grown to think of as kin.[19]

Selecting a *hunka ate* for each of the eight adoptees was not as easily accomplished as identifying the adoptees. First of all, tradition mandates sponsors to be "good" Oglala and to have had *hunka* relationships established for them in the past. Second, the *hunka ate* should know the Lakota

traditions. Third, the sponsors should also have personal resources sufficient to provide for additional children, for, if the status roles are to be
carried out literally, an adopting *hunka ate* is responsible for guiding the
hunka into adulthood. This obligation can have major psychological as well
as financial costs. Charlotte needed to choose her children's *hunka ate*
wisely.

When Charlotte let the community know that she would sponsor a
Hunka ceremony for her family that summer, two of her relatives followed
Oglala tradition by not only offering to be *hunka ate* to one of the initiates
but also by informing Charlotte of the person with whom they wished to
have a *hunka* relation. Therefore, Charlotte's middle-aged, full blood
Oglala niece, who lives with her husband and his family on Indian lands
in Southern California, chose to adopt Charlotte's grandson, Jesse. His
hunka ate reasoned, since she lived in California (as did he for parts of
each year), she would be close at hand to advise and assist him whenever he
was in need of counseling and his Lakota grandmother was 1,600 miles
away.

Charlotte's full blood Oglala former daughter-in-law announced her wish
and right to be in a *hunka* relation with Charlotte's granddaughter, Naomi.
Now living at Pine Ridge after many years in Los Angeles, the Lakota
speaking, powwow dance contest winning, political activist had watched
Naomi, the children's powwow dance specialist, grow up ever since the
child, still in diapers, came to live with her grandmother in Kyle. Special,
emotional and experiential bonds already existed between them. As the
woman was daughterless, she would take Naomi as her fictive own.

The sponsors for Charlotte's grown children had few demands placed
upon them by the *hunka* relationships. Charlotte, with little difficulty, was
able to find two upstanding members of the Oglala community willing to be
hunka ate to her two grown sons.

Finding sponsors for the two youngest grandchildren was as easy. Just
toddlers and essentially unformed as social beings at the time of the *Hunka*,
few people knew Madison and Jonathan (much less their personalities) or
had developed special relationships with them.

Powers (1986: 194) points out that, contemporarily, the *Hunka* ceremony is performed as a rite of passage from childhood to adulthood at
puberty. The summer of 1989, then, was an appropriate time for the three
older grandchildren and the foster grandchild to celebrate the *Hunka Lowanpi* as a rite of passage from childhood to adulthood. However, it was
clearly too early in the life cycles of the two youngest grandchildren to have
hunka relationships established for them and to be given their adult and
ceremonial Indian names. Charlotte's sense of personal urgency, coupled
with her responsibility as their primary caretaker for their physical and
cultural welfare, prompted the toddlers' premature inclusion in the ceremony. Ultimately, the adoptive parents for the tots were close Oglala

friends of either Charlotte or her daughter who owed debts of gratitude to or wished to do favors for the family.

The adolescent Navajo-Oglala grandson, too, was not very well known in the reservation community, as he had spent most of his twelve years either in Los Angeles or, during the summer, on his mother's reservation in Arizona. Ultimately, an upstanding male elder and personal friend of the family accepted the sponsorship of Charlotte's oldest grandson.

The hardest *hunka* relationship to establish was the one between Charlotte's foster granddaughter and her *hunka ate*. Though Charlotte had taken Kelly into her home when she was still a toddler and the girl had lived with the Standing Buffalo family, on and off, for most of her childhood, her ties with the Kyle community had become attenuated. Years earlier she had gone to live with her biological mother in off-reservation Gordon, Nebraska. Ultimately, Charlotte chose a middle aged, full blood Lakota niece who lived in a near-by reservation hamlet to be Kelly's *hunka ate*.

> To perform the [*Hunka*] ceremony properly, a shaman or medicine man should conduct it. (George Sword as told to Walker 1980: 199)

Enlisting the services of a *wakan* (a person instructed in the mysteries of and able to communicate with the spirit world) in 1989 was easily accomplished. One of the most famous and respected Oglala *wakan*s, Frank Fools Crow (Mails 1979), lived just down the road from Charlotte. Although he happily agreed to attend the *Hunka*, Fools Crow was close to (if not already) in his 90s at the time. In fragile health and unable to stand unassisted for any length of time, "Grandfather" Fools Crow's blessed presence was all that could be expected of him at Charlotte's *Hunka*. She, therefore, needed to secure the services of a second Lakota ritual specialist to officiate throughout the lengthy ceremony.

She asked her brother-in-law to provide the spiritual guidance and ritual authority for the event. Spry, feisty, a traditional tribal chief and political activist, Oliver Red Cloud, great grandson of the world famous Oglala war and peace chief of the same name (Hyde 1984), even at 75 years of age, could be trusted to endure the rigors of what would be a grueling, three-hour ceremony under a blazing August sun.

Curiously, when Charlotte first explained the proposed ceremony to me, she downplayed the "making of relatives" aspect of the *Hunka Lowanpi* ritual. Rather, she emphasized the importance of and purpose for ensuring that her descendants had their Lakota names.[20]

> Every time they use their Indian names, it will be a reminder of me and their Lakota heritage. Having an Indian name will keep them tied to their Indian culture. It will help them remember who they are.

Name giving in later life is mentioned briefly in the ethnographic literature (W. Powers 1973: 95, 1977: 57; M. Powers 1986: 60; Walker 1980: 180, 192). Only summary descriptions of ceremonial behavior associated with the event are available. Powers (1973: 95), for example, asserts that "the naming of a child was an important occasion among all the tribes – one highlighted with the giving of gifts by the parents, feasting by the entire village, and all-night dancing to the songs honoring the newly named."

A person's adult name was often given at puberty. As prescribed by the *Hunka* origin myth, it was supposed to be based on some characteristic personality trait, physical feature, or historical marker in the life of the young person (Powers, W. 1986: 60). Therefore, the Lakota name given to Charlotte's part-Navajo grandchild by his adoptive father translates as "Turquoise Boy." The name was chosen both because he lives "at the edge of the blue sea" (the Pacific Ocean) and because his mother's people use turquoise so extensively in their jewelry as well as in their sacred rituals. Similarly, the name Charlotte chose for her foster granddaughter translates as "They Bring Her Home." "I think that's a very good name for her because, after all, I brought her back twice [to live with me] from her situation [a neglectful household] in L.A." (Charlotte Standing Buffalo, in conversation, August 15, 1989)

Traditionally, an Oglala *wakan* bestowed the peoples' adult names (Powers, W 1986: 57). Often this occurred during an ear-piercing cere- mony at a Sun Dance (Walker 1980: 192). There is some evidence, how- ever, that this responsibility was also associated with having a godparent (*hunka*) relationship with the person to whom the *wakan* has given an adult name (Walker 1980: 192). The *Hunka* origin myth (Walker 1980: 194) clearly reifies the giving of names as an element of the *Hunka* tradition.

Breaking with tradition, Charlotte chose the Indian names of her two youngest grandchildren because she knew them so intimately. The other adoptees' Indian names were left to the creative imagination of the people who had agreed to be in a *hunka* relationship with the older initiates and who had known Charlotte's children and her adolescent grandchildren for most of their lives.

> If such a man had much to give away, he had a big feast and everybody came and ate and sang and danced and played games.... (John Blunt Horn as told to Walker 1980: 203)

Both as the de facto powwow chairperson and sponsor of that year's *Hunka Lowanpi*, Charlotte was expected to host at least one communal meal during the three-day event. As befitted her community status, she provided a side of beef for the midday meal before the *Hunka* ceremony. The couple hundred pounds of meat was cut into fist-sized chunks and boiled in a huge vat over a fire pit two townsmen had excavated on the powwow grounds early Sunday morning. When sufficiently cooked, the meat was placed into several 50 gallon, vegetable broth-filled school lunch containers from which the mixture was ladled out to all who presented their "stew bowls" for filling.

Her children, their adoptive relatives, and all her close kin and friends who could afford to each provided some food item (corn, bread, fry bread, soda, fruit punches, watermelons, salads, *wojapi* (a traditional Lakota berry pudding) and dozens of other American picnic or traditional Lakota recipes) to the communal groaning board. By noon Sunday, four queues, 50 people deep of would-be feasters, filed by the four, food-covered picnic tables and helped themselves to the offerings of Charlotte's feast. By two o'clock and the beginning of that afternoon's powwow songs and dances, Charlotte and her contributing family members and friends had fed over four hundred community members.

Hunka Lowanpi: *the ritual process*

The Standing Buffalo *Hunka*, as expected in the contemporary perform-ance of a ritual tradition of some historical depth, combined a number of ancient ceremonial practices and objects (see Walker 1980: 212–16) with modern and, perhaps, idiosyncratically innovative symbolic processes. Cer-tain nineteenth-century *Hunka Lowanpi* practices described in the Walker documents (1980: 193–239) were not included in the Standing Buffalo ceremony. Red paint to "mark" a male *hunka*'s face or the parting of a female *hunka*'s hair "so that [a] *Hunka* could tell that he has a *Hunka*" (Sword as told to Walker 1980: 200) was not used. Nor were the horsetail wands that gave the 1805 *Hunka* ceremony its name (Sword as told to Walker 1980: 198) in evidence in the 1989 ceremony. The special *Hunka* lodge mentioned by both Walker 1980: 224–5) and Powers (1986: 64), also was not a ritual feature of the Standing Buffalo ceremony. And, while the *hunka* dyads were traditionally wrapped within a buffalo hide (Power 1986: 64), the only possible artifacts of that practice were the star quilts neatly folded over the backs of the adoptees' chairs and presented by them to their adoptive relatives at the close of the ceremony.

The mandatory distribution of meat (Walker 1980: 217), however, figured prominently in the 1989 *Hunka*. Shredded and mashed into *wahs'na* (the Lakota word for pemmican[21]), meat was ritually presented to each initiate at the close of the ceremony. And, of course, all of the attendees were welcome to share portions of the side of beef Charlotte had purchased for the *Hunka* feast by accepting a ladle-full of the communal beef stew.

Another alimentary ritual was the offering of chokecherry juice (a trad-itional Lakota food) to the *Hunka* participants. As Powers (1986: 194) explained, "A wooden bowl of chokecherry juices is then communally drunk by all the participants, but especially the children, their parents, and the medicine man and woman." When offered, the tangy bitterness of the drink was a welcome treat for the adopters and adoptees at the end of the *Hunka Lowanpi* and before the beginning of Charlotte's "give away."

Other ritual acts included the spiritual leader's "address[ing] the people, extolling himself and the ceremony and admonishing them to observe the precepts taught by it" (Walker 1980: 228). After his opening prayers to the spirits, Oliver Red Cloud delivered a moving admonition about the personal and historical significance of the ceremony that was about to begin, as well as the need for all assembled to continue these traditions for the future generations.

The tying of a white eagle plume to the hair of each child (Powers 1986: 195) as a "symbol of constancy and virtue" (Walker 1980: 218) was another prominent traditional feature of the 1989 ceremony. Standing behind the ritual leader and emulating his every move, the eight sponsors held the feathers they were about to bestow upon their adoptive children to the four directions. After Red Cloud had delivered his words of Lakota wisdom to the assemblage, the adoptive adults tied the blessed feathers to strands of their adopted children's hair. Throughout, Red Cloud admonished the adoptees to "keep these feathers with you forever so that they will remind you who you are."

Powers (1987: 59–72) explicates the symbolic importance and ritual power of the number four in Oglala ritual.

> Both the number 4 and the number 7 have the capacity to symbolize a sense of natural and cultural fulfillment. When one "reaches" the end of the ritual line, so to speak, one gets off the ritual bus at either of these arithmetical stops. Both numbers not only establish a sense of fullness or completion but are statements of denouement.

The No Flesh origin myth (Walker 1980: 194) established the rationale for the prominence of the four-fold ritual replication sequences in the *Hunka Lowanpi* (the death of the mythic chief's four sons and the discovery of the "lone tipi" "on the fourth day" of the chief's journey). Four replications of a ritual segment occurred throughout the Standing Buffalo *Hunka Lowanpi*. The head drum group[22] repeated the *Le Hunka* song four times as the Standing Buffalo family and their adoptive parents entered the ceremonial arena. Red Cloud ritually acknowledged the four directions by turning clockwise to each of them before repeating his prayer to the spirits. And, at the end of the ceremony, Shirley Apple Murphy, a full blood, middle-aged, Lakota woman and the *hunka ate* of one of the children that day, offered and held back the bowl of pemmican mix three times before ritually feeding a spoonful of the mix to each *hunka* at its fourth offering. All of these repetitions are certain references to the Lakota belief in the power of the sacred number four to imply "the unfolding, the development, the evolution of important events" (Powers 1987: 66).

Innovative aspects of the Standing Buffalo *Hunka* included the primacy of the grandmother in its initiation, planning and fruition, and the increased involvement of the senior members of the *hunka* dyads in the actual ritual leadership and performance. The senior members of the relationships, for example, took turns describing, in exquisite detail, their commitment to their newly adopted children, the personal qualities that made them exemplary *hunka ates*, why they had chosen the particular Lakota names for their adoptees, and to what extent they meant to fulfill the responsibilities of the *hunka* relationships.

The "give away"[23]

> If a man had plenty and his friend's child pleased him he would say, "I will take this child as my own." And ... then he would ... give away his meat and his robes and his skins ... If a man did this, he was considered a generous man and everybody gave him something. (*John Blunt Horn as told to James Walker 1980: 203*)

Charlotte had been planning her *Hunka* "give away" for years. Fully a year earlier, she had begun to make, purchase, and store her "give away" items. Blankets, bed linens, hand-stitched quilts, dance shawls, beaded moccasins, pouches and key holders, pots and pans, lawn chairs, storage trunks, and scores of other practical as well as decorative items overflowed her bedroom closet and were piled high on her dresser, chests, floor, and bed by the time the film crew and I arrived at her home a week before the ceremony. Charlotte confided she had spent nearly two thousand dollars on the "give away" gifts alone.

Concerned she might appear insufficiently generous, she fretted about her stockpile of gifts not being enough and the possibility that she had forgotten someone. About mid-week before the *Hunka* ceremony she talked about and finally took "a run up to 'Rapid'[24] to pick up a few more things for the 'give away,' just in case ... "

Apparently she had gathered more than enough "give away" items. After the newly made relatives proceeded together in an honoring dance around and out of the arena, Charlotte's hour-long "give away" began. The gifts were formally presented, one at a time, to a prescribed list of *Hunka* participants, assistants, relatives, and family friends. Even the prisoners in the local jail who had helped with the cleanup after the feast and perfect strangers were recipients of Mrs. Standing Buffalo's largesse. Charlotte's "give away" was pure ritualized gifting in accordance with the mythically and historically chartered public demonstration of generosity (a central principle of the Lakota value system) at every *Hunka*.

Charlotte's ceremonial duties ended with her "give away." Her de facto powwow chairperson responsibilities, however, mandated she remain on the grounds until the end of that evening's dancing. She, therefore, stayed for final dance contests and even got up from her lawn chair and (wrapping her fringed shawl around her shoulders) took part in a couple of her favorite social dances.

Around ten o'clock, however, Charlotte was visibly spent. Yawning, nodding off from time to time, complaining of chest pains and informing us that her "heart medicine" was back at home, she packed up her powwow gear and left the arena. Her ceremonial duties to family and community now fully exercised, she drove home to her now gift less bed and first good night's sleep in weeks.

Sustaining Lakota Elderhood: Aging as a Career

Clearly, the contemporary *Hunka Lowanpi* is still the process by which the Lakota attempt to ensure the cultural, if not physical, survival of their descendants. As in the origin myth, the Lakota attempt to perpetuate themselves as a society through ritual extension of their tenets of kinship relations to people "who have no blood ties but, even stronger *Hunka* ties to each other" (Sword as told to Walker 1980: 198). If the 1989 Standing Buffalo *Hunka* is any indication, the ceremony also appears to have become the public arena in which personal status and prestige level passages (absent to participating and middle-aged to elder/sage membership) in the Oglala community are performed and reified through witnessed ritual process.

A number of thematic issues in aging studies are illuminated by the previous description of contemporary Lakota ritual. Myerhoff and Simic (1978: 240) introduced the concepts of life's career and the work of aging to describe the experience of elderhood that, in certain ways, contradicted the, then, prevailing stereotype of American old age. Rather than a rocking chair retirement from life, several contributors to the Myerhoff and Simic volume found old age to be "a period of activity, participation, self-movement, and purposefulness [work]" and that "aging [had to be understood] as the product of a building process typifying the entire life span" (240). Further, contributors explain that "career" assumes a diachronic perspective relating to long-term goals spanning an entire life time; that is, it constitutes a process by which the individual builds, or fails to build, a lasting structure of relationships, accomplishments, affect, and respect that will give meaning and validation to one's total life at its close" (240). The resources one has at hand in old age "may be material, while others may be intangible, such as knowledge, honor, or a sense of intimacy and commonality with others" (240).

Since I had known her, Charlotte Standing Buffalo Ortiz exemplified the successful aging careerist. She understood the status choices her tribal community held open to her in old age. She worked hard at doing those things that validated and ensured her status as a community elder. She purposively used the resources (personal savings, cultural knowledge and familial and community networks) at her disposal to do the work of Lakota old age. This included the ritual cementing of her descendants to their Lakota identity and community membership.

In the nearly 30 hours of video tapes from which the 90-minute edited version of the *Hunka*[25] ceremony was created, the viewer sees the septuagenarian grandmother directing her family to their chairs, advising them of what to expect next in the ceremony, what to say when asked to speak, and giving away a bounty of earthly possessions to family and friends. With her total ritual involvement that weekend, she demonstrated to observing neighbors that, even after 27 years in Los Angeles, she was still true to Lakota ways. Through the authority of her ceremonial directorship, she proved the viability of her membership in her homeland community, not as an "elderly," but as a ritual specialist and respected "elder."

The ritual status and roles the elder Lakota woman publicly performed were not capricious or idiosyncratic choices. Rather, they were mandated by Lakota myth as the responsibility of community elders. As No Flesh explained to Walker (1980: 195), the *Hunka Lowanpi* was initiated as tribal practice only after a shaman admonished the old chief who had found and adopted the two orphans in the lone tipi; "Now [that] you are an old man, do this for your people."

Myerhoff and Simić (1978: 232) also recognized the importance of one's sense of cultural continuity (the implication of "contact with, and access to, a coherent and relatively stable body of ideas, values, and symbols") in old age. Charlotte not only fully recovered this with her return to reservation community life, she also felt the need to impart some semblance of Lakota social and cultural continuity to her children and grandchildren. She had done so through example, by exposing them to Lakota social life when in her care, by sponsoring the *Hunka Lowanpi* ceremony for them, and by initiating the creation of the videotape of the ceremony as permanent record of that event – as their personal biographical object.[26]

Elsewhere, I have described five American Indian grandparenting styles: cultural conservator, custodial, fictive, ceremonial, and distanced (Weibel-Orlando 1997: 139–55). In real ways, Charlotte had chosen or been forced, by residence choices over which she had no control, to experience all five grandparenting styles. Her decision to hold a collective *Hunka Lowanpi* for eight of her children had been impelled by these experiences.

Mrs. Standing Buffalo, for long periods of time, was the custodial grandmother (Weibel-Orlando 1997: 148–9) for all four of her daughter's children. Her labor of love (foster grandparenting) on behalf of her tribe's

social services program led to her informal "adoption" and the establishment of "fictive" grandparent/grandchild relationships (Weibel-Orlando
1997: 147–8) with the Lakota youngsters who had lived with her.

Her experience as a distanced grandmother (Weibel-Orlando 1977:
144–5), however, was at the root of her sense of urgency and concern
about her California-based sons' and grandchildren's loss of ties to their
Lakota cultural heritage. Native American ceremonies are practiced widely
in southern California (Weibel-Orlando 1999: 129–98). Charlotte and her
Los Angeles-based family members, in fact, had participated in these
ceremonial events both before and after her return to reservation life. The
southern California powwows, however, are pan-Indian ritual syntheses
rather than unadulterated Lakota tradition practices (Weibel-Orlando
1999: 132–52). If her Los Angeles-based grandchildren were to learn
about Lakota ceremonial traditions, Charlotte reasoned, she had to be
the one to engage them dramatically and permanently in them.

For these reasons Charlotte resolved to provide her children and grandchildren with some lasting memory of what it means to be Lakota. She did
this by involving them in the *Hunka Lowanpi* experience and through the
presentation to them of a videotape of the event. This, the biographical
object, would be theirs for all time. To it they could turn periodically to
effect a reintensification of a sense of their Lakota selves. By creating this
contemporary Lakota mnemonic device, Charlottes was enacting what she
felt was a critical aspect of Lakota grandmothering.

Her status as the family's cultural conservator (Weibel-Orlando 1997:
149–52) was paramount. To fulfill the roles of that status was to be the last
work of her old age career as a Lakota elder. Sponsoring and directing a
ceremony central to the Lakota way of life and emblematic of its value
system and making her children the central foci of that ritual process would
be the final acts of a Lakota elder consumed with the need to see her
beloved cultural traditions survive in and sustain her children just as they
had nurtured her throughout life.[27]

How representative is this remarkable woman's old age experience? Is
this the profile of a single, indomitable, and culturally atypical personality?
Or can the works of Charlotte's aging career be generalized to include most
Oglalas? Does her elderhood represent a Lakota way of aging?

The ethnographic record suggests that both the statuses of cultural
conservator and ritual specialist, as prerogatives of Native American old
age, are more widely cast than this single example. Powers (1986: 98)
underscores the historical and contemporary involvement of Oglala
women in tribal ritual into old age or "as long as they were strong enough."
The general ritual authority of community elders (both male and female)
was clearly expressed in the 1989 *Hunka*. All of the ritual specialists that
day (the master of ceremonies, medicine man, the ritual specialist, the
sponsoring grandmother and the eight *hunka ate*) were older-to-aged

members of the Oglala community. The fact that most local families had sponsored *Hunka* ceremonies at the Kyle Fair for as long as the annual community event has existed, and continue to do so each year, underscores this ceremony as a cultural continuity.

Community elders and, specifically, older women, have been identified as ritual specialists in a number of other American Indian societies as well ([Navajo] Benally 1999: 26, [Otoe-Missouria] Schweitzer 1999: 167–9, [Tewa] Jacobs 99: 130). The pan-tribal assumption by grandmothers of the status and work of being the family cultural conservator is well documented (Schweitzer 1999). It is clear, therefore, that Charlotte Standing Buffalo Ortiz's great investment, in old age, of her time, energy, cultural lore, social cachet, and monies in the sponsorship of a ritually accurate *Hunka* ceremony for her descendents, was as much driven by cultural imperative – a Lakota way of attaining and sustaining elderhood status – as it had been by personal motivation and invention.

The inclination, in old age, to pass on one's sense of the importance of tribal identity, ritual knowledge, and community involvement, and the need for the generations who will follow to continue the perpetuation of a sense of tribal self, still exists. Not only is it the work of old age among the Oglala, specifically, and the Lakota, in general; it also is the old age imperative of a number of other North American tribal societies. Fearing the cultural encroachments of twenty-first-century technocracy, residential dispersal and tribal exogamy, and foreseeing their detribalizing effects on their children and grandchildren, aging Native Americans seek to instill and perpetuate their tribal legacy and identity in their future generations through the power of ritual process, participation, and sanctification.

Notes

1 Our relationship spanned twenty years in which Charlotte was my research interviewee and assistant, the subject of two ethnographic films and four articles, and a friend.

2 The ethnographic film "*Going Home: A Grandmother's Story*" (1986) is an account of Charlotte's return to her reservation. It is distributed by the Center for Visual Anthropology at the University of Southern California.

3 In spring, 1989, Charlotte was six months shy of the average life expectancy for Native Americans (71.1 years). Though greatly increased since 1940 (51.4 years of age), average life expectancy was still lower for Native Americans at that time than it was for the United States white population (74.4 years of age) (Snipp 1989: 68).

4 Diabetes mellitus is an escalating Native American health problem. From 1982 to 1984, it was the fifth ranking cause of death in Indian elders. By the period 1994–6, it had become the third highest cause of death among Indian elders, surpassed only by cancer and diseases of the heart (D'Angelo 1999: 2).

5 In all three time periods for which there are health data and as reported in the National Indian Council on Aging, Inc. report (D'Angelo 1999: 2), the category, diseases of the heart, was the number one cause of death among Native American elders.

6 "Outsourcing" patient referrals was and continues to be a common practice across the often understaffed IHS hospitals and clinics. The nearest cardiologist was located in the off-reservation town of Gordon, Nebraska, an hour's drive from Charlotte's home.

7   Many rituals associated with the traditional Lakota belief system are still actively practiced. Tobacco ties are composed of two-inch squares of colored cotton cloth filled with
tobacco (traditionally the plant product used in sacred ceremonies to commune with the
spirit world) and tied, one at a time, onto a long (two feet or more) string. The "tie" is
usually attached to some open-air object to which the spirits can come to admire and
partake of the offering. For a comprehensive description of contemporary Lakota ritual
practices see Powers' *Oglala Religion* (1977) and *Beyond the Vision* (1987).

8   Traditional healers (medicine men and women) are still active on many reservations
(including Pine Ridge) and some urban centers (see especially Chapters 5 and 6 of
Powers' (1987) *Beyond the Vision*). When still living in Los Angeles, Charlotte, annually,
spent her summer vacations visiting friends, relatives and the medicine man (a person 30
years her junior) who she, through personal observation and word-of-mouth recommen-
dations, had come to believe had special powers to heal.

9   The 1989 Kyle Fair planning committee wanted Charlotte to head its powwow preparations that year. However, and because the Kyle Fair presidents have always been male,
the committee, instead, elected Charlotte's 10-year-old grandson, Jess Munoz, to the
position. Sagely, they reasoned that the child, though bright and well acquainted with
powwow traditions, could never take on the organizational responsibilities of the post and
Charlotte would have to step in as the de facto president for the sake of the community
and to save family face.

10   Native Americans in Los Angeles constitute the largest urban Indian population in the
nation. Over 180 tribes are represented. For a comprehensive description of this urban
ethnic community see *Indian Country, L.A* (Weibel-Orlando 1999).

11   Powwows are pan-tribal social events that have as their foci a number of sacred, honorific,
competitive and thoroughly social dances. An honoring dance is usually performed to
show respect for particular community member (veterans, recent graduates, esteemed
elders). At each powwow two people (the head male and head woman dancers) are
designated to lead processions such as the honoring dance. For a description of Los
Angeles-based powwows see Weibel-Orlando (1999: 132–52).

12   In the 1970s approximately eight Los Angeles neighborhood bars were frequented by
Native Americans with such regularity that they became known as "Indian bars" even
though the majority of their customers were not Native Americans (See Weibel-Orlando
1999: 120–1).

13   Charlotte was fully aware that the Anthropology Department at the University of Southern California had initiated a Masters of Visual Anthropology Program in 1985 as
Thomas Fleming (one of the first students in the program) and I had spent a week at
her Kyle home that summer videotaping events in her life that formed the nucleus of the
film "*Going Home: a Grandmother's Story.*"

14   Since 1984, the research team of Myerhoff, Simić, and Weibel-Orlando had conducted
aging research funded by a grant from the National Institute on Aging.

15   Stephen D. Grossman, Jennifer Rodes, and Kate Ferraro are the three USC visual
anthropology graduate students who accompanied me to Charlotte's 1989 *Hunka* ceremony.

16   By the mid-eighteenth century, several Plains Indian groups had developed the ethnohistorical mnemonic device known as a "winter count." At the end of each year (during
the winter months), the major event of that year was drawn and painted onto a buffalo
hide in sequence after the mnemonic pictograph for the previous year (Walker 1982:
111–57).

17   Afraid of Bear's recollection is historically correct. When European explorers first
encountered the Sioux in the late seventeenth century, they were in what is now the
state of Minnesota and living in lakeside settlements in the piney forests of the eastern
woodlands culture area. The Sioux moved out onto the Great Plains in the first decades of

the eighteenth century, fully a century before the first visually recorded *Hunka* ceremony was held in 1805 (Hyde 1984: 3).

18 As both men who fathered Lorraine's children are Mexican-American, all four of her children are one-quarter Lakota and three-quarters Mexican-American.

19 Charlotte's oldest son Ben (a full blood Lakota) had received his "Indian name" when he returned from armed service in the Vietnam War. His Creek/Sioux daughter and Charlotte's daughter, Lorraine, had been given their Lakota names in earlier *Hunka* ceremonies.

20 Even the Kyle Fair master of ceremonies that year, began the *Hunka Lowanpi* by announcing to the powwow attendees that they were about to witness a "Lakota naming ceremony."

21 Pemmican is a traditional food not only of the Lakota and Sioux Nation, but also, of a number of other nomadic Great Plains societies. It is a mixture of ground, sun-dried meat, corn meal (another traditional symbolic element of the *Hunka* ceremony), chokecherries, animal fat and other wild seeds and roots which Plains women traditionally gathered. When migrating from one hunting territory to another, individuals carried balls of pemmican in leather pouches on their person. The Lakota, with a wink, say they invented "trail food."

22 The Pine Ridge Reservation is home to numerous organized groups of traditional Lakota drummers and singers. To be asked, by the sponsor of a traditional Lakota ceremony, to be the head drum of an event is a major honor. While other drum groups may participate and "spell" the main drum group, the head drum is responsible for the performance of all of the ritual musical elements of the ceremony.

23 Generosity is a core Lakota value. It is reified through regular, ritual redistribution of goods and monies at powwows throughout the year. These formal gifting events are called "give aways."

24 This abbreviation is used by most Lakota to refer to Rapid City, South Dakota, the nearest city and commercial center to the Pine Ridge Reservation. Most residents of Kyle (Charlotte among them) regularly make the 90–minute drive from Kyle to "Rapid" to do their major household shopping.

25 The video is entitled *Le Hunka: Lakota Naming Ceremony*. Copyrighted in 1990, it is distributed by the Center for Visual Anthropology at the University of Southern California in Los Angeles.

26 For a definitive work on biographical objects, see Hoskins (1998).

27 Charlotte Standing Buffalo Ortiz had a tenacious hold on life. She lived another nine years before succumbing to heart disease in September, 1998.

References

Benally, Karen Ritz. 1999. "Thinking Good: The Teachings of Navajo Grandmothers." In Marjorie M. Schweitzer (ed.), *American Indian Grandmothers*. Albuquerque: University of New Mexico Press, pp. 25–52.

D'Angelo, Anthony J. 1999. *What Kills Indian Elders*, National Indian Council on Aging (Monograph Series 1(1)). Albuquerque, NM: NICOA.

Densmore, Frances. 1918. *Teton Sioux Music*. Bulletin 61. Washington, D.: Bureau of American Ethnology.

Geertz, Clifford. 1973. "Thick Description: Toward an Interpretive Theory of Culture." In Clifford Geertz (ed.), *The Interpretation of Cultures*. New York: Basic Books, pp. 3–30.

Hoskins, Janet. 1998. *Biographical Objects How Things Tell the Stories of People's Lives*. New York and London: Routledge.

Hyde, George. 1984. *Red Cloud's Folk A History of the Oglala Sioux Indians.* Norman, OK: The University of Oklahoma Press.

Jacobs, Sue-Ellen. 1999. "Being a Grandmother in the Tewa World." In Marjorie M. Schweitzer (ed.), *American Indian Grandmothers Traditions and Transitions.* Albuquerque: University of New Mexico Press, pp. 125–44.

Mails, Thomas E. and Dallas Eagle Chief. 1979. *Fools Crow.* Garden City, NY: Doubleday.

Myerhoff, Barbara G. and Simić, Andrei. 1978. *Life's Career – Aging: Cultural Variations on Growing Old.* Beverly Hills/London: Sage Publications.

Powers, Marla N. 1986. *Oglala Women: Myth, Ritual, and Reality.* Chicago and London: The University of Chicago Press.

Powers, William K. 1973. *Indians of the Northern Plains.* An American Indians Then & Now Book, Earl Schenck Miers, general editor. New York: Capricorn Books.

Powers, William K. 1977. *Oglala Religion.* Lincoln/London: University of Nebraska Press.

Powers, William K. 1987. *Beyond the Vision: Essays on American Indian Culture.* Norman and London: University of Oklahoma Press.

Schweitzer, Majorie M. 1999. "Otoe-Missouria Grandmothers: Linking Past, Present, and Future." In Marjorie M. Schweitzer (ed.), *American Indian Grandmothers Traditions and Transitions.* Albuquerque: University of New Mexico Press, pp. 159–80.

Snipp, C. Matthew. 1989. *American Indians: The First of This Land.* New York: Russell Sage Foundation.

Walker, James R. 1980. *Lakota Belief and Ritual.* (Edited by Raymond J. De Mallie and Elaine A. Jahner.) Lincoln and London: University of Nebraska Press.

Walker, James R. 1982. *Lakota Society.* (Edited by Raymond J. De Mallie.) Lincoln and London: University of Nebraska Press.

Weibel-Orlando, Joan. 1989. "Elders and Elderlies: Well-being in Indian Old Age." *American Indian Culture ad Research Journal,* 13(3 & 4): 323–48.

Weibel-Orlando, Joan. 1997. "Grandparenting Styles: The Contemporary American Indian Experience." In Jay Sokolovsky (ed.), *The Cultural Context of Aging: Worldwide Perspectives.* Westport, CT/London: Bergin & Garvey, pp. 139–55.

Weibel-Orlando, Joan. 1999. *Indian Country, L.A.: Maintaining Ethnic Community in Complex Society.* Urbana, IL: University of Illinois Press.

Chapter 3

Claiming Identity in a Nursing Home

Debora A. Paterniti

Living out the end of life in a nursing home is an increasingly common way of aging. Sociologist Erving Goffman (1961) has described the rigid and uniform social world of such "total institutions" as places where persons pass time with little interference from the outside world. In this view, nursing homes homogenize residents' lives so that their separate biographies become the common story of the one-dimensional subject to whom nursing services are provided. This leaves residents undistinguished and their experience framed in terms of the daily practices of "bed-and-body work" – the routine cares of nursing assistance in such facilities (Gubrium 1997[1975]). It is a story bereft of personal meaning, which in the case of the nursing home, dissolves residents' individuality into institutional identities.

The picture becomes more complex, however, when we alter this perspective to take account of the diverse biographical claims put forth by the residents, claims related to what they were earlier in life and who they currently try to be. Residents convey their identities in a world where staff simultaneously construct their own work-related versions of who and what residents are. These accounts tend to focus on the difficulties that staff members encounter in caring for and managing residents. While residents often celebrate their abilities in what they say about themselves, staff commonly recognize resident deficiencies in their own accounts. In nursing homes, residents' personal claims exist against a backdrop of institutionally prescribed understandings that tend to pathologize, if not just homogenize, their actions.

In this chapter, residents' identity claims are distinguished from staff labels in order to reveal how nursing home residents describe their lives on their own terms. As we will see, residents don't leave their pasts behind after they've been admitted to a nursing home, but use past identities, skills, and preferences to bring significance to their present lives (Gubrium 1993). As transitory as this sometimes is, they construct identity and personhood within, and often against, the descriptive imperatives and tendencies of the institution (Paterniti 2000). Seeing the nursing home experience in this way presents residents as biographically active in designating what it means to be a nursing home resident. This, in turn, makes them visible in terms other than those promoted and favored by the institution and its staff.

In the following pages, we meet several residents of Merimore Chronic Care Center whose pseudonyms are Louise Jackson, Mary Kay Lewis, Joan Allen, Lucy van Ives, Nellie Wood, and Billy Brazil. Their lives are framed both institutionally and through the liberating force of their own claims to identity. Merimore is a nursing home for aging and disabled persons. Routine care in the facility includes bathing, feeding, toileting, and exercise. But residents are not merely the objects of such care. If sometimes only momentarily, they actively construct who they are as nursing home residents in their own ways. Nellie tells stories about strange friends and the mishaps she had as a child. Lucy, a singer, moves up and down the halls in her wheelchair encouraging staff sing-a-longs. Louise, in her Oklahoma accent, tests knowledge of television trivia. Billy, a guitarist, still plays his instrument, as he did when he was a member of a famous country-western band.

Residents' accounts of their lives and circumstances are embedded in the daily caregiving routines of institutional life. Their personal narratives distinguish the residents and their identities from the categories and labels staff use to characterize these very same people. In their insistence and complaints, the residents show that being a nursing home resident draws as much from claims to personal meaning as from the institutionalized depictions of bed-and-body work.

Life in an Institution

Upon first entering Merimore to study its way of aging for residents, I took my lead from Goffman and oriented my observations to life in a total institution. I figured I was about to view this way of aging and hear its residents' stories and accounts for their actions in institutional terms. Staff categories and their sense of this world were the points of departure.

Merimore Chronic Care Center, a private, for-profit, long-term care facility principally for the aged and mentally ill, was a facility with modest accommodations and few private rooms. It was recognized as one of the best chronic care facilities in the county where it was located. While some Merimore residents spent as little as a few weeks in respite or recuperative care, most came to the institution to live out the rest of their lives. With the exception of a dozen or so regular family members, who visited weekends or on regular weeknights after dinner, the staff were residents' primary source of interaction.

Although many staff members worked double shifts, in contrast to the residents, staff left the institution to pursue other rounds of life. The ability to leave the institution provided staff a kind of freedom unknown to residents, where the physical walls of Merimore defined the totality of social life for all but a few. Goffman (1961) described total institutions like Merimore as places whose confines prescribe a distinct way of living. The institutional walls of Merimore drew lines of demarcation between the world inside and the world outside. For residents, most of what was outside remained there.

Merimore residents lived in a social world of which I had little knowledge at the time. As I entered this world, I struggled to make my own sense of it. Early on, I noted that breakfast was served as the nurses' aides moved bins of dirty linen to the laundry room, which was repugnant to me at the time. Colorless paint and faded wallpaper provided the backdrop for dozens of bodies seated in the open entryway, some wearing brightly colored robes, others dressed in washed-out patterns, seemingly camouflaged against the faded wallpaper. An older man with dark skin sat tied in his wheelchair with a three-inch webbed belt surrounding him; he had wet his pants. The sight of his pants intensified the smell of urine. The man attempted to move himself down one of the many corridors with his right leg, casting it out in front of him and pulling it back as he leaned forward in a feeble effort to forward his body with the aid of the chair. He stopped his chair next to the post where I stood. As I tried to get my bearings, he tried to maintain his balance. He took a couple of deep breaths, then loudly cleared his throat and spit at the post as I moved past him. I heard a woman scream and looked around at others who seemed either deaf or accustomed to the noise. I heard the man behind me begin to clear his throat again as I disappeared behind the heavy wooden door marked "Staff Only."

Initially, I had come to the facility for summer employment and became involved in the daily lives of many of the individuals I describe here by way of my work as a nurses' aide. I combined this with my role as a participant observer, jotting notes throughout the workday, not only for residents' charts, as my job required, but also to document what it meant to be a resident and in need of care. Maintaining these dual roles wasn't easy. I kept track of the fast pace and the flow of work in the home by monitoring schedules and staff routines. I took notes while waiting for meal carts or at staff meetings, in the laundry room, and in the employee break room.

I carefully recorded the accounts staff provided one another about the residents and about aspects of their work with them.

In time, I focused on residents' own accounts of their experience in the institution, initially out of sheer curiosity. So I started listening to their stories, watching and noting who they were and how they got along. At the end of each shift, I dutifully completed my nurses' aide's notes. Later each evening, I wrote out detailed notes about the institutional lives of those with whom I was working and of the residents I was both providing care and observing.

It wasn't long before I realized that residents told stories that significantly contrasted with those that staff might tell about who and what the residents were. These were accounts and claims that differed in meaning and intention from how staff members often framed their intentions and their lives. Both residents' own narratives and staff members' accounts, not just the latter alone, were part of the Merimore experience, a realization that began to tell me that there was more to this way of aging than simply living out life in a total institution.

Residents as Contingencies of Bed-and-Body Work

First, let me lay out the different ways that residents' lives were viewed and described by staff members, whose principal orientations were to residents as part of their routine work. I focus on the particular residents mentioned earlier. Following this, I'll turn to these residents themselves, especially to their comments and claims in relation to staff's bed-and-body work, which cast an alternative light on the total institution perspective.

At a staff orientation early in my employment at Merimore, the director informed all trainees that we should think of the people at Merimore as "residents," not as "patients." She asked us to use this language so that we might begin to consider Merimore the residents' permanent home. In retrospect, this might have seemed like a humanizing move by the administration, one that might have broken the hold of bed-and-body work on staff's relations to the residents.

I soon learned that it was more rhetoric than fact. First of all, from the staff perspective, residents came to Merimore because they could not meet the physical or psychological requirements necessary for independent living. They could not walk without assistance and had difficulty bathing and dressing themselves. Many could no longer prepare their own meals and required special diets consisting of food that, it turned out, was all the same color or of a mushy consistency. From this perspective, even while they were viewed as "residents," they were significantly bodies in need.

During orientation, new staff members received a photocopied page they would see repeatedly at the end of each shift. It specified the time they were to spend with each resident, in effect defining interactions in terms mandated by institutional rules and State law. The page organized staff members' eight-hour shifts into a series of boxes to be checked when they finished each task. If the boxes were not checked when the head nurse examined the residents' chart, the work was viewed as incomplete. (See Diamond 1992 for a discussion of charting as it relates to interaction with residents.) Staff training emphasized the importance of completing the work designated in the boxes.

The result of the box-based directives was that staff related to residents by their specific categories of resident deficiency. In practice, the categories helped to structure their daily work routines. Residents became a particular type and amount of staff labor and were labeled as such. As contingencies of bed-and-body work, some residents were "feeders;" others fed themselves. Some were "morning showers"; others had their showers during the evening shift. Some residents were "bed-bound"; others wandered aimlessly and were known as "wanderers." The catalog of staff categories or types was extensive and conveyed the contours of staff members' daily concerns and caregiving preoccupations.

Time consumers

Louise Jackson, for one, fell somewhere between the most independent and the most deficient of Merimore residents. No one really knew if Louise could walk, as she spent her entire day and evening in bed. Louise was referred to as a "morning shower" and was frequently dragged by her aide to the shower room in a rolling plastic shower chair under noisy protest. Louise could feed herself, but she mostly picked at her food, stirring it around so it looked as if she tried everything on her tray. A few extra dollars from her monthly social security check afforded her a small stash of sweets, which she ate sparingly. The sweets were probably the only thing that kept Louise's weight close to ninety pounds.

At predictable intervals, Louise laid claim to one of her deficiencies, as the following incident recorded in my field notes illustrates. Note how Louise's claim dominates the aide's work routine.

> "I'm wet!" Louise screamed from her room, as the nurse passed with the medicine cart.
> "I'll tell your aide, Louise," responded the nurse. The nurse looked up near the ceiling as she counted out pills for the resident in bed 14B. She called out, "Louise, press your call light, honey."
> "Oh never mind that, I'm *wet!*" Louise shouted.
> Louise's aide passed the room and shook her head at the nurse. "I heard her," the aide mumbled, "I just changed her sheets an hour ago."
> Spotting her aide, Louise cried out, "Hey, *get back here.*"

The aide called back, "I hear you, Louise. I'll be there in a minute."
"You already had your minute. *I'm wet!*" Louise yelled back.
The aide disappeared around the corner, following the voice of a kitchen worker announcing, "D Ward, your meal cart is ready. D Ward?"

As a patient and later as a ward attendant, sociologist Julius Roth (1963) kept track of the routine work of staff members in tuberculosis sanitariums. Roth noted that in these institutions, "the urgencies and peculiarities of patients must be worked into staff-oriented schedules" (p. 31). Control of residents by staff consisted not only of scheduling tasks, but in defining what was important enough to be scheduled. (Also see Lyman 1993 for a discussion of caregiver control.) At Merimore, this meant that Louise would have to wait until her aide finished the work of lunch, distributing meal trays and assisting "feeders" with their food before attending to Louise. With regard to the completion of such work, staff recognized different types of troublesome residents. One type was a resident who requested too much, luring staff into their rooms to engage them in time-consuming tasks or conversation. Louise Jackson was such a resident – a time consumer.

Feeders

Merimore nurses and aides realized that attending to "legitimate" deficiencies, such as feeding a "feeder" during mealtime, could constitute reasons for not attending to time-consumers such as Louise. Louise finally pressed her call light, but her aide was no longer around to answer it. The kitchen's announcement that the D Ward cart was ready meant that it was time for Louise's aide to feed Mary Kay Lewis.

Mary Kay lay quiet, contracted in her hospital bed. The sheets surrounding her remained undisturbed by bodily movement, precisely the way the last nurses' aide had left them. Some aides were more meticulous than others when they made the bed, changing and charting several changes in a day. They turned Mary Kay not just to her left and right side to prevent bedsores, but propped her up in different positions, even turned on the television set for her. Others left her in one position, peering under her sheets only to see whether a ring of urine would be a telltale sign of Mary Kay's neglect. Near the end of their shift, these aides would change the bedding to make it appear to the staff on the next shift that all of the work charted had actually been completed.

A family picture propped on Mary Kay's bedside table showed her standing outdoors near a large tree, her arms around a woman who could have been a younger version of herself. Crouched beside the two women were a tall, brown-haired man and three blonde, smiling children. That was Mary Kay before her life at Merimore. She was now a withered woman, half the person in the picture, missing most of her teeth and her smile. The picture suggested that she had a family, yet no one visited Mary Kay. In her current state, she was hardly able to take pureed food from the tip of a spoon because of the constant involuntary movement of her tongue. It required a patient aide to feed her.

Mary Kay, a feeder, exemplified the highly burdensome care receiver; the severity of her deficiencies demanded extra and tedious staff time. Mary Kay's twice-weekly shower usually occurred only once a week; her contracted body resisted easy transfer and movement and made showering her difficult. Similarly, changing her bedding required the presence of an additional aide, which was hard to come by in the facility because of high turnover and understaffing.

Troublesome behavior

At Merimore, aides repeatedly encountered behavior they labeled "troublesome," such as Louise's frequent calls to change her bed linens during mealtime and Mary Kay's difficulty eating. Troublesome behavior increased the burden of work, demanding extra tasks and usually involving extra time. Such behaviors were hardships that workers had to learn to manage so that they were only minimally intrusive to their schedules. Leaving a full tray by the bedside or a resident in wet sheets could always be justified by the need to perform other tasks. As a result, Louise waited in a wet bed for her sheets to be changed, and Mary Kay frequently went without food.

Staff members invoked their responsibility for completing other tasks or shortages of time as accounts for leaving work undone or for doing a partial job. It was acknowledged that "everyone knows" certain tasks take precedence over others. What everyone knows was part of the taken-for-granteds of institutional culture, providing reasons for confining work routines to what was viewed as important. It was in this context that residents such as Louise and Mary Kay were time-consumers and feeders, which reduced who and what they were to the demands of bed-and-body work.

Residents as Bed–and–Body Information

Nurses' aides and other staff members were required by law to keep daily records of residents' care and health status. The house physician and residents' individual doctors regularly reviewed this information and also received condensed verbal accounts of residents' status by the head nurses during their monthly visits to the facility. Nurses, aides, and other staff members also passed along bits of information about residents to each other. They communicated this information while waiting for meal carts, while exchanging dirty linens for clean ones, as they made beds, and even while feeding, dressing, walking, and showering residents, often talking about them as if, although bodily present, they were not there at all. Bed-and-body information especially was carried across work shifts. The day shift reported to the evening shift about the happenings during the daylight hours, the evening shift reported to the night shift, and the night shift, in turn, reported to the day shift.

In the context of such information and its flow throughout the facility and between shifts, residents were further depersonalized. As such, what it meant to be a nursing home resident was, simply put, a matter of record. Because records and the flow of bed-and-body information centered on work assignments and task completion, residents in effect became bits of work-relevant information.

The following field notes illustrate how nursing staff informationally framed some resident activities and interactions. Notice how skeptical the framings can be, conveyed as if residents' claims about themselves, their needs, and their possessions were fictional, not part of alternative realities of bed-and-body work. While some residents were indeed confused and demented, the overall tenor of related information tended to frame legitimate complaints as irrational or unwarranted demands on staff time.

> After the head nurse on the day shift reported the overall shape of the day to the evening nurse, she remarked that Joan Allen, a ninety-year-old resident, claimed she was "missing four dollars." The evening nurse added that Joan also had recently complained about missing clothing to the night nurse.
> Later, the head nurse explained, "Beth [the night nurse] left you a note about the missing clothing, right before [the incident of the missing money], and now it's money, huh?"
> The head nurse continued, "[Over] the weekend, she went with her son for Mother's Day and she couldn't find her pearls. She said somebody had taken them. Okay, so Susan [the nurses' aide] went into her room and *found them* in her drawer." The evening nurse shook her head in disgust.
> Later, during report time from the evening to night shift, the evening nurse added, "[Joan] told Lillian [the day nurse] that she lost four dollars, but I asked Joan about it and she said it happened a long time ago, so I don't know how come she just complained today. And then one time she said that she was missing her pearls, and Bea found them in her *drawer*. We don't know whether she is just kind of confused or her memory's failing or what."

Staff reports not only provided information about a work shift, but framed residents' claims in a particular way. In this case, collectively, the nurses came to the conclusion that Joan's definition of the situation was flawed with respect to what had actually happened. Therefore, commentary by reporting nurses indicated staff would need to question all of Joan Allen's future claims because of her potentially failing memory.

Staff seldom accepted the word of residents over that of the staff. For example, while reviewing nurses' aide notes for the previous evening shifts, a nurse noticed that Lucy van Ives had gone without a shower for two weeks. Lucy's regular shower times were Tuesday and Thursday mornings, but sometimes early in the afternoon, on the days that her aide was very busy. A month of high staff turnover meant some work tasks had not been completed. A new staff member – one already transferred to a less labor-intensive wing of Merimore – had charted that Lucy had refused three consecutive showers. Furthermore, last Tuesday's shower was not charted. Concerned about this, the nurse called Lucy's Wednesday aide to the nurses' station and the following exchange transpired.

> "I want you to give Lucy a shower today," the nurse stated firmly.
> The aide answered, "Today isn't her regular shower day. I still have one shower left." It was approaching one o'clock, and the conscientious aide grew concerned that she would not finish her assigned tasks by the end of her shift.
> "I'll sign your overtime sheet," the nurse persisted, "Lucy really needs her shower today."
> Complying with the nurse's request, the aide gave in and headed to Lucy's room and announced that she would be next in line for a shower. Lucy was in her room playing her accordion. Margaret Hyde, her roommate, was resting in bed. She came out from underneath the bed covers when Lucy stopped playing. "Tuesday is *my* shower day," Lucy refused. "I had my shower yesterday."
> "Lucy, the nurse told me that you didn't have a shower yesterday," the aide flatly replied.

The reality was that Lucy's shower had not been charted. Sociologist Timothy Diamond (1992) has noted in his work as a nurses' aide that when information is not in the chart, in practice it is as if occurrences such a showers indeed never happened. Matters of record call into question the truth claims of residents, casting the realities of their lives exclusively in terms of the staff's bed-and-body information. This was later confirmed when the following exchange took place.

> Wanting to believe that Lucy had her shower the previous day, the aide reported back to the nurse, "Lucy told me that she had a shower yester-day."
> "Oh, don't believe what she tells you," the nurse replied, exasperated.
> "I want *you* to give her a shower *today*."
> The aide plodded back to Lucy's room, arms full of towels.

Residents' Own Identity Claims

While bed-and-body concerns dominate staff characterizations of residents' lives and selves, Merimore residents did not define themselves solely in these institutional terms. Residents brought identity claims of their own to nursing home life. They weren't simply mouthpieces for bed-and-body identities, as the concept of total institution might suggest. Instead, residents framed what they were on their own terms, different from accounts of their actions conveyed by the staff. Indeed, at Merimore, residents seldom acknowledged work routines as the primary features of their daily lives or as a consideration in characterizing their actions. Consider the diverse ways that the following three residents conveyed important dimensions of their lives.

Nellie Wood

As in other settings, casual sociability was a way of passing time at Merimore. But, for physically incapacitated residents, it also permitted a measure of interpersonal contact that their bodies couldn't provide. Talk permitted Nellie Wood a freedom beyond what her crippled body could support. Partially deaf and ridden with arthritis, Nellie spent all of her time confined to her bed. Her steely blue eyes were covered with a layer of opaque film from cataracts she apparently had for some time. In spite of her interest in current events, the thickness of her cataracts kept her from reading, so she relied entirely on the minimal information delivered by the staff and nightly visits from her son, who would often read the newspaper to her. Nellie was a "twice-weekly morning shower" and a "feeder" due to her poor eyesight and gnarled hands. But, interestingly enough, Nellie was an avid storyteller. Her favorite account was the story of Hennie Teet, which is excerpted from field notes of interactions with her.

> Have I ever told you the story of Hennie Teet? I haven't? Oh, I like to tell this one. Anyway, Hennie Teet wasn't his real name; that was just a name that people in town made up for him.... When Hennie Teet came into the store, I had my back to him. He asked me for ten pounds of oats and when I turned around, I noticed that his pants were unzipped, and I could see *everything*. Well, I was so embarrassed. [Nellie laughed and shook her head] So I got him his oats, and when I turned around to give them to him, I couldn't look him in the eye, I just stared at the ceiling! [Nellie laughed] I was sure I told you that one before. I tell everybody the story of Hennie Teet.

Indeed, Nellie had told everyone the story. The famous story had become all staff members' introduction to her as a resident. Along with the story of Hennie Teet came tales of the pranks of Nellie and her friends, her work in the family store, and the escapades of her young children. Telling stories kept Nellie's mind and body alive; her eyes sparkled and her nearly fist-like hands waved enthusiastically when she discovered a newcomer who was willing to listen. Most new staff members were eager to hear Nellie's stories, which provided a reprieve from the pace of the work routine and offered information about her that could not be read in Nellie's chart or heard in staff accounts of their work. Nellie's stories made her into a nursing resident who otherwise would be conveyed exclusively in institutional terms.

Most staff members heard Nellie's story of Hennie Teet more than once. As they became familiar with her stories, veteran staff members tried to avoid them, giving staff neophytes the onerous task of feeding Nellie. Seasoned staff members found no respite in Nellie's storytelling; through repetition, the stories became old, tedious, and an impediment to the efficient completion of their caregiving tasks. The stories definitely made feeding Nellie more time consuming. They were forced to wait impatiently to force Nellie to take a few drops of food from a spoon between story lines. On more than one occasion, when it was a seasoned nurses' aide's turn to care for Nellie, I observed mounds of pureed vegetables and meat being stuffed into her mouth between breaths, hastening the feeding and quelling Nellie's storytelling in the process.

But Nellie was no pushover. Detecting the work of hasty staff, Nellie could meet them with an outstretched arm and crumpled hand. Closing her mouth and turning her head, she would announce, "That's it. I've had enough." Refusing to listen to Nellie meant that an aide would leave Nellie's room with a nearly full tray of food, with his or her work unfinished, and with little to document in Nellie's chart as completed service activity.

Residents' storytelling could literally bring residents to life in terms of qualities beyond their own deficiencies. Storytelling thus allowed the residents to transcend the institutional rhythms surrounding their daily lives. Through her stories, for example, Nellie could transform the routine work of mealtime into a social occasion, making mealtime into something other than an opportunity to play out the role of a "feeder."

Lucy van Ives

Lucy van Ives also assembled bits of her biography to carve a special space for herself within the nursing home's bed-and-body work schedule. Lucy frequently refused her shower so that she could listen to her records or play her accordion, aspects of life experience she brought with her into the facility. She characteristically would attempt to mimic songs from the latest album given to her by the activity director. It was her unique way of being a nursing home resident, something that distinguished her from other residents.

Lucy was in her sixties, was mildly retarded, and had a diagnosis of schizophrenia. She had been institutionalized since her early twenties. When the state governor ordered the hospital in which she resided closed, Lucy was moved to Merimore, a common outcome of state hospital deinstitutionalization at the time. Along with a few articles of clothing and her own wheelchair, Lucy had brought with her a small accordion, two long-playing record albums, and an old record player. Soon after she arrived at Merimore, Lucy announced that she was a singer and became the self-appointed source of entertainment for the Center's rare special events.

Lucy spent most of her days at Merimore repeatedly listening to one side of a single record and trying to play the same songs. Even though her roommate, Margaret, assisted Lucy at mealtime and on those occasions when special treats were distributed, Margaret usually stayed in the ward lounge or sat out at the main entrance when Lucy decided to play her music.

Lucy used her accordion playing to lay claim to a distinct identity in the nursing home. To herself, she wasn't simply "a shower" or "a feeder," but a singer with something to offer those who cared to listen and, she hoped, to enjoy. An excerpt from my field notes provides a glimpse of the particular way that, on one occasion, Lucy insisted on being a nursing home resident.

> Lucy was playing her accordion when the aide approached her again, making yet another attempt to finish work that wasn't yet charted.
> "Lucy, I have to give you a shower today. You don't have a choice," the aide insisted.
> Lucy stopped playing her accordion. "Yes I do. Today is *not* my shower day. I had one *yesterday*, and I won't go. I'm playing my songs right now." Lucy pulled her accordion back against her chest and resumed playing.

With this, Lucy insisted on a way of being a resident that amounted to being more than "a shower." Just as Nellie refused to eat when aides would not listen patiently to her stories, Lucy refused to interrupt her musical moments for an institutional task. More than just playing music or telling a story, Lucy's and Nellie's insistence challenged institutional demands for being a passively receptive nursing home resident and a routine institutional identity.

Billy Brazil

Billy Brazil was admitted to Merimore just after his fifty-second birthday. An attractive man, his disability made him seem at least ten years beyond his actual age. He was ambulatory, but walking was an effort for Billy. So, like many others in the home, Billy spent his days in a wheelchair.

Yet Billy was no mere wheelchair user. He had had quite a "wild life," according to his many recollections on the subject. Billy described himself as one of the best musicians in the business, playing backup guitar for famous country-western performers like Willie Nelson and Johnny Paycheck. He would tell stories about his adventures and concerts, and once commented, "Back in those days, I would play my guitar, smoke my cigarettes, and get high on speed. That's why I'm here [at Merimore] you know, 'cause that kind of life gets rough, all the smoking and the women and the drinking."

Billy was diagnosed with chronic obstructive pulmonary disease, which forced him to be on a near constant flow of oxygen. He could do without his oxygen only for short periods of time. During his twice-weekly showers, he frequently struggled for air by the time the aide brought him back to his room. Serious problems breathing required the nurse to raise his oxygen intake. It often forced Billy to spend the night sitting up in his chair. As bed-and-body work, Billy was an evening shower and someone who could feed himself. Most days, he required only minimal assistance with dressing. Staff described him as "an easy patient." He wasn't a time consumer.

When Billy came to Merimore, he brought his guitar. Although he claimed to have had a number of guitars, he argued that this particular instrument was his favorite. Billy would strum familiar tunes like Jimmy Buffet's "Margarita-ville" and Van Morrison's "Brown-Eyed Girl." On Sundays, when no showers were scheduled, there was a more leisurely work pace. Staff members from C Ward would encourage Billy to sit at the entrance to Merimore and play his guitar. At other times, in his room, Billy would take his guitar from his bed and, playing a few bars, would recount one of his numerous bus trips or wild party nights.

Life in and about Billy's room regularly took staff to places beyond those of bed-and-body work. Billy saw most people in the facility as different from himself; other residents were older, more dependent, and more troublesome to staff. Staff saw Billy as different, too. As an easy patient, being a nursing home resident for Billy captured a world that staff members who took the time entered into *with* him, on *his* own terms. Easy patients such as Billy reminded staff that the individuals they cared for were something in addition to being nursing home residents.

Accepting Residents' Identity Claims

The identities of bed-and-body work, while prevalent, did not fully determine how staff related even to troublesome residents. Being a nursing home resident was not merely a subjective reproduction of staff timetables and institutional charts, but was also shaped by staff members' recognition of residents' identity claims. If Billy Brazil was a case in point at the easy end of the care spectrum, such recognition wasn't solely directed to easy residents.

In the following account, we again find Lucy at odds with the nurses' aide concerning the need to be showered. Lucy's insistence on her own choice in the matter worked against the scheduled demands of bed-and-body work. Lucy kept playing her accordion as the aide attempted to reason with her, explaining that giving Lucy a shower was something she *had* to do, not something she *wanted* to do, even if it wasn't scheduled for that day. Lucy didn't respond to the aide, but instead played on and sang more forcefully. Stymied by Lucy's singing of a familiar melody from *The Wizard of Oz*, the aide chose to sing-a-long with her, accepting her momentary claim to personhood.

> "There's a land that I heard of once in a lullaby," the aide joined in.
> Lucy stopped singing and lowered her accordion. She closed one eye and cocked her head to the left. Still peering out of the one eye, she said to the aide, "Now quit that, you're throwing me off key." Lucy started to lift the accordion back into position.
> Seeing an opening, the aide inquired, "Lucy, do you like to sing in the shower?"
> "Yeah," Lucy nodded, looking down at her accordion.
> Trying not to sound desperate, the aide asked, "How would you like to sing in the shower with me?"
> Lucy pursed her lips and squinted both eyes, considering the offer. "Okay, take me to my room, so I can leave my accordion."

By accepting Lucy's sing-a-long and thus confirming her claim to being a singer at the moment, the aide got Lucy to consider taking a shower at a time other than her normally scheduled one. Recognition of Lucy's way of wanting to be a resident then and there allowed the aide to accomplish her work.

Legitimate claims to any system of beliefs or way of being depend on the existence of organized support for them (Berger and Luckmann 1966; Snow and Machalek 1982). While the normal routines of nursing homes generally threatened residents' personal identity claims, institutional work requirements can also complement patients' attempts to sustain personhood. Louise's strategies to attract staff to her room are exemplary. Louise was aware that staff were obliged to change soiled linens, and she knew that her wet bed offered the opportunity to interact with staff members. This provided an excellent opportunity for her to test staff's knowledge of TV trivia, and, in the process, establish herself as a trivia expert. The following incident taken from my field notes is illustrative.

> After mealtime, Louise's aide returned to Louise's room. "I'm back, Louise," the aide announced. "Oh, what do you want?" Louise replied,

postponing up her bid for attention for the moment. The nurse raised her eyebrows and started back toward her medicine cart in the hallway.

Louise nestled further down under the covers of her bed and reached for the volume knob on her 12–inch black and white television set. "Fix that, will you?" she pointed to the antennae without looking up. "Right there," she grunted in the affirmative as the fuzzy picture gained some clarity. "I think I can make it even better," the aide persisted. "There," she added.

Although the picture was still a bit fuzzy, Louise nodded with contentment. Nose pointed at the center of the screen, Louise's poor eyesight necessitated her to perch herself only inches from the screen, blocking it from view with her mussed salt-and-pepper hair. "Do you remember when he was just a boy?" she asked of Ron Howard's character, Opie, from *Mayberry R.F.D.* Louise considered herself an expert at television trivia, especially when it came to television shows with children. Louise's interest in TV show trivia set her apart from others in the facility. Louise was from Oklahoma. Her favorite characters, Opie, Pa, and Barney from the *Mayberry* series reminded her of the past. "Bring that a bit closer," she requested, pointing to the rolling bedside table supporting the TV.

The wobbly wheels made the table nearly impossible to move without lifting it completely. The aide pulled the table, and it caught the bed sheet. "Louise, would you be interested in sitting up in the wheelchair and watching your TV while I change your sheets?" the aide persisted. Louise snapped, "I don't wanna get out of bed."

"How 'bout I watch the program with you while I change the sheets?' the aide inquired. This piqued Louise's interest. Louise agreed, and the aide lifted Louise's 89–pound body out of bed and into her wheelchair, where she sat, quizzing the aide while the aide did her work.

By recognizing Louise's claim to how she wanted to spend her time – and her claim to what kind of person she actually was (a TV trivia buff) – the aide completed her own work tasks. At the same time, Louise, the TV trivia expert, found an audience to challenge. Louise's unique identity was allowed to surface as the aide managed to get her own work done.

Sometimes patient strategies for asserting personal identities backfire, however. For a while, Louise's nurse grew concerned over the number of times aides charted that they were called to Louise's room to change bed linens and refill her water pitcher. One afternoon, a nurse saw Louise pour water from her pitcher into her bed just before she announced, "I'm wet!" Being "found out" jeopardized any calls that were otherwise justified, and Louise had to wait for staff attention, her need to be who she was receding into the background in the process.

If Louise and others resisted the use of typical staff labels and conventions for defining residents, a small number of residents regularly escaped the rigid interactional parameters of routine work. Billy Brazil was one of them. Billy enjoyed his interactions with the staff and staff members enjoyed Billy. As noted earlier, he often invited them into his room during their breaks or at the end of their shifts. Billy had a private room where staff could reveal their concerns, even hide from other staff members and residents who sought them out at busy times of the day. Even staff who worked overtime visited Billy's room at the end of their long shift. Some returned after finishing their shifts, sneaking onto Billy's balcony and bringing cigarettes and beer to ostensibly share remnants of Billy's past life. Staff members appreciated Billy's company, especially when he played his guitar. Nurses' aides took Billy to be one of their own, regularly entering into his world in their more leisure moments and sustaining personhood on his terms as they did so.

Conclusion

In their encounters with staff, Merimore residents were not just puppets of institutional routine. They were also active agents in establishing their own identities. A total institution perspective shortchanges this active participation in establishing who and what residents are. Many residents struggled to maintain a sense of personhood and a way of aging that was their own, not merely the institution's. Their identities might well have been fragile and uncertain, but they were, in some measure, formulators of their senses of self.

Active and yet fragile, residents' identity claims were largely overwhelmed by the predictable institutional categories that identified residents as mere objects of bed-and-body work. Diamond (1992) notes that "patient" is a word that is close in origin to the word "passive" (p. 129). Although staff orientation taught that a Merimore resident was a person as much as he or she was a patient, work in the total institution, in practice, required residents to be passive recipients of staff care taking. Institutional categories of bed-and-body work provided convenient labels for dealing with work in the institution. Organizing patients in terms of labels such as "time consumer," "feeder," and "trouble maker" not only made work predictable, but also proved difficult for patient to challenge.

Nonetheless, Nellie, Lucy, Louise, and Billy and other Merimore residents laid their own claims to self, which, like staff categories of bed-and-body work, were a part of their day-to-day existence. These residents were not completely the passive recipients of bed-and-body work nor of the identities prescribed to them by institutional tasks. Nellie, Lucy, Louise, and Billy were active persons in the constructions of their own personhood. They were never the complete by-products of institutional routines and rationality.

At the same time, personal identity claims were not purely individual achievements. The possibilities for being a nursing home resident on one's own terms at Merimore were not only served by the claims put forth by people like Nellie, Lucy, Louise, and Billy, but were also undergirded by staff acceptance. As we recall the varied ways Nellie, Lucy, and others described their experiences and identities in interaction with staff members, we are reminded that nursing home residents' identities are products also of what institutional staff members permit them to be, providing direction for limiting institutional totality in relation to the demands of bed-and-body work.

References

Berger, Peter L., and Luckmann, Thomas. 1966. *The Social Construction of Reality*. Garden City, New York: Anchor Books.

Diamond, Timothy. 1992. *Making Gray Gold: Narratives of Nursing Home Care*. Chicago: University of Chicago Press.

Goffman, Erving. 1961. *Asylums: Essays on the Social Situation of Mental Patients and Other Inmates*. Garden City, New York: Anchor Books.

Gubrium, Jaber F. 1997[1975]. *Living and Dying at Murray Manor*. Charlottesville, VA: University Press of Virginia.

Gubrium, Jaber F. 1993. *Speaking of Life: Horizons of Meaning for Nursing Home Residents*. New York: Aldine de Gruyter.

Lyman, Karen A. 1993. *Day In and Day Out With Alzheimer's: Stress in Caregiving Relationships*. Philadelphia, Pennsylvania: Temple University Press.

Paterniti, Debora A. 2000. "The Micropolitics of Identity in Adverse Circumstance: A Study of Identity-Making in a Total Institution." *Journal of Contemporary Ethnography*, 29: 93–119.

Roth, Julius A. 1963. *Timetables*. New York: Bobbs-Merrill.

Snow, David A., and Machalek, Richard. 1982. "On the Fragility of Unconventional Beliefs." *Journal for the Scientific Study of Religion*, 21: 15–26.

Part II

Adaptation

Chapter 4

Three Childless Men's Pathways into Old Age

Tanya Koropeckyj-Cox

Parenting has traditionally been a marker and a means of entry into maturity and full adult status. For women in particular, a life course without children has been regarded as problematic and often stigmatizing (Fisher 1991; May 1995). Social norms are echoed in developmental theories of the adult life course, either assuming or prescribing parenthood as a central component of maturation in middle and old age. For example, Erik Erikson's theory of life course stages includes *generativity* – an investment in the next generation – as a crucial developmental task in middle adulthood. Parenthood is identified as a natural and "instinctual" (Erikson 1997: 52–3) pathway for achieving generativity, though Erikson acknowledges that it is neither necessary nor sufficient for adult development (1963: 267). David Gutmann's (1987; Gutmann and Huyck 1994) conceptualization of personality development and gender, on the other hand, specifically singles out parenthood as a uniquely important catalyst for moving adults through successive stages. He explicitly centers life stages around parental and post-parental transitions.

For the cohorts who entered adulthood during the post-World War II baby boom, the pressures to bear children and follow conventional life paths were especially intense. The quest for stability and security following the Depression and the war years placed a high value on domesticity and procreation, defining both men and women by their familial roles and contributions (May 1988, 1995; Coontz 1992). Adult development, maturity, and the normative life course were defined as contingent on the social status and experience of parenting; childless adults, particularly women, were pitied, regarded with scorn, or seen as psychologically deficient (May 1995). Even as attitudes became more tolerant in the 1970s, childlessness was still an unusual life path and voluntary childlessness in particular was viewed with suspicion and criticism (see Veevers 1980; Blake 1979).

Research on women over the last three decades has brought to light the consequences of these normative pressures for women and the dilemmas that they raise throughout the life course. In contrast, very little is known about the place of parenthood and the implications of childlessness for men in the life course and in old age. This chapter explores the life stories and the different ways of aging of three childless, older men.[1] As men of advanced age, they are part of an "invisible minority" within the predominantly female elderly population that has only recently garnered attention among sociologists and gerontologists (Thompson 1994; Rubinstein 1997). As childless men, they are doubly invisible. Although childless adults make up close to one-fifth of the older population, their non-normative life path and the tendency until the last decade for research on families and reproduction to focus only on women, has provided very little insight into the experiences of men who have navigated a childless life course.

The three men whose stories are presented in this chapter are all currently married, and their marriages are a focal point of their concerns and well-being in old age. Their diverse circumstances, attitudes, and decisions document the variety of ways in which men navigate adult life. Their accounts describe the non-normative life paths that led to their childlessness and the current perspectives that shape their sense of the future. For one man, an active lifestyle focused on physical pursuits and marital companionship provides the basis for a fulfilled, "child-free" life. The second man's story highlights a later life transition into volunteer work with other senior citizens, providing a social resource for himself and his wife and giving him new perspectives on vulnerability in old age. The third man's account reveals a process of deliberate substitution, as he negotiates mutual obligations and a commitment for future care with his nephews. Each life story illuminates varied meanings of manhood and aging as each man describes different ways of constructing social networks in the present and expectations for the future.

Child-Free and Couple-Focused

Ben Andrews[2] looks like a television commercial or magazine ad for "aging well." A slim, handsome man, he appears younger than his 68 years. In many ways, he embodies the idealized vision of healthy, physically fit, and active aging. Still, his child-free and athletic lifestyle represents an unusual pathway into older adulthood.

Married and living with his wife who is more than 15 years his junior, Ben has never had children. He explains that he and his wife could have become parents after they married. He was 53 and his wife, in her early thirties, was probably physiologically able to have had one or more children if they had chosen to do so. Instead, they actively prevented pregnancy, initially through contraception and then permanently, through surgery.

When asked about the reasons for their childlessness, Ben and his wife give different but complementary responses. Ben explains that at 53, he believed that he was too old to enter into parenthood. He notes that, "by the time that [children] were in their growing up period, it's better to have, say, a 30-year-old parent than a 60-year-old parent." His wife, Linda, emphasizes that it was not just the circumstance of age that determined their choices. Explaining their deliberate decision to forego parenthood, she notes that their lives were quite complete without adding children.

> The reason we didn't have children was because there really wasn't room in our lives for children, in addition to age. We just enjoyed being together so much, and we were both working and we didn't have that much time, that we just wanted to be together. Maybe it was selfish.... He always said that if I wanted a child we'd have a child. If I didn't, I didn't. I wanted one when I was first married in my other life [to my first husband], to hold a rotten marriage together. And fortunately we didn't have any.... But this one, we had so little time, we just wanted to be together. We didn't want that responsibility.

When probed about whether he had any regrets or concerns about their childlessness, Ben admits to feeling some occasional regret but it is mainly focused on his wife: "It would have been a lot better if Linda had somebody as she gets older and I'm not around." When asked specifically about any regrets or disadvantages for himself, he admits, "I haven't really given it a thought."

Still at an early, "young-old" point in his aging, Ben's life is centered on activity and a fulfilling, close relationship with his wife. Describing himself as "semi-retired," he continues to work several days a week as a professional consultant. The other days he devotes to a fairly intensive and time-consuming regimen of running, physical fitness, and related self-care routines, including frequent ice pack and other restorative treatments. Both Ben and his wife compete in local races. He enjoys the competition as well as the company of other runners, explaining, "Runners are different from other competitive athletes. They are not interested in 'did you win,' but in 'how did you do today?'...And runners seem to be a much more friendly group of people than any other sport." The focus of his competitive running is on individual improvement and performance, but the pursuit of running also represents a mutually supportive activity and shared commitment central to Ben and Linda's marriage.

At 68, Ben does not consider himself to be at all old, though he describes with a mixture of pride and annoyance the various sports injuries for which he has been treated. Indeed, his devotion to physical fitness represents a paradox in his construction of his own aging. In many ways, he describes the rigor and physical enjoyment of running, including the endorphin "high" of long-distance running, as a means of avoiding the declines associated with aging. He recounts his physicians' comments about his superb cardiovascular fitness with a sense of achievement. At the same time, he has endured multiple orthopedic surgeries to repair the cumulative, permanent damage caused by his running. This contradiction may be inherent to rigorous sport, where playing through pain and enduring the risk of injury are taken for granted and where the pursuit of performance may simultaneously deny the force of aging while compelling the athlete to face its unavoidable advance.

Ben admits that the prospect of losing his ability to run would be "absolutely devastating." When probed about his future plans and expectations, he recounts the following description by his doctors: "Ben's objective is to run forever, to be able to run forever." His doctors, however, have pointed out that he is "running against time," implying the inevitability of aging and irreparable physical decline.

Although much about Ben's lifestyle and outlook suggest a denial of the aging process, his accounts reveal a more subtle subtext of coping with chronic illness and considering his own mortality. Both he and his wife mention several times that he has chronic respiratory problems that occasionally flare up into disruptive episodes requiring medical attention. These episodes are very stressful for both of them. Although he appreciates the love and care provided by his wife, he describes his experience of the sick role and his wife's caregiving as difficult for both of them.

The most potent element in their construction of their lives together and their consideration of mortality is the unusual difference in Ben and Linda's ages. The large age gap of over 15 years is invoked in describing their pathway into marriage and permanent childlessness, but it remains a salient theme throughout their accounts, shaping their interactions with each other and their plans for the future. Dating back to the time when they were first married, Ben recounts the importance of this age gap.

> **Ben:** That was one of the considerations [future planning] when we got married. I said, "You know, there's [over 15] years difference, and unless I'm a freak . . . or unless you have an accident, I'll be gone before you are . . . . You're going to be pretty much alone." And my wife was a very meek person when we got married. People used to walk all over her. Her parents, everybody. No more. She's her own woman now.

Interviewer: Did you have anything to do with that transition?
Ben: I had everything to do with it . . . She's her own person, and that's important . . . All the financial things that I have done . . . She's well aware how it ticks. She isn't going to be lost like her mother. . . . Linda is skilled, and she knows how to do that. So she's going to be self-sufficient as an individual.

Clear in his account is the assumption that he would predecease her and leave her a widow on her own. This expectation is probably not unusual in many marriages, given that men are often older than their wives and women on average can expect to outlive men by 5 to 8 years. The particular age difference in Ben and Linda's case may only underscore this gendered expectation of female longevity and widowhood. While many men of Ben's cohort share the concern to provide financially for their wives into old age, Ben's account is striking in its description of very consciously influencing what he has regarded as his wife's ability to function independently. Within this affectionate, companionate marriage, and one that interestingly has not seen the presumed gender imbalances of parenting (a concern particularly emphasized in Gutmann's work), Ben is unabashedly candid about his role in shaping his wife's development into an assertive, independent person. Whether this admission reveals an underlying power imbalance or a progressive attempt to promote egalitarianism within this marriage is a question that cannot be fully explored with the material available.

In addition to the assumption of Linda's greater longevity, the age difference seems to be linked with an almost palpable sense of limited time. Ben and Linda are very much focused on each other, keeping each other happy and enjoying each day that they have together. Ben responds to a query about his "job in life" with the concise answer: "to make my wife happy . . . because we have such a great relationship." When asked about whether there was anything in their lives that they would do differently if they could, Linda notes that she wishes she had met her husband sooner so that they might have had more time to spend together. In a retrospective account like this, it is impossible to discern whether this sense of immediacy has been characteristic of their entire relationship or whether more recent events, concerns, or illnesses may have provoked a greater concern about Ben's mortality.

To the extent that Ben and Linda have planned for their future, their actions have focused mainly on financial security. More generally, their orientation toward the future emphasizes maintaining a healthy lifestyle as a way of staying active for as long as possible. Their hope is to avoid the physical and emotional pain of decline and disability. Given their relatively young ages and high level of physical health, it may not be surprising that they do not mention having made any practical plans or preparations for the possibilities of decline in the future. On the other hand, the difficulties that they have already experienced with his chronic health problems suggest that they would likely be hard hit by any unexpected major change or challenge. In particular, their physical fitness and Ben's older age appear to be taken for granted; the possibility that they might someday be faced with a serious disability with which they could not cope by themselves or that Ben could outlive his wife are contingencies for which they would be unprepared.

While much research on aging has emphasized the importance of social networks, Ben and Linda's accounts are striking in their minimal mention of social ties. Their social investments are focused on each other, resulting in a mutually satisfying marriage that appears to be relatively insulated from other social connections. Ben notes that he enjoys his contact with work associates, as well as the connections he and Linda have made through their interests in running, collecting coins, and participating in their civic improvement association. Thus, reminiscent of the concerns raised by contemporary social commentators (e.g., Bellah et al. 1985), Ben and Linda's social networks appear to be based on individual lifestyle choices; they constitute a set of relatively weak social ties that are contingent on specific interactions or involvements and represent minimal commitment. There is little mention of relationships that might transcend specific involvements, raising the question of whether they would have anyone in their social networks to whom they could turn in an emergency or for a long-term problem. Theirs is a close marital relationship within the context of a loose social network of peers with shared interests or location. Such a pattern may be satisfying and sufficient in the present, but other research on older childless couples has suggested that the greater insularity and isolation of childless marriages may leave the partners more vulnerable to loss or decline (Johnson and Catalano 1981).

On the other hand, Ben and Linda's way of aging – actively and athletically – may be at the vanguard of the future of aging. Physical activity is seen as a positive lifestyle choice that is encouraged by physicians and health professionals, though certainly not with the kind of rigor that the Andrews undertake. Activity has been associated with decreasing the risks for particular health problems, and longitudinal studies of older adults suggest a potential advantage of physical fitness and healthy lifestyles for increasing longevity. Among the cohorts born since the 1930s and 1940s, the decline of infectious disease and overall improvements in nutrition and lifestyle may represent the potential for new ways of aging – with significantly more years of active life and overall life expectancy compared to earlier cohorts.

Husband–Provider and Community Volunteer

At 67, Dennis Kroft has experienced a very different life path, defined by a long, steady blue-collar career and valued social connections and commitments. Dennis dropped out of high school to join the army during World War II. His four years of service represent a significant part of his life story, and his status as a war veteran has remained an important part of his identity and social life. Both he and his wife have a long history of active involvement with the local branch of a war veterans' organization, and he spends several hours every Sunday tending the bar at the Knights of Columbus hall. Dennis had a variety of blue-collar jobs before spending 38 years working as a mechanic in a manufacturing company. Now retired, he describes himself as financially independent and is pleased with this security after a steady career of hard work.

Dennis and his wife, Ellen, have been married for over 40 years. He describes his wife as the most important person in his life, and he regards taking care of her and himself as his primary responsibilities. Although relatively talkative in his interview, Dennis does not reveal much about his private life. His account does convey the importance of his marriage to him, but he doesn't elaborate much. The overall sense is one of satisfaction and stability. For example, when asked about the happiest times in his life, he identifies his return from the war but notes that "everything else [in his life] was normal." Unlike Ben and Linda's open affection and inward focus, Dennis and Ellen have pursued interests and involvements, both separately and together, with an orientation outward to their community. They joined a local senior center together, and they are both active in its activities. They seem to be embedded in a wide network of social relationships, including cherished, long-term friendships with their current and former neighbors.

When asked about his childlessness, Dennis explains that he and his wife had always assumed that they would have children. They had tried once, but his wife had a miscarriage – "it just got messed up physically or internally or something like that. And we just couldn't have any children. Not that we didn't want them." He notes that he has felt both regret and satisfaction with his childlessness: "I'd say 50–50, you know. Sometimes you wish you have. And sometimes you're glad you didn't have." When probed about his wife's feelings, he answers, "I don't know – she never mentioned it." Dennis and his wife have long accepted their unanticipated childlessness, and his accounts suggest that the childless status has not been problematic for them or their marriage.

Dennis does not recall feeling stigmatized or marginalized because of his childless status, in part because of close social ties that he and Ellen have maintained with friends and their children: "All my friends had kids. And I could say that you took care of those children. . . . [When they were in their 30s and 40s] there was another couple the same age as us. Their kids were over our house more than they were in their own house." As those friends' children have grown older, Dennis and Ellen have remained in contact: "They still come back to us, the kids. Even though they're grown and have their own kids . . . They still come back to us. It was more or less just like we were their aunt or uncle, or something like that." In addition to these fictive kin ties, Dennis and Ellen have always remained close with their nieces and nephews. Thus, Dennis and Ellen feel that they have influenced a younger generation even without having been parents themselves. Dennis also believes that he and his wife could depend on their nieces and nephews for help if they should need it in the future.

A significant aspect of Dennis' current activities and self-identity is the volunteer work that he began several years ago as a driver for a local agency that serves senior citizens. Two days each week, Dennis drives a van that picks up elders from their homes and takes them to senior centers, medical appointments, and shopping trips. The service is subsidized by funds from the state lottery, providing an affordable resource for elders who cannot drive. More importantly, Dennis explains, the service is a social and practical lifeline for isolated and frail elders.

> It's amazing the service it provides. I mean, I never realized people can't get out of the house. If it wasn't for us picking some of these people right here up, they would never get out of the house, . . . even to go grocery shopping. . . . Go to the hairdressers. Go anyplace. They'd never get out of the house . . . . And the kids don't care, . . . don't care about them at all. It's really pathetic.

As most of the elders he serves live alone, he recounts several episodes in which he has found elders in need of help or medical attention. With no one else around to check on them or assist them, Dennis has been their first line of help.

After a long career in blue-collar positions, Dennis has found this volunteer work to be particularly gratifying. As he explains,

> It's a great service, this place [the senior center] and the [transport program]. And it's enjoyable. I worked for a big manufacturing company for 37 years. Very seldom anybody ever thanked me for doing something. [Now] every one of them gets on and off that bus everyday – thanks you for bringing them. It feels like you're doing something helpful. I mean for them, if they can't get out of their house, you're providing a touch with the community for them. You're helping them keep going.

He notes that his volunteer work has "opened his eyes" to the realities of aging and the vulnerability of frail elders. He is glad to be able to help those who need it. At the same time, he does not view his involvement as a responsibility, but as a fully voluntary commitment – something special that he does because he can and because he enjoys it.

From the point of view of his own life course, Dennis's experience as a driver has given him a new perspective on aging, family, and childlessness. He has seen many elders who are alone and without much help or support despite being parents with grown children. He explains that often the families are not aware of their elder's needs or health declines, and he describes circumstances when the social worker at the senior center has been the one to recognize a problem and convey it to the elder's family members. He has watched how she informally monitors the status of the seniors at the center and attends to any signs that they might need help in taking care of themselves. Dennis's criticism makes clear that adult children, if available, have an obligation to provide such monitoring and to maintain frequent contact with their aging parents. Although he was not a caregiver for his own parents, his sister provided most of the direct care that his parents required in their old age.

For Dennis and Ellen, social connection and activity have been very important throughout their adult lives. They value their relationships with other people. Based on his descriptions of their friendships, senior center involvement, and the veterans' organization, their social ties appear to be strong and stable. Dennis does not explicitly speak of these ties as potential resources to draw on later if needed; however, it is clear from his accounts of the frail elders that he finds their social isolation most disturbing. When probed about his own expectations, he identifies his nieces as potential resources for help if they should need it; he feels that he and his wife could count on them if they really needed to, but he hopes that won't happen. He assumes that he will leave money and other assets to his nieces when he and his wife die, but this is not something that they have ever talked about with others. Indeed, it does not appear that Dennis and Ellen have ever spoken with their nieces and nephews about what might happen or what they might expect in the future. As collateral kinship ties are fairly ambiguous in their obligations and expectations, it is unclear whether their implicit assumptions regarding their nieces represent a realistic consideration of future resources. On the other hand, a single interview with Dennis may not provide adequate information about the kinds of interactions that really constitute and maintain his and Ellen's relationships with kin, friends, and others, including with each other.

It is only in the area of finances that Dennis articulates a clear sense of preparation for the future. He is proud of his financial independence, which reflects a lifetime of steady work and savings. He expects that he will be able to provide for himself and his wife and that they will remain secure as they grow older. He also underscores the importance of planning for his wife's future, making sure that she is taken care of when he passes. His planning, however, appears to be entirely focused on material well-being; he does not report considering any other plans for the future, such as residential moves or other accommodations for their future aging.

Interestingly, Dennis and Ellen's social activities may represent a valuable, latent form of preparation for advancing age. For example, their membership in the local senior center affords them contact with their contemporaries while also integrating them into a network that includes well-trained and concerned social service professionals. Through his work as a driver for the senior transport program, Dennis is also gaining first-hand knowledge of the kinds of assistive services available to community-dwelling seniors. He is observing and learning about many of the specific concerns and exigencies of aging. Even if he does not explicitly plan for or anticipate these situations in his own life, his exposure may raise his awareness of their possibility and potential responses.

Finally, Dennis and Ellen's community involvements not only keep them socially connected in the present, they offer a level of integration that is likely to be of benefit even if their activities and abilities were to decline in the future. Whereas Ben and Linda's social ties appear to be specific to particular activities – work, hobbies, and athletic competitions – Dennis and Ellen's connections are not as clearly contingent on their continued activities or abilities. Their friendships, kin ties, and veterans' organization membership seem to represent a level of personal investment and durable connection that are not only likely to continue but might even intensify in response to potential future needs. Their more recent decision to join the senior center, motivated mainly by current social interests, is even more clearly amenable and potentially responsive to changes and declines that they may face in the future. And although Ellen plays the main role of kin-keeper in maintaining social ties with family, Dennis is fully involved in each of their networks in his own right, not depending on his wife for the maintenance of social ties like many men of his generation.

Planning for Contingencies

Michael Grodsky's family immigrated to the United States when he was very young. As Orthodox Jews from Eastern Europe, they settled in a major East Coast city and his father worked as a clothing salesman in a small store. Michael remembers growing up very poor, but he did well in school and his academic achievements were strongly encouraged by his family. By the age of 18, however, he had rebelled against his family's expectations of becoming a rabbi. Continuing his education in secular institutions, though never completing college, Michael opened his own store as a young adult and then trained for a career in business.

Now in his early eighties, Michael considers himself "very, very lucky," especially given the poverty he experienced in his childhood. "I never was in want of anything. I had plenty of money. I always had nice people, very good friends .... I was very lucky considering I come from a very poor family." His 40-year career as a businessman afforded him financial security throughout his adulthood, and he was able to provide economic assistance to both his parents and his in-laws in their older years. By his own account, he lived conservatively and had begun saving for retirement with his first paycheck. He has always been concerned with planning ahead for his future, first with an eye toward having and providing for his own family and then toward planning for retirement.

Married at 27, Michael and his wife remained permanently childless because of repeated delays in childbearing until the time was right. Their delays were profoundly influenced by circumstances outside their control, first the Great Depression and then Michael's military service during World War II. Throughout this period, Michael's wife, Rachel, continued to work for a department store. His parents had openly objected to her working outside the home, but Michael and Rachel felt that the economic uncertainties of the time justified her employment. Indeed, as Michael explains, "I didn't care if she worked or not . . . . She had such a nice job. They loved her." She had progressed up the career ladder until the store unexpectedly closed and left her unemployed.

Upon Michael's return from service in World War II, they tried more seriously to start a family, but they were unsuccessful. As Michael recounts,

> The reason why we didn't have children is because I had to struggle at the beginning. And we didn't think about children for 4 or 5 years after we got married. Then when we started thinking about children, my wife went to a doctor and she was unable to bear children. . . . And before you know it, I was in the service. We got down . . . it was getting to us. So when I got back, I was pretty old and she was too, so we decided – no, we did try. But we were in our late forties. Nobody wanted to give us – the adoption agencies would rather have 23-year-olds, 24-year-olds. You know what I mean? And they made it very, very difficult for us. They wanted to give us older children. We didn't want any of that.

The adoption agencies considered them too old to adopt an infant, so they remained childless. Their pathway into inadvertent childlessness, resulting from repeated fertility delays, represents the most common reason for childlessness and one that was particularly prevalent among adults of their birth cohort who entered into adulthood during the Great Depression (Rindfuss, Morgan, and Swicegood 1988).

Michael explains that his economic success compared to his siblings allowed him the opportunity to assist them and become involved in an extended kinship network:

> Being as how I was in business and doing very well, everybody felt in the family that I'm in a position to help these [relatives]. So that's what

I did. I helped them financially, and we became friendly with all the kids. And we watched them grow up. We really became part of their life, their social life.

Michael and his wife celebrated most holidays with their siblings and the children. As the nephews grew up and got married, Michael and Rachel started their own tradition of entertaining all of their nieces and nephews at Thanksgiving. This annual holiday event continued for nearly 25 years, eventually expanding to include their spouses and the next generation's children. Michael valued the opportunity to have a role in his nieces' and nephews' lives and to maintain a connection with them, though he had to stop the holiday dinners about five years ago because of his wife's declining health. He is pleased, however, with the frequency of their visits in recent years since his wife's health had begun to decline: "We have a very nice relationship with all our nephews. And that's mainly the basis of my social life right now." His days are full now with staying on top of chores, taking care of his wife, reading books at home, and making frequent trips to the public library.

When asked about the saddest times in his life, Michael cites the health crises that he and his wife have faced. Michael describes his own bout with life-threatening cancer 20 years ago. Fortunately, the tumor was successfully removed through surgery, and he has been in remission ever since. Then a year ago, his wife fell and broke her leg. The past year has been very difficult for both of them. Her mobility has been severely limited, and she has found herself suddenly frail: "She's had a very tough time. At her age – she is almost as old as I am – right there for her to come back. She's trying hard. She's a very meticulous person, and I have to be careful that she don't get morally upset – depressed. She gets depressed." After years of traveling together, they have had to give up on travel, adding to the losses with which they have been coping in recent years. They have had to greatly curtail their social activities and have lost touch with many of their friends and associates from earlier years; their social contacts now are limited mainly to visits from their nieces and nephews.

Michael has focused much of his energy on preparing for the future, saving his money and managing his investments. His most important concern is taking care of his wife's needs for as long as she is living. He admits that his holdings are "very complicated" and has designated a particularly skilled nephew to coordinate his financial matters and estate if he should predecease his wife.

Michael speaks quite candidly about his strategies for substituting resources – cultivating relationships with his kin in order to help him and his wife should they need it later. Money is part of this picture. He describes his considerations in the following passage:

Most of my nephews are heirs. All on a different scale. It all depends how close I am to them. 'Course, I had a problem which I don't think I've been able to solve because I've asked several people who were in line to explain what's the right attitude to take. For instance, do you leave more of my money to a person who at this moment is needy? Or to a person who is close to you? What would you say? . . . What would you do? I have certain nephews know of this. A nephew – I just took them . . . to a restaurant to celebrate her birthday. They are [wealthy], but they're very, very close to me. Now if I leave them some money, what good is it? So I just gave them – she said she'd like to have this [music box] . . . . Right now my will is written in a manner I leave some to charity and the remainder is equally divided among most of my nephews and their families. . . . I'm not exactly satisfied now. . . . There's some of my nephews who are struggling. I'd like to give them more. But yet I never even see them. . . . How about if you have a nephew who is a stinker, to put it bluntly. One that never calls, never cares about you. Would you leave him some money?

Michael describes using gifts and money in the present, as well as the promise of money from his estate, as a way of reinforcing relationships and setting up a sense of obligation to reciprocate in the future. When asked specifically who might provide assistance to him and his wife in the future, he notes,

I always felt that if I needed anybody there's a few of my nephews that I'm *sure* – especially if they know there's money involved – I have to qualify it. It occurs to me, you know, I told my wife if I die, I want you to be *very generous* with your nephews. Give them. Keep giving them money. Don't be stingy . . . . So they'll take care of you. So that's what I'm thinking. I'm sure there's a few nephews who are well-to-do. I'm sure if I was in need, they would take care of me.

Later he adds more bluntly, "It's important, you know, take care of family. If you've gone mental, they know that they're going to get some money when he dies, it's easy to love him."

Of the three childless men whose lives are featured in this chapter, Michael and his wife are the oldest and have had to face the most serious setbacks, particularly her physical decline and disability. Not surprisingly, Michael has the most clearly articulated plans and concerns about coping with current challenges and preparing for future exigencies. His emphasis on cultivating his nephews' involvement provides direct acknowledgement that his situation as a childless man places him outside the boundaries of conventional care obligations, in which the normative focus is mainly on the spouse and the parent–child bond. Recognizing his situation as potentially precarious, his response is proactive. Striking is his open discussion of bargaining with his nephews, both subtly through informal gifts and dinners and more explicitly through consideration of his future bequests.

The candid articulation of his strategies may be unusual, but it reflects a remarkable awareness of the mechanics and limitations of social norms in American society. Lacking the normatively strong and more clearly prescribed parent–child relationship, Michael realizes that the strength of his own familial network and its value as a potential social resource depend on continuous investment – materially, socially, and affectively. He is actively constructing a web of familial obligations with the expectation that his nieces and nephews will reciprocate in the form of future instrumental and emotional support.

Michael's observations and actions echo the comments of a number of scholars who have described the fragility and the contingency of postmodern kinship bonds; the uncertainty of contemporary kin relations requires continuous reflection and tending, but the stresses are often balanced by the benefits of voluntary, actively cultivated relationships (see, for example, Giddens 1991; Weston 1991; Stacey, 1991). Interestingly, although American culture offers only informal substitutes for filial bonds (and formal, paid services), childless older couples in Japan are able to utilize legally recognized methods for "adopting" adults to act as their own kin. Through a process of designating an heir and often sharing a residence, these Japanese elders are able to formally cultivate substitutes for the crucial parent–child relationship; in exchange for inheritance, the elders are assured the instrumental help and physical care they may need in advanced age (Hashimoto 1996).

Discussion

What can we learn from examining the lives of these three childless men, who are members of a distinctive, non-normative, and often marginalized group? Never having experienced fatherhood, their life paths do not fit into developmental schemas and life course theories that have assumed the centrality of procreation and parenthood. The "doubly invisible" lives of these men offer a view of several different ways of aging, each man encountering a different landscape and constructing a unique path through later life.

Although defined in these analyses and in the original interviewing process by their childless status, we must ask first, how important is childlessness in their lives? Addressing this question is difficult due to my secondary reading of the transcript materials and the method of the original study, which usually involved only a single in-depth interview session of about two hours. Each man was interviewed within his chosen surroundings – Ben and Michael were interviewed at their homes, while Dennis arranged to hold his interview at the senior center. Only Ben was interviewed with his wife present, allowing for some observation of their interactions with each other. Further, the interview questions themselves had emphasized the key concepts of generativity in the life course and the meanings of childlessness. This provided for focused discussion of these issues in the lives of these childless men, but also slanted their self-presentations and assessments to emphasize and elucidate their childless status.

Based on the telling of their life stories and answers to specific queries about childlessness, we get only a limited view of what William Marsiglio (1998) has described as men's "procreative consciousness." Both Dennis and Michael depict their early expectations as being centered on the assumed progression into fatherhood. Their early identities (and Michael's early financial planning) reflected the importance of the husband-provider and father roles that were shaped by the normative expectations of the time and the construction of life plans that they had shared with their wives. Ben, on the other hand, married late and seems to have been indifferent to the notion of prospective fatherhood. By the time he had married, he saw himself as being outside the normative and preferred boundaries for entering into parenthood.

All three of these men, however, recount their own participation in the process of procreative decision-making and in the resolution of the permanent childless status. Dennis and Michael describe their early hopes and expectations for parenthood as well as their participation in the process of trying to have a child – not in terms of their sexual participation, but expressed in terms of their concerns and support for their wives. The combination of Ben's age-related reservations and Linda's desire not to bear any children is reflected in their mutual decisions to contracept and then later to seek surgical sterilization. Thus, all three of these men relate a sense of responsibility and active involvement in procreative considerations.

Research on women, including my own parallel analyses of interviews with childless women, has consistently emphasized the centrality of childlessness to women's self-identities (Fisher 1991; May 1995; Koropeckyj-Cox 1998). Childlessness is experienced by women as a problematic, non-normative status, frequently provoking questions and requiring justification in a variety of social settings (Houseknecht 1987). In other words, the normative importance of motherhood for women requires childless women to explain themselves. In the childless women's interviews, a narrative about the childless status consistently emerges out of their own, open-ended telling of their life story. Although they had been told that childlessness was a primary topic of the research study, their elaborate and self-reflective narratives suggest that they were probably well-practiced in constructing and relating an account of their childless status.

For the men, on the other hand, childlessness is not a strong theme in their interviews, and their status does not seem to require explanation as in the women's interviews. Despite the emphasis on generativity and parental status that framed the interview process, none of the three men mentions his childlessness when asked to provide an open-ended narrative of his life. Their accounts of childlessness emerge only when specifically probed on the topic by the interviewers. When they do provide descriptions of their pathways into the childless status, their accounts of the reasons for childlessness reside primarily outside of themselves. Dennis describes the physical complications that prevented reproduction, centered in his wife's body and manifested in her unexpected miscarriage. For Michael, the impact of historical circumstances, namely the Great Depression and World War II, are implicated in his childlessness, though he also cites his wife's diagnosed infertility as well as the adoption agencies' assessment that they were too old to become parents. Only Ben clearly describes both the decision and the ability to bear children as shared by both his wife and himself. He recounts their open discussion and decision-making concerning the choice to remain childless and how they each participated in the steps of preventing pregnancy.

For all three men, neither the process of remaining childless nor the status itself is seen as reflecting on their own self-identities or social standing. They do not regard childlessness as having influenced their views of themselves or their relationships with other people. These observations suggest a lesser salience of parental status in the life stories and self-assessments of older men, but more research is needed in this area, including the employment of a variety of methods and observations across different contexts and time periods. For Dennis and Ben, their current stability and high levels of health and activity may help to minimize some of the potential, practical consequences of childlessness with which Michael must cope more directly. Also, the implications of the childless status for self-identity and masculinity may have changed over time and across circumstances for each of these men in ways that are not revealed through a retrospective interview process. Further exploration and elaboration of gender-focused theoretical perspectives are needed to better understand the meanings and salience of childlessness for men throughout the life course.

The open-ended life history narratives provided by each of these men are structured around their individual paths through education and work. The dominant themes for all three men are the importance of independence, establishing professional competence and economic security, and being good providers for their wives. These themes, not their childlessness, are repeatedly referenced as key aspects of the men's self-identities, and they reflect the central components of masculinity as it has been defined for their cohorts. The themes very closely match Carolyn Heilbrun's (1988) list of the primary areas of self and societal assessments of men's lives. She argues that gender shapes the life story in basic and pervasive ways, providing different pathways and opportunities, different referents for assessing the life course, and different expectations of what is important. Ruth Ray (1998, 2000) has further elaborated this argument through her conceptualization of gender-based scripting in life history narratives. She has observed that the content, structures, and assessments of men's life stories are fundamentally shaped by the specific scripts of achievement, independence, and responsibility that are associated with masculine success. This normative masculine script is particularly evident in each of the three men's narratives concerning their worries and plans for the future. Each man frames his concerns about the implications of childlessness primarily from the point of view of providing for his wife's future needs. The role of the husband as provider and protector is a major component of the social expectations that they have internalized and the definitions of masculinity that have shaped the men of this cohort.

By studying the lives of childless men, we can begin to elucidate how life paths, relationships, and identities are continually refined and negotiated over time (see Holstein and Gubrium 2000). A more time-extended research approach is needed, however, to further explore how these processes evolve in response to specific events, transitions, and social interactions at different times in the life course and over longer periods. In many ways, forging a non-normative life path may require more explicit and self-conscious navigation through social expectations, reactions, and evaluations, and may provide a window for better understanding the processes through which individuals' life courses are continually constructed.

Finally, the different ways of aging presented in this chapter may provide some clues to what may lie ahead for many Americans in the future. The "non-normative" childless life path has increased in its social acceptance and prevalence since the 1960s. It is estimated that around a quarter of the adults born during the baby boom era will have entered their fifties without ever having biological children, and a higher proportion than ever will regard their childlessness as voluntary. Further, current cohorts approaching old age will have experienced diverse family and relationship histories, including a higher incidence of divorce, remarriage, and step-relations as well as some novel pathways into family life, such as the use of assistive reproductive technologies or artificial insemination. The life stories of Ben, Dennis, and Michael provide a glimpse of the kinds of creative adaptations and different pathways that contribute to the construction of a meaningful old age.

Notes

1 The chapter is based on analyses of in-depth interviews and life histories collected by Robert L. Rubinstein and his colleagues at the Polisher Research Institute of the Philadelphia Geriatric Center between 1989 and 1994. The original data collection was funded by two grants from the National Institute on Aging. The author gratefully thanks Dr. Rubinstein for access to his archives and for his encouragement and advice in the analyses.

The current research was made possible by generous dissertation funding from the Murray Research Center, Radcliffe College/Harvard University, and from the Boettner Institute, the School of Arts and Sciences, and the Department of Sociology, all at the University of Pennsylvania. Further work was completed during the author's post-doctoral fellowship in the Demography of Aging at the School of Hygiene and Public Health, Johns Hopkins University, funded by the National Institute on Aging.

2 Pseudonyms are used throughout.

References

Bellah, Robert, et al. 1985. *Habits of the Heart: Individualism and Commitment in American Life*. Berkeley: University of California Press.

Blake, Judith. 1979. "Is Zero Preferred? American Attitudes Toward Childlessness in the 1970s." *Journal of Marriage and the Family*, 41: 245–57.

Coontz, Stephanie. 1992. *The Way We Never Were: American Families and the Nostalgia Trap*. New York: Basic Books.

Erikson, Erik H. 1963. *Childhood and Society, 2nd edition*. New York: W. W. Norton.

Erikson, Erik H. 1997. *The Life Cycle Completed, (extended version)*. New York: W. W. Norton.

Fisher, B. 1991. "Affirming social value: Women without children." In D. R. Maines (ed.), *Social Organization and Social Process: Essays in Honor of Anselm Strauss*. New York: Aldine De Gruyter.

Gerson, Kathleen. 1985. *Hard Choices: How Women, Decide about Work, Career, and Motherhood*. Berkeley: University of California Press.

Giddens, Anthony. 1991. *Modernity and Self-Identity: Self and Society in the Late Modern Age*. Stanford, CA: Stanford University Press.

Gutmann, David. 1987. *Reclaimed Powers: Toward a New Psychology of Men and Women in Later Life*. New York: Basic Books.

Gutmann, David and Huyck, Margaret H. 1994. "Development and Pathology in Postparental Men." In E. H. Thompson, Jr. (ed.), *Older Men's Lives*. Thousand Oaks, CA: Sage Publications.

Hashimoto, Akiko. 1996. *The Gift of Generations: Japanese and American Perspectives on Aging and the Social Contract*. Cambridge, UK: Cambridge University Press.

Heilbrun, Carolyn. 1988. *Writing a Woman's Life*. New York: Ballantine Books.

Himes, Christine L. 1992. "Future Caregivers: Projected Family Structures of Older Persons." *Journal of Gerontology: Social Sciences*, 47: S17–26.

Holstein, James A. and Gubrium, Jaber F. 2000. *Constructing the Life Course*, 2nd edition. Lanham, MD: AltaMira Press.

Houseknecht, Sharon. 1987. "Voluntary Childlessness." In M. B. Sussman and S. K. Steinmetz (eds), *Handbook of Marriage and the Family*. New York: Plenum Press.

Ireland, Mardy S. 1993. *Reconceiving Women: Separating Motherhood from Female Identity*. New York: Guilford Press.

Johnson, C. L., and Catalano, D. J. 1981. "Childless Elderly and Their Family Supports." *The Gerontologist*, 21: 610–18.

Koropeckyj-Cox, Tanya. 1998. *The Conditional Benefits of Parenthood (or Childlessness) for Subjective Well-Being in Older Adulthood*. Unpublished doctoral dissertation. Philadelphia: University of Pennsylvania.

Marsiglio, William. 1998. *Procreative Man*. New York: New York University Press.

May, Elaine T. 1988. *Homeward Bound: American Families in the Cold War Era*. New York: Basic Books.

May, Elaine T. 1995. *Barren in the Promised Land: Childless Americans and the Pursuit of Happiness*. Cambridge, MA: Harvard University Press.

Ray, Ruth E. 1998. "Feminist Readings of Older Women's Life Stories." *Journal of Aging Studies*, 12: 117–27.

Ray, Ruth E. 2000. *Beyond Nostalgia: Aging and Life-Story Writing*. Charlottesville: University of Virginia Press.

Rindfuss, Ronald, Morgan, S. Philip, and Swicegood, C. Gray. 1988. *First Births in America*. Berkeley: University of California Press.

Rubinstein, Robert L. 1986. *Singular Paths: Old Men Living Alone*. New York: Columbia University Press.

Rubinstein, Robert L. 1997. "Foreword." In J. I. Kosberg and L. W. Kaye (eds), *Elderly Men: Social Problems and Professional Challenges*. New York: Springer.

Stacey, Judith. 1991. *Brave New Families*. New York: Basic Books.

Thompson, Edward H., Jr. 1994. "Older Men as Invisible Men in Contemporary Society." In E. H. Thompson, Jr. (ed.), *Older Men's Lives*. Thousand Oaks, CA: Sage Publications.

Veevers, Jean. 1980. *Childless by Choice*. Toronto: Butterworths.

Weston, Kath. 1991. *Families We Choose: Lesbians, Gays, Kinship*. New York: Columbia University Press.

Chapter 5

Constructing Community from Troubles

Christopher A. Faircloth

In an increasingly fragmented world, community seems to elude us. In place, instead, are nostalgic images of a strong communal past. Cultural movements, such as the birth of neo-traditional architecture – perhaps best represented by Seaside, the "perfect" community in the Florida panhandle that served as the backdrop for the movie *The Truman Show* – point to communal desire, but not to actuality, in vivid detail. Some commentators, such as Robert Putnam (2000), tell us that we have indeed lost this precious commodity and it is only a return to traditional values and folk-ways that can revive community today. Whether it is an orientation to earlier forms of communal solidarity or concerted attempts to establish the semblance of community in architectural design, hope seems to over-shadow reality.

Community has traditionally signaled likeness and consensus, from which the search for community takes its point of departure. But perhaps we do ourselves an injustice by looking for it solely in these terms. Can community be formed from aversion and complaints? Can it be built out of what has traditionally figured to be its opposite? These are the questions that grew in pertinence as I undertook the research that led to the story of Shady Grove, a senior public housing complex in the Southeastern United States. As I became acquainted with individual residents, interviewing them and observing their daily lives, I was surprised at how communal they were when nothing about the setting would lead one to think it possible. Indeed, the residents seemed to be such sources of irritation to each other that I would never have guessed the complex housed anything other than socially isolated and complaining individuals.

Shady Grove's physical setting seemed to work against togetherness, if it didn't preclude social interaction. There was little park area, nor any outdoor benches. The environs had no architectural enhancements encouraging residents to mingle. The living units were arranged so that their occupants' comings and goings were easily hidden from each other. The porches in front of each unit were small and bare of furniture. In many cases, latticework had been erected between unit porches or trees and hedges grown to maintain privacy. Just as Arlie Hochschild (1973) initially figured in her study of Merrill Court, a San Francisco bay area housing complex for seniors, nothing about the Grove's setting appeared to encourage community life.

But as I focused on the incessant conversations that I came to call "troubles talk" (Faircloth 2001, 2002), a form of community life unexpectedly appeared. I began to notice the troubles residents posed for each other, which they communicated by constantly complaining about other residents. This was a source of continuous interaction and produced distinct personas and social types, each of which served as a basis for shared identities and sentiments. Surprisingly, the elderly residents of Shady Grove formed a way of aging by constructing community from the everyday troubles of an otherwise isolating social environment. Just as surprising, this had little to do with the infirmities and disadvantages of old age. As this chapter will show, Shady Grovers developed a way of aging that didn't center on issues that relate necessarily or distinctively to old age.

Troublesome Individuals

The talk and interaction surrounding two residents was key to my initial understanding of community. These residents – Donna and Orin (all names have been fictionalized) – were predominant sources of troubles talk at the Grove. They were viewed by many as the most troublesome, if not the most nefarious, characters in the complex. Their mere presence prompted endless complaints. By way of comparison, residents established who they themselves were, but more importantly who they were *not* and what they did *not* want to become. Donna and Orin provided a shared communicative anchor for the expression of common resentments, which, in being shared, actively elaborated the local sense of what those who resented them shared in common.

Orin and Donna were a source of hate, ridicule, apathy, and even bafflement. Donna's poor and erratic behavior eventually dominated discussions between residents during my tenure in the neighborhood. When

I entered the Grove, Donna was full of energy, affable, and talkative. As time passed, however, she experienced a sharp descent into depression, fueling talk among the residents about what was viewed as grossly erratic behavior. Orin presented a different set of troubles. His everyday activities drew annoyed attention to himself, exasperating many residents and frustrating others. He, in turn, seemed to relish the attention. Both Donna and Orin, in their own ways, inspired the troubles talk that formed the Grove's community life.

"Always sticking his nose where it doesn't belong"

To many residents, Orin was strange and annoying. He was different from other residents and relished the resulting celebrity, if not the notoriety. Typically, every day at the crack of dawn, Orin mounted his three-wheeled bicycle and "gallivanted," as the residents put it, around the complex and neighborhood, running his errands. The bicycle was "a work of art," with large handlebars and bright colors, proudly displaying a garish flag in support of a local university. Orin stood out like no one else, was proud of it, and this disturbed many residents. Orin also was known to many of the students who lived around the complex. In a discussion, one group of students actually asked me if I knew the "bike rider," taking for granted that such a sight was noticed by everyone. According to one of them, "You can't miss him. He rides all through the apartment complex, waving to everyone."

Orin lived for the moment, full of energy and spunk. He was vivacious and outgoing, but evidently his presence was just too much for many. "That boy just got a little too much get up and go, I think," Dan, another resident, once pointed out. Perhaps not surprisingly, Orin's flamboyant behavior and garish appearance also led to his sexuality being questioned. John, the maintenance director of the housing authority that manages Shady Grove, described Orin this way:

> What is there to say? [Laughs] He's a fruit, too. Always something wrong with the toilet. Kept calling last year all the time about that damn toilet. There was something a little fishy. Think he just wanted to look at Rick's [a maintenance man] whacker. I don't know, Orin's always been a little strange riding that bike around and shit.

Orin regularly intruded into the resident affairs. Many times this occurred when, according to Orin, he was actually trying to provide assistance. But the residents didn't see it that way. As one of them, Mae, remarked, "I shouldn't talk like this, but he's always putting his nose up other people's ass." Most saw Orin as constantly needing to be the center of attention. The result is that his actions, along with others' responses, have created a persona for him from which it is impossible to escape. At the same time, being a source of troubles talk, the persona is a shared source of related social interaction for residents and their complaints about him.

This regularly plays out in casual conversation, such as in the following discussion between resident Donna and me, as we took the walk that became our daily ritual. Donna and I recounted an incident involving her and Eve, another resident, in which Eve had reacted angrily.

Donna: Have you heard anything from that woman [referring to Eve]?

Chris: Which woman?

Donna: You know, the one that wouldn't let us in last time.

Chris: No, but I'm going to visit her today.

Donna: I don't know what got into her. It was rude and disrespectful, Chris, and it still bothers me. I had just seen her before Christmas and gave her a Christmas card. I saw her after that and she said it was the perfect card, "That it suits me perfectly." I don't know, I just buy cards, but Eve said it fit her, then I guess it fit. [Laughs] So I don't know what's wrong, Chris. There's never been anything between us.

Chris: You think Orin had anything to do with this?

Donna: [Sternly] Oh, I know he did. Well, I don't know for sure, but I'm pretty sure of it. He's always over there talking with people. I don't say anything to him anymore. I saw him the other day, and just said "Hi" to him and that was all. He knows I know now. I'm not sure how, but he knows what happened. Somebody told him.

Chris: Orin gets around here, huh?

Donna: Yeah he does! I'll tell you, when I was moving in here in my old place, I had my whole family helping me, my sons and all. Big, large muscular boys. You saw Butch that day, right? Well, Orin comes gallivanting up and asks if he can help. Comes back four or five times! I don't need his help. I'm really sick right now, but I have my boys to help and they are doing everything. I don't need to deal with him. Orin keeps coming by, asking me if I want his phone number? So he runs off and writes that, telling me if I ever need anything, just to let him know.

The incident with Eve was something that all Shady Grovers knew a great deal about and had shared many opinions and complaints. The particulars are not as important as the fact that it was a widely discussed event. Equally important, it was an event that focused considerable troubles talk on Orin's annoying behavior. Donna was quite sure that Orin was involved, although in the preceding exchange she does offer some initial uncertainty. Upset, she complains that Orin is untrustworthy and an instigator. To Donna's chagrin, Orin is aware of her every activity, which as an intrusion on her privacy, she figures I and other residents understand perfectly.

In this exchange, as in others, Donna uses a well-known event involving a resident, Eve, to construct Orin as someone who knows too much. Orin is a "troublesome person," who deserves the complaints leveled against him. Oddly enough, he is a person too willing to assist others, often overstepping the bounds of shared concern between neighbors and friends. Donna depicts Orin as someone who insists on doing too much, something quite discomforting to her. She makes it perfectly clear that she wishes to have no contact with Orin.

Donna isn't alone in expressing such feelings towards Orin. The sentiments are widely shared. According to many Grovers, Orin is too energetic for a man his age. As one of them put it, he has too much "get up and go for his own good." Another remarked, "He's too busy, ya know. Always sticking his nose where it doesn't belong." But, if his high energy level and amount of activity are troublesome and deeply resented, they also prompt talk and interaction linking this well-known figure with shared feelings of animosity. Curiously, hate and difference are, at the same time, leading to common identity in reaction.

Another resident, Margaret, provides further evidence on this score. Margaret has little respect for Orin, complaining of his rumor-mongering and, at the same time, implying that Shady Grovers are basically genuine folk, not as phony as Orin's behavior depicts.

> He's always spreading rumors about you or anybody else, talking in his slick way. I'd love to just tag him one. My son taught me some things. I may be little but I'll stand up for myself. He [Orin] always talks about how he used to work for a lawyer, using those big words to impress you. But I worked for a law firm too, and they taught me how to spot a phony. I guarantee you, Orin fits that description. We'd all be better off if he'll just leave or die or something. I know I would.

The complaints, heard in one form or another throughout the Grove, are points of departure for many related stories. As the preceding comments convey, according to Margaret, "He's always spreading rumors about you or anybody else, talking in his slick way." For Margaret, this sets the stage for further troubles talk, presented as following logically from the start. Margaret complains about the way Orin presents himself and his past, a past she thinks is false: "He always talks about how he used to work for a lawyer." Orin is presented as an individual who spreads falsehoods, something "we'd all be better off without." This scenario is a setting devoid of such troubles – what Shady Grove ostensibly would be if only Orin weren't around. Cohesive community is constructed from the wished-for absence of a well-known figure whose conduct seems to destroy it.

"Just a bitch"

Early in my fieldwork, I attended a neighborhood barbecue hosted by the managing housing authority. I sat at a table at the rear of the party. Four women were seated there talking about various happenings in the neighborhood. When Donna approached the table, the women became excited. They appeared to be very pleased to see her. I should note that at this point in the fieldwork, Donna seemed to be outgoing, vivacious, and well kept. The women gathered around, asking countless questions and showing great respect for her. Donna had recently undergone a heart transplant and was recovering from the operation. She was like a heroine in the neighborhood and the residents were proud that she had worked valiantly to overcome her heart failure.

Donna's success seemed to give residents a feeling that they, too, could overcome the ravages of old age. Donnas was a source of inspiration in this regard. Her example seemed to tell residents that they could struggle on successfully and dare to muster hope against catastrophe. As Diane, another resident, told me, "You know, Chris, all of us women, we're proud of her. She's made it back. You should have seen her before. It makes me think sometimes and I try to do it."

Donna's resulting good health didn't last for long. After a routine medical exam turned up some serious problems, Donna seemed to come apart, both mentally and physically. She fell into a deep depression, rarely, if at all, emerging from her unit. Her sons would visit, bringing food and other goods, but for long periods of time Donna was otherwise reclusive.

It was the extreme difference between the "healthy Donna" and the "ill Donna" that made her such a remarkable object of troubles talk. There was the Donna in whom the residents expressed such great pride, the Donna who had overcome a major obstacle to good health. But there was also the Donna who was depressed and reclusive. The extremes produced myriad "before-and-after" stories about Donna herself and about her relations with neighbors and family. The contrasts punctuated complaints about what Donna had become, making uncommonly vivid the troubles talk shared about her by residents.

Margaret, a close friend of Donna's when she was well, drastically changed her feelings toward Donna when Donna's behavior worsened with the depression. Her new concerns over "Donna's antics," as Margaret put it, were representative of many others' changes in attitude. This poignantly emerged one day as Margaret and I chatted on her front porch. At one point, Margaret underscored her complaints by stating, "Donna is just a bitch and that's all there is to it. I feel sorry for her, don't get me wrong, but she just needs to stop." Margaret's comments were full of both anger and compassion.

In contrast to the troubles talk centered on Orin, Donna's behavior conjured up mixed emotions. Poignancy and the resulting sentimental solidarity of the complainers rested as much on what Donna was before her surgery as on the troubling character she became afterward. While talk of Orin was almost always negative, the troubles talk surrounding Donna came in sharp contrasts. The key here is that community can be built out of reversals of the traditional positive sentiments that bring people together.

Troublesome Groups

Troubles talk at Shady Grove was not exclusively focused on individuals. Groups of residents also were the butts of continuous complaints, especially those called "animal people" and "cooped-up women." Here again, as with troublesome individuals, Grovers found common cause in casting aspersion on what they most generally referred to as "those people."

"Animal people"

One afternoon, as I stood in the Grove's back parking lot conversing with a number of residents about a tenant in the complex, the animal people came into focus. At one point, I asked if the residents could provide an in-depth description of the people they were at that point rather nebulously complaining about. One of them sarcastically replied, "Oh, she's just one of those damned animal people. There's tons of them around here. They just love animals." I later heard similar remarks and soon figured that shared thoughts and sentiments derived from a loathing of animal lovers. In time, I learned that, among Grovers, you are either one of the animal people or you are not, to put it simply. Gradually, I learned that there were finer distinctions. Troubles talk related to animal people varied according to whether the targets of complaints were bird feeders or pet owners.

Shady Grove is located between two ponds of water. The pond to the West is well kept, bordering a student apartment complex. Geese and ducks frequent the area in great number, using Shady Grove as a pathway to the other pond, which is dirty, untidy, and the source of complaints by the residents. While referred to as a pond, the second body of water is actually a water drainage area for the larger neighborhood surrounding Shady Grove.

The result of this arrangement is that in moving between ponds, birds linger in the complex to feed on the bread, seed, and other morsels left for them by the residents. This is a source of considerable consternation for some. Those who feed the birds see them as nice creatures or, as one told me, "cute little things." One resident, Erica, noted, "They sure are pretty, Chris. Just look at 'em! Brighten your day right up when you see them comin'." The nonfeeders have a quite different view, calling the ducks and geese "dirty" and "vile." Some Grovers view all birds with disdain, detrimental to the overall quality of life in the neighborhood. The "bird feeders," as these residents see it, are direct contributors to poor quality of life. Without these animal people, birds wouldn't linger in Shady Grove, scrounging for food and making a mess.

I first happened upon bird feeder troubles talk when Diane and I returned to the complex after a short walk. Soon after arriving, a large flock of ducks seemingly appeared out of nowhere, walking near us. I pointed to the birds and Diane reacted negatively.

Chris: Look, there are those ducks everyone talks about.

Diane: I have to stay away from them, too. They have a lot of fleas.

Chris: So you don't want them around then? Some people feed them though, don't they?

Diane: Yeah, some of us like them out here and some don't. They live in that pond there. [She turns around and points as the ducks get closer to us.] Shoo ducks, shoo! I've got to stay away from them. Mike [a female resident] even feeds them. She says she doesn't, but I've seen her. Told her about it, too. But that's Mike, she does what she wants and there's nothing that is going to change her.

Periodically, angry moral battles break out among Grovers over the presence of these birds in the neighborhood. The statement "some of us like them here and some don't" is a poignant reminder of the dissension that abounds in the Grove over the issue and the residents who are troublesome because they contribute to the problem. For Diane, complaints are complicated by the fact that Mike is Diane's friend, provoking a personal dynamic that extends into this social division of the neighborhood. Diane complaints are noticeably ambivalent since Mike seems to be presenting an identity that is at odds with what Diane sees as reality. Mike might claim otherwise, but Diane is sure that she does feed the birds, putting Diane on both sides of the shared sentiments this produces.

Mike focuses on the problem differently. For Mike, there are birds and there are birds, so to speak. She has a large bird feeder by her front porch and often jokes about her attempts to keep squirrels away from it. Mike evidently truly enjoys birds, including ducks and geese. She once quipped with me, "I love to watch birds, Chris. They brighten us up some days. Especially when us old ladies are drunk." But this doesn't extend to the migrant ducks and geese that steal seed from the other birds, as the following conversation between Donna, Mike and myself indicates. As we talked, we noticed a number of ducks eating the seed surrounding Mike's feeder. Mike presented a wide range of feelings about birds and their place in the neighborhood.

Mike: Those damn things are always around. There's nothing you can do about it. They weren't eating out of the feeder were they? [I shake my head no.] I hope not. I like to see the birds and they make such pretty sounds, unlike those damn ducks.

Chris: Some of ya'll like them and some of ya'll don't, right?

Mike: That's right. I don't care; they just need to get rid of the things. We need to get the watch-a-ma-call-it, the Humane Society or something, to come pick them up.

Donna: [The housing authority] can do it, Mike. John and them can pick them up.

Mike: I called before. They said they're not allowed to do that or something, I don't know. Orin, though, he caught 18 of them one time, but he couldn't catch the male one, so they keep breeding.

Chris: [Laughing] How did Orin catch them?

Mike: Put him a trap out. The male was too smart for him though. [Laughs] They come from that water over there and they travel across here to get to that other pond. Someone told me that there's another pond way back there, but I haven't seen that one

Donna: They're so ugly too. Disgusting.

Mike: I know. They're not pretty like those mallards. They have a Spanish name, can't remember what it is, some Spanish name.

If, in other conversations, Mike expresses warm feelings towards the ducks, she now communicates disgust, differentiating one species of duck from another in the process. In so doing, she refines the trouble and the troublesome group in question. With this, the category animal people shrinks in application, and so do the shared communal sentiments that result. While the communal borders constructed from troublesome individuals shift with their changing characterization, animal people, and troubles talk about them, expand and contract in relation to the animal habits in question.

Pets and their owners are also a source of annoyance, if not anger. While pet ownership is not officially permitted in the Grove, the restriction is ignored. As with the mixed sentiments of bird complaints, trouble talk here is socially complicated.

Troubles talk centered on pet ownership can be caustic, as shown in the following conversation between Donna, Opal, and myself concerning Opal's next-door neighbor, Mae, and her large pet cat.

Opal: [Angrily] The cat shits on the front porch every night and Mae has to wash it off in the morning. I see her doing it.

Chris: Why would she do that?

Donna: I don't know. The cat poops everywhere and it's just nasty.

Opal: It used to be real mangy, flea-bitten. I wouldn't let [her grandson] near it.

Chris: She doesn't have a litter box?
Donna: I guess not and the cat doesn't even cover it up when they're done. I know it doesn't. Go in her house, it smells awful. You've been in there? [I nod]. The thing has sprayed everywhere. Once a cat does that, you can't get it out.

Still, Mae is a popular resident. Mae has lived in Shady Grove for a long time; only Mike has lived in the complex longer. Residents, including Donna and Opal, helped Mae through an assortment of physical and emotional traumas, including a stroke. Donna, Diane, Erica, Mike, and Opal, among many others, call Mae a friend and often stop by her unit to chat. But Mae's pet cat complicates these relationships, causing friends at the same time to view Mae as a troublemaker. Solidarity gained from complaints against pet owners clearly has its limits.

Once started, the social momentum of troubles talk can take on a life of its own, expanding what is shared in the process. This was apparent as I sat in on a cat-related conversation between Opal and Diane. While the conversation began with complaints about Mae and her cat, with Opal telling me "it shits everywhere dammit, on my car, on the porch, on the sidewalk," troubles talk soon extended to other pet owners. Referring to someone whose name she was unsure of, Opal lodged additional complaints.

I think they call her "Gypsy." She lives over there by Dan. Across from him. She's got at least four cats and they are always out roaming, getting into things. The problem is the cats are out-and-about, getting into things.

In conversation, one extension of troubles talk tends to lead to another, which simultaneously builds the communal contours of exchanges.

"Cooped-up women"

Years ago, in her book *The Unexpected Community*, Arlie Hochschild (1973) described residents who were called "poor dears." The term referred to those Merrill Court residents who stood socially below their peers in the local scheme of things. Residents located themselves in relationship to each other within a hierarchy of advantage related to the misfortunes of age and family life. Hochschild explains:

There was a shared system of ranking according to which she who had good health won honor. She who lost the fewest loved ones through death won honor and she who was close to her children won honor. Those who fell short on any of these were often referred to as "poor dears." (1973: 58)

Poor dears were a vital part of the social contours of community life at Merrill Court. The term apprised residents of who they were in the local social scheme of things, providing a shared basis for assigning identity. Hochschild notes that the "hierarchy honored residents at the top and pitied 'poor dears' at the bottom, creating a number of informally recognized status distinctions among those who, in the eyes of the outside society, were social equals" (1973: 59).

The term "cooped-up women" operates similarly in Shady Grove, although usage by Grovers is more elastic than applications of the term "poor dear" appeared to be at Merrill Court. Like the use of poor dear, those who refer to others as cooped-up women invidiously distinguish between residents who mingle with others, and as a result are not cooped-up, and those who are viewed as detrimentally keeping to themselves and, as such are cooped-up. At the Grove, those who are cooped-up typically are women.

The term can be used categorically to complain about certain groups of socially isolated women or to Shady Grove as a whole. For example, a female resident might feel superior to other women in the complex because she ostensibly is more "vivacious and outgoing." Another resident might embrace a more global connotation. For instance, resident Audra once mentioned to me that she thought all Grovers were too cooped-up, which presumably would include every resident.

Applications of the term can be controversial. Residents might talk of a group of woman as certainly being cooped-up, but these women, in turn, might provide sound evidence that they are not. The term has considerable rhetorical cache in practice. But the important point regarding community life is that, regardless of application, the term works to recognizably differentiate residents, allowing them to orient to each other as the troublesome groupings in this regard they are to each other. While disagreement is prevalent over who these cooped-up women actually are, the shared recognition and widespread use of the term and category adds to what these residents hold in common, enhancing community in the process.

Consider, once again, the female resident named Mike. Her status as cooped-up illustrates the community membership she shares with other cooped-up women. She is the only resident of Shady Grove who has lived in the complex since its inception. For many residents, she epitomizes the reclusive woman, someone who frequently is used as a basis for comparison in this regard. Mike is 83 years old and has lived at the front of the complex for the past few years, after having lived "in the middle of it" for an extended period of time before that. Her unit is surrounded by a wood fence, a high hedge, and a tall fir tree, all of which feature the social isolation that is a common source of complaint about her and others in the complex.

Mike doesn't often venture outdoors. Even while I sought her out for conversation many times, she only occasionally is seen walking about the complex. The physical isolation of her unit and her reclusiveness showcase what others mean by being cooped-up. At the same time, and for the purposes of drawing other social distinctions, Mike's social isolation can be overridden by her energetic relation with family members, as well as her assertive attempts to be herself. The following illustration sorts this into its facets.

One morning I sat at the kitchen table with resident Dan, who lives directly across the street from Mike. As we talked about recent happenings around the Grove, I remarked that I had just tried to visit with Mike but she wasn't home. This was surprising to me since Mike is usually in her unit, being the cooped-up woman others complain about. Dan just waved his hand as if it really wasn't a problem, saying that it certainly was nothing to worry about. This short conversation followed:

Chris: When did you last see Mike around, Dan?
Dan: Oh yeah. She was over here the other day.
Chris: Good. I was worried about her. She doesn't come to the door when I knock and she's usually there when I come to visit.
Dan: Oh, she's just hiding out. She's hiding from her family or something. Always hiding from something. Surprised I ever see her to tell you the truth. Got family problems or something like that. Plus she's got the black butt. She watches them movies till about 6 or 7 in the morning. Them old movies. And then she sleeps all day. I'm sure she's asleep when you knock over there.

Dan's comments combine references to the assertively private Mike with a subsequent description of the cooped-up woman who is "hiding out." The illustration teaches us something about the shared nature of troubles talk – it has more general acknowledgement than its individualized evidence would warrant. Cooped-up is a *social* type generated out of complaints about others. Its shared application doesn't depend exclusively on the personal facts that do or do not support it, but rather on common usage.

Further to the point, shortly after my chat with Dan, I ran into a group of other female residents. They were gathered together outside Margaret's unit, taking a break from helping Margaret place her furniture into a moving van. Margaret was moving in with her daughter to help care for her newborn and was leaving the Grove after many years. I volunteered to help them carry the heavier furniture. As we loaded and chatted, Donna arrived and questioned me in an abrupt and derisive tone, "So I hear you are taking Mike to pay her phone bill?" This triggered an extended discussion centered on Mike's place in the social hierarchy of the neighborhood, further complicating the shared meaning of cooped-up.

Chris: I didn't think so. I told her that I'd talk with her today on the phone, but she didn't mention anything about me taking her to pay any bills.

Donna: [In a progressively angry tone] Well, that's what I heard. She shouldn't be using you for that. I told her that before. She used to walk all over the place paying things and now you have to give her rides. She needs to stop that. She can do it herself.

Opal: Well, I sort of feel bad for her. The last two times I've been over there, she hasn't come to the door when I've knocked.

Donna: She's been in there. Holed up.

Chris: Dan said what it was.

Donna: What is it?

Chris: Something about how she's been staying up until 6 or 7 in the morning watching old movies or something and then sleeping all day.

Opal: I tell you what it is. She's got Alzheimer's. [Margaret nods in agreement.]

Chris: It wouldn't surprise me if she has it in the early stages.

Opal: Every time I go over there and knock on her door, it's wide open. She comes up there and asks who it is, like she don't know me from Adam's house cat. She knows me and after I tell her, she always says, "Oh, I knew that."

Through its twists and turns, this conversation brings Mike to light in various ways. Initially, Donna expresses anger because she feels that Mike is taking advantage of me, which depicts Mike as a troublesome individual. But this soon develops into a complaint about a member of a well-known troublesome group. The inklings of this emerge when Opal points out that Mike has either not been at home or has refused to answer her door. Confirming Opal's point, Donna conjures the cooped-up woman as she portrays Mike as "holed up," a variation on this social type.

Explaining this as possibly the result of Alzheimer's disease, Opal recasts the trouble in question as medical rather than moral, reducing the negative force of the complaint in the process. Interestingly enough, Mike herself uses the term cooped-up to describe others. While she shares use of the category with them as a term of reference for a troublesome group, she doesn't always cast the trouble in moral terms either. As the following incident illustrates, sometimes cooped-up women "can't help it."

This incident occurred at the start of my fieldwork in the Grove. A small number of residents were showing me around and introducing me to the other residents. When Donna tried to introduce me to Eve, Eve responded rudely, slamming the door in our faces. Noticeably upset, Donna suggested we discuss this with Mike, Eve's neighbor, who might know why she behaved this way. We arrived at Mike's and, following a brief description of what had just occurred, Mike explained to us how cooped-up Eve was.

As her explanation unfolded, we learned that Mike provides assistance to her "needy" neighbors, Eve and Olga. In communicating this, she portrayed them as cooped-up, but not to be complained about for the same reasons as others, because Eve didn't deliberately act reclusive.

> She's [Eve] always been a little strange but was nice enough. She's fallen and she's isn't doing well. Basically stays to herself back there, all cooped up in there. Her and Olga both. You never see them. Just like recluses. Olga used to put her garbage out but she was really sick, you know, and couldn't get it in very well, so for a long time someone would put it out for her. I don't know who. It could have been her, I guess, but then I would take it back for her. God, that went on for the longest time.

Reclusiveness is a shared concern, one to complain about. For many residents, Mike epitomizes this as a source of complaints. Insisting on being socially isolated, such cooped-up women work against what Shady Grove otherwise could be – a community of individuals who share life in the complex. At the same time, while widely used to reference this kind of trouble, the term, like the use of animal people, can be constructed more positively. Still, regardless of which valence is emphasized, its leading presence in the local culture of complaining at the Grove makes it as effectively communal as "poor dear" is at Merrill Court.

Conclusion

Community signifies places and domains of shared understanding, locations of everyday life that assign common meaning and recognizable identities to those who live, work, or otherwise spend time there. But geography can only be shorthand for the "we-ness" that marks community life. As an official neighborhood, Shady Grove would seem to represent the geographic boundaries of shared identity for residents. But, clearly, the residents actively construct the sense of community and its boundaries. They are not just members of a community that simply exists. At the Grove, residents use troubles talk to build community and to construct the identities of the residents themselves.

As noted at the start, the design of the complex would seem to work against sharing anything. But community at Shady Grove centers on much more than location. What is activated and shared works despite location and design. Community life at the Grove is something accomplished, built from talk about the troubles that residents produce and hear from one another. In this regard, Shady Grovers are actually "doing" community as they interact with one another on the premises – even if their interactions center on troubles.

Curiously enough, I've hardly mentioned old age in this chapter. While Shady Grove is officially a senior public housing complex and the conversational substance of the later years does take place there – such as talk of dementia or of being chronically ill – the language of later life isn't much used to construct this community and its way of aging. Grovers are certainly old, some are sick and dependent, and more than a few are impoverished. But the local culture of community isn't so much a reflection of these conditions, as it is a construction assembled out of the troubles talk Grovers share through complaints about one another. As a community, the Grove is not an adaptation to the typical problems of old age. It's an adaptation and outgrowth of the troubles residents bandy about in their everyday interactions.

References

Faircloth, Christopher. 2001. " 'Those People' and Troubles Talk: Social Typing and Community Construction in Senior Public Housing." *Journal of Aging Studies*, 15: 333–50.

Faircloth, Christopher. 2002. "The Troubles with Celebrity: Community Formation in Senior Public Housing." *Ageing & Society* XX: xx–xx.

Hochschild, Arlie. 1973. *The Unexpected Community*. Berkeley: University of California Press.

Putnam, Robert. 2000. *Bowling Alone: Collapse and Revival of American Community*. New York: Simon & Schuster.

Chapter 6

Family Lives of Aging Black Americans

Colleen L. Johnson and Barbara M. Barer

Two views of the contemporary black family are prevalent in popular and academic commentary. One is problem-oriented, while the other portrays the black family's superhuman resilience. The first perspective presents a discouraging picture of high divorce rates, matriarchal dominance, and the peripheral status of men. The other portrays an exaggerated adaptability in family relations. Contrary to these one-sided views, our research has found greater diversity in the family lives of black Americans. Using case material from interviews, this chapter examines the lifestyles that characterize these families and the experiences of individual members. Some aspects of the families described do seem problem-ridden, but they also appear to be quite functional in other aspects. A more nuanced perspective indicates that black families combine elements of both negative and positive qualities in different ways in response to their particular social circumstances.

Two research projects conducted in the San Francisco Bay Area of California provide the data that illustrate related ways of aging. First, in the late 1980s, 129 African American adults, 65 years and older, were part of a study of the social dimensions of health care among inner city residents. Using open-ended interviews, we found much variation in their family lives, which contradicted the common narrow stereotypes about blacks (Johnson and Barer 1990). Typical respondents faced a variety of challenges in adapting to the aging process; they were often poor, and as members of a minority group, faced a situation referred to as "multiple jeopardy" (Dowd and Bengston 1978; Jackson 1980, 1985). Most lived in public housing or small dark apartments, and many had to contend with the restrictions of crime-ridden neighborhoods. They were usually supported by a small social security check or supplemental security income. Despite these disadvantages, however, their sense of well-being was high, a finding that at least in part can be traced to their supportive families.

A second source of case material comes from a longitudinal study of the oldest old, which included a sample of 122 blacks over the age of 85, who were interviewed several times in the course of the research. These data present the life course trajectories and aging experiences of African Americans who were born in the rural South in the early nineteenth century. In late life, most of them displayed a keen sense of survivorship. They were proud of having overcome difficult early lives and the effects of prejudice and discrimination.

In recent years, an impressive set of findings on black families in later life has come from large-scale surveys that offer alternatives to the problem-focused stereotype (Taylor, Jackson and Chatters 1997). The case material presented in this chapter is meant to augment this recent quantitative turn in perspective, to further fill the gap in information about the complex tenors of African American family life.

Our objective is to present the lives of blacks in their own context rather than through the lens of white culture. The findings focus on the diversity in life experiences, particularly on how the family affects the aging process. Rather than assuming that the standard nuclear family is the norm or model for comparison (Smith 1993), we offer a kinship model of family. This takes into account the importance of active, multifunctional extended family relations in shaping the aging experience of many black Americans. The level of social integration differs among these respondents. There are, for example, those who grow old without family and those who remain isolated from family and friends. This extends to those who are childless, who must find substitute supporters when the disabilities of old age occur. Taken together, the case material shows that the family lives of aging black Americans are anything but either purely dysfunctional or superadaptive in their characteristics.

Multifunctional Extended Families

Large, close-knit extended families are the most common family type presented in our material. For the very old, there is pride and status in being the progenitor of three and four generations (Barer 2001). As one respondent put it, "I'm the last link of the old folks on either side. I'm a six times great great grandmother." Multigenerational families offer the opportunity to both give and receive various forms of emotional and material support. The phenomenon of "fictive kin," which entails the elevation of friends to family status, runs through these reported experiences. Fictive kin are people with whom one feels kin-like but who are not related by blood or marriage (Chatters, Taylor, and Jayakordy 1994). Anthropologist Carol Stack (1974) noted years ago that this serves to further expand family networks, especially among African Americans, extending both emotional and material support in the process.

Members' narratives represent how family involvement gives meaning to life, providing a basis for identity and generativity. Such households have been singled out as very adaptive in the migration of blacks from the South to large Northern cities (Martin and Martin 1978). The following three cases illustrate how reciprocity in the exchange of goods and services, as well as emotional support, takes shape in multifunctional extended families. These cases also show how the mutually supportive activities of such flexible, inclusive social units contribute to the positive aging experiences of older blacks despite the sometimes serious malfunctioning of some family members.

Mr. Marshall

Eighty-nine-year-old Mr. Marshall lives in a large extended family household that has flexible boundaries and a changing membership. While some family members live troubled lives, the group as a whole sees that his needs are well met. Mr. Marshall is a distinguished-looking, well-groomed man. When he was interviewed, he was wearing a striped dress shirt, tailored pants, silk stockings, and shiny polished black leather shoes. He has short brown, barely gray hair and is clean shaven with a neatly trimmed moustache. He lives in his own home in a somewhat dangerous urban neighborhood with his now wheelchair-bound wife of 66 years, along with various transient family members. Overall, Mr. Marshall is sustained by his religious convictions and his pride in "still being alive."

Typical of his generation of black men born in the South, Mr. Marshall came to California during World War II to work in the war industries. He started out with the Southern Pacific Railroad laying tracks and then worked at a Navy supply center where he reports having earned 89 cents an hour. He added, "I've really been disappointed my whole life. Never made the money I would have liked to have made – it didn't amount to nothing. You just don't have what you want, you just make out with what you got." Commenting further on his finances, Mr. Marshall notes, "I live on Social Security and SSI. I'm paying $190 a month for graves and burials for both me and my wife, one grave together." However, Mr. Marshall is also proud to have been ordained a minister in the Church of God and Christ, where he led a small neighborhood congregation well into his later years.

Mr. Marshall's father, who was part Indian, "did lots of different kinds of work, hard work." He describes his parents as being very strict. "That's why I never got in trouble," he explains. Such is not the case, however, with his own descendents. He and his wife raised two sons. Both died prematurely of alcoholism, leaving behind young children whom the Marshalls raised with the help of welfare funds. Some of these grandchildren now see that Mr. Marshall receives attentive care. Nevertheless, his family members' lives are fraught with the problems of substance abuse, crime, and prison sentences. Among their several grandchildren, one grandson died early of cirrhosis of the liver and another committed suicide at the age of 35. The granddaughters seem to have fared better and provide both material and emotional support to the Marshalls. Of his grandchildren's children, one died at the age of seven in a house fire, and three great grandsons are incarcerated, one with a double life sentence. He laments, "I didn't know that they were doing what they were doing. They got in with the wrong crowd. It hurts me pretty bad."

Still, Mr. Marshall's own daily life seems full, much of it supplied by family members. On a typical day, he says, "I sit around and watch TV mostly, the fights and the news. I be dressed and out every day. In the morning I walk to the corner, just to be walking. I cut a little grass, pick up the paper, the leaves, and stick around and watch my wife. We're really one now." The household is busy, with a granddaughter coming daily, paid by the County, to provide personal care to his ailing wife, and to prepare breakfast. A service worker also arrives daily, at noon, to tend to housekeeping chores and to prepare the evening meal. Additionally a great granddaughter and her son are temporarily living in the home, and a grandson, who is described as "a wino," lives on the property in an outlying structure.

Of Mr. Marshall's siblings, only one brother and a sister are still living and they and most of his nieces and nephews remain in Louisiana. In the course of the study, Mr. Marshall's wife passed away and his sister's daughter in Louisiana began urging him to live with her, saying she would come and get him. He felt that it was "too late to move. They all call me from the South to refresh their minds on things that happened 75 to 80 years ago that I recall. I have a good memory." Meanwhile, his brother's stepdaughter in a neighboring community telephones him nightly.

Mr. Marshall takes pride in the fact that "I'm still living," having suffered his first heart attack at the age of 74. He has undergone several surgeries for various conditions, has visual and hearing problems, and reports having "a blood clot around my heart. Still, I eat like a mule. I don't feel no older than when I was twenty, but I know I'm old."

Asked how he sustains his sense of well being, Mr. Marshall responds,

> I'm pretty hard to upset. I've been through so many trials and tribulations for so long that I don't pay attention to problems any more. You learn more through experience than education. I don't get angry so easy. I guess I'd be gone if I did anger easily. I still believe in God.

Everyone ought to believe like that – some kind of super being. It's a beautiful life, sick or well. I'd rather be living than dead.

Mr. Marshall's story typifies a black man who sustained a steady work history and a long marriage, along with a range of family troubles. Yet, despite disappointments with his past earnings and family difficulties, he views his struggles from the perspective of a long-time survivor. He has learned from his life experiences to no longer get angry or worry. His strong religious convictions also contribute to his peace with aging. Mr. Marshall's sense of self is evident in his careful grooming and meticulous dress. While his domestic life resonates with many of the negative features presented in the image of the problem-riddled black family, it also provides a workable life-sustaining context for his present well-being.

Mrs. Edwards

Mrs. Edwards is an example of a strong family matriarch, who, at the age of 76, still gives more than she receives. She is immersed in her large extended family, providing a home base where some of her children and grandchildren live, and where others are constantly dropping by. In spite of poor health, she remains active in community associations.

Mrs. Edwards lives in a small Victorian house in the inner city with her son Harold and three grandchildren. Most of her ten children, her 52 grandchildren, and "about" 20 great grandchildren live nearby. Her ten children have a broad range of work histories, from semi-professional jobs to one son who is in jail. She herself is a retired practical nurse who has been widowed for "a long time." During her interview, one son, who is a parole officer for the city, stopped by dressed in a white shirt and tie. Another son, who was unemployed and dressed informally, also dropped by.

Mrs. Edwards met us at the door in her bathrobe and nightgown. She is a short vivacious woman who later said that she enjoyed the interview and wanted us to come again soon. She has sparse gray hair, the result of chemotherapy for breast cancer. The interview was conducted in her bedroom just off the living room, where she could easily observe what was going on in the rest of her active household. The room was dominated by a king-sized bed and a large television set at high volume during the interview. The room was cluttered and in need of cleaning. There was an empty whiskey bottle under a chair, open packages of food, and cigarette butts strewn on the floor. A cockroach was crawling on the bed.

Four years ago, Mrs. Edwards developed breast cancer and is now facing a bout of cancer for the second time. Despite this serious illness, she is active in her church and with her many descendents. She has public vouchers to take taxis around the city to visit her children and to go to church activities. At one point in the interview, she comments on her busy lifestyle, showing the extent that a supportive family plays into this.

> After this interview, I will go to my daughter's for dinner. I can get up and go any time I want. I'm not nervous about my health now. I have cancer, so I can't say my health is excellent, but it is not poor. I guess it's fair. I don't worry about it. I'm more concerned about starting my fruitcakes for Thanksgiving dinner than I am about the cancer. The whole family will be here.
>
> I am fortunate that I have enough money. My children help me when I'm sick. I get social security and a pension, and my children give me money. The only help I had after surgery was a visiting nurse who stopped by to show my son and daughter-in-law how to change the bandages. The social worker wanted to give me a nurse and someone to clean my house, but why should I pay for that when I have so many children and grandchildren to help me? My daughter gave me four nightshirts. She said she'd kill me if I was sitting up in bed in an old sweater.

Mrs. Edwards recounts her earlier family life in detail, this time indicating the support she received along the way.

> I was first married to Mr. Houston. I had eight children by him. Then he lost his mind, so I had to divorce him. After that, I came to San Francisco and met Mr. Moore. I had two sons by him. He's been dead for quite awhile. I had divorced him before he passed. My parents came to San Francisco long after I did. Father died at 92. He lived with me for years and years. When I was still in Texas, my mother had a house in the middle, with my sister and me living on each side of her house and my cousin was down the street.
>
> I'm still in touch with Mr. Houston's daughters by his first marriage. They came for my oldest son's marriage. One has died, but there's Ginna who has a child named "Johnny." Leala is called "Baby." I was there two years ago. Ginna had a car and drove me all around. I stayed with them for two weeks. I also have contact with Mr. Moore's children by his first marriage. I keep in touch with everyone.

Describing her children in equal detail, Mrs. Edwards once again reveals that both problems and support come from her extended family. It is as functional to Mrs. Edwards and some other members as it may appear to be dysfunctional for still others.

> My eight children by Mr. Houston include my eldest son who lives in Kentucky. He has a son who is a pediatrician. Next, I have a daughter

who works for the phone company. My third son has lost two children. A daughter died of crib death and a son died in an automobile accident. My fourth, a son, works for the State. His son got killed. Someone shot him over a drug deal. My fifth is Raymond who has three children. He is a parole officer. His daughter, Angela, is asleep upstairs. Lots of my grandchildren drop by to spend the night. My sixth is David. He has a son who is a paraplegic who lives here. His other son is in prison. I don't know when he'll get out. My seventh son is Kenneth who is also in prison at Vacaville. When I took sick, my doctor wrote a letter requesting he be transferred to a closer prison, but that didn't work out. As it is, I don't get to see him much. He has a wife and two children. My eighth son by Mr. Houston I can't think who it is. Let's see ... Oh, it's Richard. Richard came in the other day with a bottle of brandy and passed out on the couch. I took his brandy and hid it. It's what I need for my fruitcake. I talk to his wife every day. My daughter and son by Mr. Moore are also around here a lot.

We noted earlier that Mrs. Edwards gives to her family as much as she receives. She is a strong older black woman who is head of a large extended family household. The description of her ten children suggests a wide range of life trajectories, which she takes in her stride. Her practical nature and sense of humor help to sustain her, as when she puts to use her son's bottle of brandy, or at another point in the interview jokes about her daughter's disapproval. Even at the age of 76, and in poor health, she cooks and hosts holiday dinners for her many offspring. It's clear that her family life defines her and provides meaning for her life.

A follow-up interview found Mrs. Edwards much the same. She was still actively involved with her very large family and in the community. Some of her children and grandchildren moved out only to be replaced by other children and grandchildren. When asked about her large family, she brought out a big book in which she had recorded family information, many birth announcements and wedding invitations, her cab vouchers for which she pays $9 for $90 worth of cab rides, and a watch which was a retirement gift from the Visiting Nurse Association. It was inscribed, "We love you, Elizabeth."

Mrs. Edwards has a new color television and her idea of a good day is simple:

Nothing hurting and I can lie down and watch TV. I've lost a lot of weight, so I get a little bit depressed. I am also distressed about my son in prison. At least he didn't kill anyone. I read that the punishment is strict for that. But freedom and your health are the best things in life. If your freedom is taken from you, you have nothing.

An hour later, Mrs. Edwards clearly wanted to get back to her "stories" on television. She got up from her seat in the living room and went to her bedroom door to watch a soap opera while answering our final questions.

Mrs. Edwards typifies someone with a large multifunctional extended family, whose home provides a base that is flexible in taking in those in need. As some children and grandchildren move out, others move in. She still manages to maintain close relationships with the stepchildren of both of her late husbands. She also takes in her stride the fact that she has one son and one grandson in prison, part of the social experience of many poor black families. At the same time, her other children are most attentive to her needs. The problems of her domestic life are balanced by its persistent positive contributions.

Mrs. Edwards is an emotionally strong woman. Despite two bouts of cancer, her spirits are high, and she stands ready to help her children and grandchildren. She has adequate financial resources that permit her to offer generous hospitality to her family. She adapts to family problems by distancing herself from the problems, such as having a son and grandson in prison. Yet, she carries on in a domestic context that effectively works for her in old age.

Mr. Jackson

Mr. Jackson represents those blacks who were born in the South on poor farms that required the hard work of all family members. He differs from the majority, however, in that he left home to become a catcher on a black minor league baseball team. During most of his work life, he was employed with one company, which now provides him with retirement income and benefits. He is a homeowner whose neighborhood has changed over the years and now is crime-ridden and unsafe. He is actively involved with family and friendship networks that provide a rewarding social life in his old age.

Mr. Jackson is a 78-year-old widower who retired after 33 years at a local company. Describing his work history, he comments, "I started as a janitor, but I worked my way up doing all sorts of things in maintenance." He has lived alone since his wife's death. Although the exterior of his house is in need of painting, the inside is lovely, with expensive traditional furniture, oriental rugs, marble tables, and many pictures of family members. Everything is neat and clean, the result of Mr. Jackson's care and attention. He is an expansive talker who thoroughly enjoyed his three-hour interview.

The day of the interview, Mr. Jackson mentioned that it was his birthday. He will be seeing friends and then will go to his son's house for dinner. He is very close to that son and his wife. The memory of his own wife lingers on: "It's been two years and a day since my wife died. We had been married fifty years, ten months, and one week." Mr. Jackson has two other sons from a previous marriage, who live in Chicago. He maintains a distant relationship with them. He spoke with one son a month ago and to the other three months ago. He last saw one son in 1977, and the other son has not visited since 1957.

Mr. Jackson's father died when he was ten years old, so he had to quit school and go to work.

> I was one of many children in a very poor family of sharecroppers. As a young man, I left home and became a catcher in the Black Baseball League. In those days, blacks and whites weren't playing together. In my early twenties, I met my wife and we married and went to live in Chicago. I worked as a chauffeur for an army officer, and my wife was their maid. At one point, I had to drive him to San Francisco. I liked the city, so we decided to move here. It took me only four days to find a job here.

Over thirty years ago, Mr. Jackson had prostate cancer but has never had a recurrence. "I take care of myself pretty good. I watch what I eat and I keep my weight down. I view my health as excellent," he points out. In responding to a question about his economic status, he says,

> I get all my bills and insurance. Some times I make it through the month and sometimes I don't. But I don't need anything. I do up breakfast by 8 or 9 o'clock and then scrub and vacuum the house. I also do gardening, carpentry, and projects around the house.

These comments indicate that, while he has some health problems and can't live extravagantly, he makes do and enjoys his life.

Mr. Jackson maintains an active social network. He sees his son every Friday night and also drops by the son's home several times a week. He helps out his son by taking his grandchildren to the doctor, giving them money when they need it, and shopping for them. Detailing his relations with other family members, it's evident that family for him extends to several fictive kin.

> I am very close with my son and his family here, but I'm distant from my sons in Illinois. I am probably closer to their children, my grandchildren there. I talk to them on the phone more than to their fathers. I love my grandchildren who live here. I keep some toys for them here, so they can play when they come by.
>
> I have a brother and two nieces in Oakland, who I see every month or so. I am really closer to my friends than to relatives. I have very special friends, two men and three women. We've known each other it seems like forever and we're close like family. Mrs. Walters lives right down

the street. She is like a sister to me. She wants me over today for a birthday dinner. I will go there after our interview for a meal and then have another dinner at my son's tonight.

His friends have been elevated to the status of kin, a common practice in black culture. When friends become very close, they are referred to as "like family." In some cases, actual kinship terms are used to formally recognize particular kinds of familial relationship, such as being "like a sister to me."

Mr. Jackson concluded his second interview speaking about religion, which the following comments indicate is a significant part of his everyday life.

I don't go to church every week, but I'm very religious. I believe you got to do your talking while you have God's breath in you. When the heart stops beating, you won't be able to talk to someone a foot and a half away. When you read the Bible, you see that the soul is your breath. The soul goes back to the Lord when you die.

Mr. Jackson illustrates a lifetime of stable employment despite an abbreviated education after the early loss of his father. In his old age, he is comfortable with his retirement income, he is a proud homeowner, and he is actively involved in family and friendship networks. He had a long-term compatible marriage until recently widowed. Family, for Mr. Jackson, appears to be as functional as they come.

The Childless

Just over 45 percent of the older blacks in the samples from our two projects never had children or had outlived all of their children. Some had to take care of younger brothers and sisters upon a parent's early death. Others did domestic work minding white children. Over an extended time, it became too late for some to have children of their own. In comparison to childless white elderly, however, the childless elderly blacks in our studies were more integrated into an extended family; siblings, nieces, and nephews often substituted for children of their own (Johnson and Barer 1995). Nevertheless, a diminished social life is more prevalent among the oldest old who are childless, as the following cases indicate.

Mrs. Page

Mrs. Page is 89 years old and childless. She has no extended family support nor does she have close friends or fictive kin. Commonly, blacks in that situation single out a friend and elevate that individual to kinship status.

However, Mrs. Page has not taken advantage of this practice. Economically, she is better off than many, because she is financially independent. Aside from close relations with her brother's widow, who lives on the same street, Mrs. Page has few contacts and complains of loneliness. Her loneliness has left her vulnerable to exploitation, both from transient relationships and from some of her siblings' children.

Mrs. Page lives alone in her own home in a rundown urban neighborhood. Nearby homes are surrounded by chain link fences, while others are unoccupied and boarded up. The front entrance to her home has double metal doors with double locks that take her some time to maneuver. Inside, her small two-bedroom home is well maintained. Several family photos of siblings, their children, and grandchildren are in evidence, as well as numerous religious artifacts and a collection of storybook dolls.

Mrs. Page is a tall woman who walks unsteadily with a cane because of her "bad knees." At our initial meeting, she was dressed in somewhat soiled slacks, a pastel striped blouse, with several strands of gold chains around her neck, dangling earrings, and multiple rings on her fingers. Her gray hair was disheveled and she wore glasses. She complained,

> I'm just annoyed that I can't do what I used to do. I hear well for my age. I don't eat as well as I used to. I fix things for myself and then don't eat them. The dirt and filth of the neighbors causes me distress, sort of a sinus condition that I have. I spit a lot.

Mrs. Page was born in Louisiana, the oldest of nine children in an intact family. Five of her siblings are still living. She has no idea how many nieces and nephews she has. At the age of five, she moved with her family to Oklahoma where she finished high school and started college. "I had to leave college because the cotton got bad and my father couldn't sell the cotton any more," she explained.

Mrs. Page married young and came to California with her husband who was seeking work with the railroad. Two pregnancies ended with a miscarriage and a stillborn birth. "My husband and I raised three little girls, my brother's daughters. He and his wife separated and he wasn't around that often. We kept them well up into their teen years and then their mother came in and took over and wanted to keep them away from me." After 50 years of marriage, Mrs. Page has been widowed 22 years. All through her marriage she worked for the Federal Government, starting as a stenographer and retiring as a department supervisor. She proudly recounted that "I had to be cleared by the Secret Service for the work I did in supplies in World War II."

A typical day for Mrs. Page consists of doing crossword puzzles in the morning, and reading the paper and the Bible. She offers further details, some of which are truly gruesome.

I do the washing and go outside to water the grass, but I mostly walk around and look out the window. I used to like to quilt, but now I can't see the hole in the needle, or I put something down and I can't find it. I sit on the porch and watch the men go by. My sister-in-law, my brother's widow, lives down the street, and we walk together or go to something at the church. Friends are mostly gone. It's so bad to even go to the neighborhood store here for a Lotto ticket. All the neighbors are afraid they'll get a gunshot through the window. There is drug dealing in the house next door, and yesterday there was a stabbing on the street. A woman stabbed a boy and he had his guts in his hand.

When asked about her extended family, Mrs. Page responded, "They're all married with their own families. They don't visit, but they help when needed. People are not what they used to be. If I need them they come." One niece broke off contact after Mrs. Page refused to co-sign a loan for her. She explained,

I loaned her $500 four years ago, and she never paid it back. Now she asked for $1,500 for a down payment and wanted to put my name on the loan. At my age you don't co-sign for anyone! First thing you'd find is that you won't have a house any more.

Out of loneliness, Mrs. Page had befriended a young couple in the neighborhood who frequently spent evenings with her. In exchange for their companionship, she provided them with food and beer and often gave them money. After they moved away she admitted being uncomfortable with their behavior. "They got too familiar with me." Apart from daily contact with her sister-in-law and twice-weekly Bible classes, Mrs. Page is alone.

I get to feeling very sad and lonely. There's nowhere to go and nothing to do any more. That's very difficult for all elderly people. We go to church, but need other things to do, too. Thank God that I'm here this long and no more problems with illness than I'm having. I can drive, eat, and sleep but nowhere to go and nothing to do but look at the four walls. That's very depressing.

As the research progressed, Mrs. Page continued to express concerns about loneliness. "I walk the streets. I don't go no place but to church and the store. I go driving (a 1971 Chevrolet) just to get away from home. No one comes over very much. Everyone is afraid of everything now." Mrs. Page remains quite isolated, expressed fears about her badly deteriorating neighborhood, and worries about the possibility of having to relocate. Yet, curiously enough, not all is grim in this otherwise dismal picture.

Page maintains her spirituality and manages to see herself as better off than others her age. She takes pride in her independence, her life experiences, work accomplishments, and having survived to such an advanced old age. At our final interview, Mrs. Page was upset. "They put out the neighbor I had next door. She lost her house – couldn't keep up with the bills. Also, there's been a lot of shooting around here, a lot of disasters." A dilemma for her is the prospect of having to move. "I don't want to sell my house and live in a home for the elderly where they don't treat you too good. I'll just stay here and drink coffee, eat pie, and have a beer once in a while."

The quality of Mrs. Page's family life is complicated by both her undesirable surroundings and her insistent independence. There are negatives to be sure, but there is also persistent resilience in managing on her own.

Mrs. Howard

Mrs. Howard was also 89 years old and childless at the time of our first interview. She fares somewhat better than Mrs. Page, mainly because of her close relationships with her siblings' children. In contrast to Mrs. Page, Mrs. Howard's extended family members often intervene to make the lack of support from being childless less pronounced. Having helped her siblings raise their children in the past, these nieces and nephews now provide Mrs. Howard with material and emotional support. However, given her advanced age, it is not surprising that some of her younger relatives are themselves senior citizens experiencing their own physical limitations. Similarly, long term survivorship means outliving one's peers, so that Mrs. Howard is bereft of contemporaries. Nonetheless, Mrs. Howard is still socially active. The practice of creating fictive kin serves Mrs. Howard well. Her relationship with her "play daughter," for example, is very meaningful to her. She uses the term "play" to signify that she and the individual in question "play" at being related.

The availability of subsidized senior housing, supplemental security income, Medicaid, and government home care provisions allow Mrs. Howard to remain living in the community. Despite declining health and bouts of loneliness, Mrs. Howard uses positive comparisons to improve her mood. In recounting her early childhood years and her current long life, it's evident that she maintains a positive attitude by thinking of those who are worse off.

Mrs. Howard was born in Texas, one of eight children mostly raised alone by their mother. She recalls those years, initially remembering her mother:

> She was strong, a hard worker. Compared to others, we always had enough to eat and a comfortable place to live. Papa died when I was nine. He was a farmer, growing cotton and corn, and he was also a

preacher going from church to church. I was brought up in the church. Being the oldest girl, I had to do more than the younger ones. I began cooking, washing, and ironing before they did. I didn't mind it.

In the early 1940s, Mrs. Howard followed her younger sister to California where she met her first husband while both were working in the shipyards. "I worked for the government doing laundry, ironing sheets and soldiers' uniforms." Twice married and widowed, Mrs. Howard remained childless, having had a hysterectomy in her early twenties.

Now Mrs. Howard lives alone in a neat and orderly one-bedroom apartment in senior housing. She relocated from her own home where she used to live with her now-deceased sister. The two had lived together for many years, sharing the care of her sister's son and daughter. This nephew now provides considerable support. "I'm like a parent to him. They are both really like my children," Mrs. Howard explains. In fact, before leaving Texas, Mrs. Howard helped her mother raise one of her brother's children. "My oldest brother's son does a lot for me too, I think because he's retired and has time. I also have a very close grandniece who lives nearby." Other nieces and nephews, of which there are many, live in Texas and most of them have physical limitations. As she reported, "Some are in worse shape than I am."

In addition to consistent and attentive support from her nephews, Mrs. Howard receives help from her play daughter. "She claimed me as a play mother when I first met her. We lived in the same building for ten years. She calls me mother and brings me cakes, figs, greens, and candy because she knows I like sweets." Mrs. Howard also views two long-time friends to be part of her family. "I feel just as close to them as to my nieces and nephews." She differentiates these relationships from her church "sisters." "That is what we call one another in church, Christian sisters who are church ladies. That's different than a play sister."

A slender woman with a gentle manner, Mrs. Howard was attractively dressed during the interview. She still participated in some church and senior residence activities. Her typical daily activities consisted of fixing herself light meals, doing a little housekeeping, some visiting, making telephone calls, and watching TV, favoring game shows and baseball games. "Sometimes I walk up and down the hall or go to the store." She considered her health to be "fair," mainly because of suffering from lifelong migraine headaches. Still, she comments, "I thank the Lord he spared me to get to this age. I can still get around, dress, bathe. Lots of people are in nursing homes, I haven't got there yet."

Five years later, we interviewed Mrs. Howard again. During the intervening years, her health had deteriorated. She began to have dizzy spells, and falling episodes, two of which resulted in emergency hospitalizations. By the time Mrs. Howard was 94, she no longer dressed daily, nor was she able to walk in the hallways. "I can't do like I used to. Sometimes I'd like to be goin'. Not being active worries me." She spends most of her days "resting" and her personal care and housekeeping help had to be increased from three hours daily to six. "I keep having new girls. They send so many different ones. I used to have the same one for three years but she left."

Mrs. Howard laments the loss of her siblings:

> I'm the last one alive of my immediate family. I get to thinking about my people sometimes and be sad – all of them gone but me. I miss my sister very much. I miss my people. I do get depressed sometimes. It don't make me feel good when I can't do the things I want to do and could do when I was young.

Nevertheless, a positive outlook prevails. "I'm still looking for the picture to be better for me. I haven't given up. I been blessed, everyone has ups and downs. People are nice to me."

The contrasts between Mrs. Page and Mrs. Howard are striking, illustrating not only differences in family solidarity but differences in desired level of sociability. One woman without children leads a busy family life, while the other is lonely and isolated. The two women have responded to their childless status in markedly different ways. Mrs. Howard maintains relationships with her siblings' children who are attentive to her needs. As her disabilities increase, she continues to manage a very positive view of her life and her future. Unlike most elderly and childless black Americans, Mrs. Page has no close friends or fictive kin. Her only relative is her brother's widow. Her temperament also differs. She tends to view most areas of her life in negative terms, and she is fretful and lonely, albeit she prides herself on her independence and survivorship. Most important of all for the theme of this chapter, the contrast between them belies the one-sided negative view of black family life. The contrast shows that a childless family life can be as positive for some as it is negative for others.

Social Isolates

The presence of children does not necessarily result in an actively supportive family. The following cases offer examples of those who had children but rarely saw them, or elderly persons who were completely alienated from their families. In two of the cases, respondents reported that they avoided their children because the children exploited them. Their children visited only when they needed money or food. Among those social isolates with a large number of children and grandchildren, alienation from children was often the result of their offspring's own distractions or difficulties in surviving the problems of inner-city living. Here, as for other elderly black

Americans, the social circumstances of poverty had its own effect on the family lives under consideration.

Mr. Smith

Seventy-seven-year-old Mr. Smith fathered seven children, but that was no guarantee of social support in old age. Even though he has six surviving children, ages 28 to 42, 15 grandchildren, and 2 great grandchildren, he is unable to ask anyone for help. "It's all they can do is to help themselves. They all got debts and other problems." Only two live nearby, and he is convinced they would help if they could. "We don't get together on holidays. They don't have anything to eat themselves. They can't feed me."

Mr. Smith's relationships with his offspring range from affection for a daughter who just moved away, to rather troublesome contacts. He explains: "One son stops by if he can find something to eat or find some money to buy drugs. I don't fool around with them. They don't know I'm thinking that way, but I really do." Mr. Smith does not know the names of all his grandchildren or great grandchildren. "I wouldn't know the greats if I seen 'em. They holler for me to help them, but I wouldn't go around any of them."

The only person Mr. Smith can turn to is a woman with whom he has had a 40-year, off-and-on relationship. Although her health is precarious, she is his sole source of support. "I can count on her. She understands me better than my mother did." Despite his lack of support and the limited sociability with his children, Mr. Smith says that he is still satisfied with the relationship he has with them. "I wouldn't want it no better. I wouldn't think it be right." He values his self-sufficiency independent of both family and friends. The kind of family life he maintains, it seems, is adequate for him to get along. Remaining sequestered in his small dark apartment, he describes his daily routine, "I don't visit nobody, and nobody visits me. I stay right here night and day." According to Mr. Smith, this is one way to deal with the hazards of his neighborhood. "If you go outside, they could be stealing and knock you up on the side of your head." A terse comment suggests he's made peace with the ways of his world: "I see things going on in the street and I don't see them."

Mrs. Davis

Although Mrs. Davis maintains some social relationships and lives in senior housing, she complains of being isolated. She is a 67-year-old widow who lives in an attractively furnished apartment. Her sister lives in the same building and they are very close. After their parents separated, the two spent their childhood being "shifted around." They continue to be intimate and mutually supportive. Neither of them has contact with their

88-year-old mother, because, as Mrs. Davis notes, "She wasn't much of a mother." Four surviving siblings live nearby and they, too, are rarely seen.

Mrs. Davis married at age fifteen and had four children. She left them with their father, because she thought he could better provide for them. It's clear to her that they now certainly couldn't provide for her.

> Now they are in their forties. They're around here, but I don't see them. I don't approve of their lifestyle. They just want to disrupt my life. I hadn't seen them for years but then I decided to get to know them. But that didn't last, they only wanted to get money out of me.

She remains estranged, thus protecting herself from their exploitation. She does know that the eldest passed away and left one daughter who has two girls.

Mrs. Davis' relationship with her son by a second marriage is different. He is married with three children who all live in the Midwest. He maintains contact by telephone and sends birthday cards and gifts. Every few years they get together, an event Mrs. Davis looks forward to. Meanwhile, her sole source of support is her older sister, who is quite disabled. "We spend three to four hours a day together, just looking out the window. I don't do much for fun. There's lots of senior citizen stuff downstairs, but I don't go."

Holidays are spent with Mrs. Davis' sister's daughter and granddaughter rather than her mother or her own children. Still, Mrs. Davis says she is satisfied with her family life, and she appears comfortable with having no contact with her descendents. She describes herself as a loner and appears comfortable with her solitary life. Like a few others, she maintains no relationships with her children, because she disapproves of their lifestyle. Although a large number of relatives are nearby, they do not form a support network. By choice, Mrs. Davis does not have friends. "To tell the truth, I don't have any friends. I've never had any. I've always been a quiet person. I didn't like to interfere with others. I don't want to be bothered with other people."

Mrs. Rose

Mrs. Rose is a 71-year-old woman who also lives in senior housing. Although she complains of poor health, she is a volunteer visitor to the housebound several days a week. She has ten children, seven of whom live in the area. She is not satisfied with the limited contact she has with them, her 28 grandchildren, and 12 great grandchildren. She explains:

> I love them very much, but it looks like everybody got their hands filled. I don't see them all. I see one daughter sometimes, but not for a month

now. I do talk to her on the phone every day. My son calls every other day but don't ask me how often I see him. I don't see none of them a lot. Every once in a while, I help out a daughter. She doesn't have a husband. I help her out with food.

Mrs. Rose herself is one of ten children, and although dispersed throughout the country, the siblings maintain contact through letters and telephone calls. "Recently we all were together for mother's funeral. Ever since my mother died, it seems like I'm all alone." Occasionally she spends a weekend with a second cousin in the area. Her holidays are spent with her children.

Mrs. Rose has few friends and the few she has are in poor health and are unable to get around. She details this, too.

We stay in touch by phone and sometimes we see each other at church. One dear friend lives next door; we turn to each other when we need something. My children are not available to help. They don't have to. I can do for myself. My children tell me my energy is better than theirs.

These three respondents, who complained of social isolation, have children or siblings living nearby. This could potentially lessen their isolation, but such is not the case. Both Mr. Smith and Mrs. Rose had seven children living in the area, but maintained little or no contact with them. In both cases, the children were struggling with poverty or were distracted by other problems. Mrs. Davis complains of social isolation even though she spends most of her days with her sister. This bond developed in early childhood after the breakup of their family. This bond became so close that she left her husband and children to go back to her sister. Living in a dangerous neighborhood is one factor that keeps older people in their homes alone. Others are isolated because of temperament; they prefer to be alone. Also, early alienation or social distance from family members can become more accentuated in later life with the onset of disabilities. Taken together, these case studies of social isolation once more provide a family picture more complex than commonly believed. There are problems, indeed, but there's also functional adaptation.

Conclusion

These case studies of aging black Americans show considerable variation in family life in the later years. These individuals tell stories of being born in the early 1900s, mostly into large families in the rural South. Their childhood was generally marked by poverty, early loss of parents, and limited educational opportunities. During World War II, they came to California seeking work in the shipyards and various war industries. Now in old age, many have a positive attitude about their lives, even while there are enduring hardships. These stories lead us to some important observations about the lives of aging black Americans.

Family diversity

The ways of aging we have considered have been presented in the context of family life. A range of family types was found, from large, close-knit extended families to abbreviated families with little contact between members. As we noted at the start, two stereotypes of black families are common today. On the positive side, this social unit is seen as an infinitely flexible, loosely bound group that readily incorporates outside members who are in need. On the negative side, a problem-focused perspective concludes that the family is likely to be immersed in a "tangle of pathology," with unstable marriages, female-dominated households, a peripheral status of males, and out-of-wedlock births. Our case studies, in contrast, present a range and variety of families that defy these one-sided views.

Certainly, there were respondents in our studies who were in three-generation extended families. While problems affected individual members, the family often worked to satisfy individual needs. Although some families fail to meet the needs of its older members, one can still find impressive family solidarity among blacks. Childlessness is common, but its effects have varied outcomes. For example, Mrs. Page is lonely, isolated, and bereft of family contact. Mrs. Howard, however, is actively involved with her siblings and their children as well as with church and friendship networks.

Also reflected in respondents' stories is a sense of equanimity and contentment, despite the hardships of lives that are far from perfect. There is life satisfaction in the face of their minority status and the effects of prejudice and discrimination. Positive comparisons also enhance life satisfaction. "Somebody is always worse off." One man commented on his contentment with life, "I was born with a roof over my head. As soon as I was old enough, I had a job. I was never out of work. I never laid down hungry, and none of my children did either."

Pervasive life themes

Five life themes resonate in these case studies. First, the extended family among black Americans can indeed be an actively functioning unit. Its members can be in frequent contact, and they exchange supports when needed. A norm of reciprocity is commonly endorsed; one should help others and they will help you. Unlike many white families, where lineal relationship between generations dominate, black extended families also emphasize collateral ties between siblings and nieces and nephews. Sibling solidarity is strong and naturally facilitates relationships with siblings' children, in turn enlarging the network of support among these families.

Second, the church is very important in the lives of these respondents. Their religion consists of a belief system that gives immediate meaning to their lives. Not only does the church provide a center for spiritual uplift and sociability, it is also a source of support to those who need it most. This echoes throughout the case material, further specifying the diversity of black family life.

Third, survivorship is a common theme. As many comments indicate, several of our respondents have overcome the disadvantages of early deprivations and have lived far into old age. When asked what was the best time of their life, the majority said the present is better than the past. They commonly mentioned, "Life has been hard, but I am comfortable and secure in my old age."

Fourth, the case material points to the important effects that psychological factors play in adaptation. Temperament and personality traits define the level of optimism and contentment versus pessimism and unhappiness that individuals presented in the interviews. In some cases these traits seem to be connected to an unstable disrupted childhood, but in others loom forth to designate the variety of individuals around which family life is centered.

Fifth, and finally, the patterns of black family life presented in this chapter differ from those found among aging whites in the same age group. Statistical comparisons found that blacks are significantly more integrated into kinship and community networks. When they need support, kin and fictive kin are often available to help. In fact, older blacks are three times more likely than their white counterparts to have a caregiver available if the need arises. Moreover, these black respondents had significantly more positive scores on their subjective well-being. All told, we hope that the case material included here elucidates the remarkable diversity of black family life, steering us away from both negative and positive stereotypes.

References

Barer, Barbara M. 2001. The "Grands and Greats" of Very Old Black Grandmothers. *Journal of Aging Studies*, 15: 1–11.

Dowd, James J. and Bengtson, Vern L. 1978. "Aging in Minority Populations: An Examination of the Double Jeopardy Hypothesis." *Journal of Gerontology*, 33: 427–36.

Jackson, Jacquelyne J. 1980. *Minorities and Aging*. Belmont, CA: Wadsworth.

Jackson, Jacquelyne J. 1985. "Race, National Origin, Ethnicity and Aging." In R. H. Binstock and E. Shanas (eds.), *Handbook of Aging and the Social Sciences*, 2nd edn. New York: Van Nostrand Reinhold, pp. 264–303.

Johnson, Colleen L. 1995. "Adaptation of Very Old Blacks." *Journal of Aging Studies*, 9: 231–44.

Johnson, Colleen L. 1999. "Fictive Kin Among Oldest Old African Americans in the San Francisco Bay Area." *Journal of Gerontology, Social Sciences*, 54B: S368–S375.

Johnson, Colleen L. and Barer, Barbara M. 1990. "Families and Networks Among Older Inner-city Blacks." *The Gerontologist*, 30: 726–33.

Johnson, Colleen L. and Barer, Barbara M. 1995. "Childlessness and Kinship Organization: Comparisons of Very Old Whites and Blacks." *Journal of Cross-Cultural Gerontology*, 10: 289–306.

Johnson, Colleen L. and Barer, Barbara M. 1997. *Life Beyond 85 Years, The Aura of Survivorship*. New York: Springer.

Martin, Elmer P. and Martin, Joanne M. 1978. *The Black Extended Family*. Chicago: University of Chicago Press.

Smith, Dorothy E. 1993. "The Standard North American Family: *SNAF* as an Ideological Code." *Journal of Family Issues*, 14: 50–65.

Stack, Carol B. 1974. *All Our Kin*. New York: Harper and Row.

Taylor, Robert J., Jackson, James S., and Chatters, Linda M. 1997. *Family Life in Black America*. Thousand Oaks: Sage.

Part III

Change

Chapter 7

Aging and Change in a Religious Community

Sarah Matthews

Social arrangements are never static. When they change significantly, as they did during the twentieth century, the resemblance between social circumstances in childhood and old age may seem remote to those who have lived through them. This chapter describes the lives of nuns who lived through World War I or its aftermath, the Roaring Twenties, the Great Depression, World War II and the Korean War, post-war affluence including the baby boom, and the anti-Vietnam war and civil rights movements of the 1960s and 1970s. These nuns experienced the widespread adoption of motorized transportation, urbanization that increased both population and ethnic diversity in cities, new ideas about the roles of women and men in society, the invention and adoption of communication networks including radio, television, and computers, and the expansion of education at the primary, secondary, and college levels. While these massive social changes directly affected the nuns' lives as individuals, they also had profound effects on the religious community to which the nuns had committed themselves in their late teens. These changes, in turn, sent additional reverberations through the nuns' personal lives.

The women who were interviewed for this study entered the convent between 1912 and 1941, in most cases immediately after graduation from a Catholic high school staffed by the nuns of the religious order. Although a span of thirty years may seem too long to define one age cohort, prior to 1941 the socialization or "formation" of the nuns into religious life was relatively static. After 1941, however, their living arrangements made continuation of the old ways all but impossible. Nuns who joined the community after 1941 encountered quite different circumstances from their predecessors and as time passed these became even more radical. When the nuns interviewed for this project were old, the contrast between their early life in the convent and that of the recent recruits was staggering. Rather than defining the cohort using birth dates, then, the boundaries were derived by examining the actual experiences of members of the community (Rosow 1978).

The subjects of this research participated in life history interviews for a sociological study of aging in a religious community that was conducted by a younger member of their community. She had shared religious life with them for more than thirty years.[1] Thirty-two nuns participated, approximately one-third of the survivors of the cohort who were well enough to be interviewed. Data were collected in the late 1980s when 4 of the nuns were in their late 60s, 16 in their 70s, 10 in their 80s, and 2 in their 90s. Their voices are heard throughout the chapter and illustrate how this way of aging, like others, is shaped by long-term societal and biographical influences. As we hear their voices describe the changes they've experienced, it's evident that who and what they are – their very identities as "women religious" – are also changing. For some, life-long identities are on the verge of disappearing in their later years.

Early Days in the Convent

Between 1912 and 1941 when the nuns entered the convent at the ages of 17, 18, and 19, they joined a cloistered religious community whose way of life had changed little since the early 1600s. Although living in the twentieth century, their formation and their way of life during their first years in the convent in many ways was still medieval.

Life in the monastery

Members of the religious community wore long, heavy, full black habits, which hung to the floor and had sleeves that extended below the fingertips. Undersleeves extended from the wrists to the elbows or shoulders. When sleeves were in the way of work, they were pinned back but the undersleeves were not removed except within the convent. A starched white shoulder covering or guimpe[2] and an elaborate headdress, including a veil, accompanied the habit.

The nuns' days were highly routinized, with everyone in the community participating in the same schedule: "Everything, of course, was by bells." On weekdays, they rose by five in the morning in order to be in chapel for half an hour of prayers and meditation before the six o'clock Mass. Except for a "reading," silence prevailed during breakfast. Days were spent either teaching on the grounds of the monastery and in nearby parochial schools, or with other duties on the convent grounds. The newest nuns were also engaged in instruction, a "canonical year," to prepare them to take their vows. The nuns ate supper in silence while listening to a reading. Compulsory recreation in which all the nuns met together followed. This was the *only* time in which "unnecessary" talking was permitted. Following recreation, all the nuns lined up in the hall by seniority, with the newest nuns at the front of the line and the general superior at the end. They folded down their veils and tucked their hands into the long sleeves of their habits. Following a short prayer said in unison, everyone filed into the chapel to fill the stalls and benches for night prayers (Gayer 1990: 93–94). The final hour of the evening was devoted to preparation for the following day. Lights were turned off at 10:00 p.m. and a "grand silence" commenced.

The nuns who were in the monastery on week days, primarily the newest nuns in their canonical year, also said five "offices" at scheduled times between breakfast and the noon meal and four offices in the afternoon. Those away from the monastery were expected to say the offices at the appropriate times. In addition, the nuns were required to say other prayers during the day. Sisters who had been too busy stayed in the chapel after night prayers to "finish up their prayers."

There were clear ranks within the community,[3] with the newest members being the lowest. In previous centuries, there had been two classes of nuns, one that was educated and taught girls and one that was illiterate and performed domestic work. The latter class had been phased out by 1920. Elimination of the "servant" class meant that the housekeeping tasks – cleaning, cooking, serving and laundry – were shared by all of the nuns. Most of these tasks, however, fell to the newest members.

> My job was to see that there was bread for each meal. You'd slice it and put it in big cans and then you were responsible to see that the tables were set and the towels that were used were washed. During the meal you served and you were just constantly going.

The young nuns were aware, however, that with increased religious age or seniority, their current responsibilities would be shifted to those who came after them (Gayer 1991: 79–81).

A general superior governed the convent. The vow of obedience was one that pervaded the nuns' descriptions of their early years. They were expected to do without question as instructed by anyone who had authority over them. The young nuns were learning the meaning of the vows of poverty, chastity, and obedience, which they would take in the near future, and what living in the religious community meant, as two of them remember.

You never had a voice to speak. Everything was very traditional. You were never able to express yourself. But that was our mode of life, I think. We were never asked our opinion on anything. We just did it. It was traditional. You don't break tradition. So there were many times we didn't feel as though it was fair, some of the things that were being done. But we had no voice to speak about it. We'd be held back from profession if we did.

＊ ＊ ＊ ＊

You couldn't go out at night – never to anything. All those years you had to be in at six o'clock. We couldn't even call our relatives. We never had a vacation. We didn't have any funds to use – like a budget. You couldn't manage your own things, couldn't determine your major in college. You had nothing to say about where you would teach or what you would teach.

Family members could visit the nuns at the monastery on Sundays, but the nuns were not allowed to go home except under rare circumstances.

Some of the sisters reported that blindly following rules had been difficult during their early years in the convent.

The months of my postulancy were easy and comfortable with Mother Coretta. Later with Mother Adrienne, the routine became rigid and repressive. I'm not sure about the term "formation." "Blind obedience" was the watchword and I wasn't exactly of a nature to dumbly fall into line like a robot. We had a few explosive differences of opinion but somehow the community kept me and I survived.

Others reported that adjusting to the strict communal schedule imposed on them was trying.

I hated to be regimented in the chapel and in the refectory [dining hall]. And I hated sitting and meditating after I had been read to, because I didn't remember what was read. I only remembered the nasal voice of the person who was reading. There was something about it that I didn't like. And it was very irritating.

The nuns who were in their canonical year and, as a result, were in the monastery during the day, were the "workforce" of the convent (Gayer 1990: 83):

So every Monday morning or afternoon we'd have to gather up the laundry in the burning hot attic room over the laundry and sit there and clap and wring and then straighten them out getting them ready to hang. They were wet and then when they were straightened, they'd hang them up to dry.

Ironing with a mangle was especially onerous because of the guimpe and elaborate head cover that the nuns wore.

The machine was a big flat mangle. It was a great big machine. It was not easy to run. You worked it with your foot and you pulled on the top. That's when I got my back [trouble], too. And you had to leave it on the guimpe just for a few minutes, and then you lifted it up, and then you turned the guimpe. Electa and I used to be careful that one side would be shiny and so you started on the wrong side. You had to be careful because those things would tear, you know. We were always very careful to get the ears nice and straight. It all took time.

The guimpe was difficult to maintain in its starched form. Humidity and rain often caused a "limp guimpe," as the nuns jokingly referred to it. It also got in the way of eating: "You had to have enough guimpes, because it took hours and hours [to launder them], and you could have it on for two seconds and drop berries or something [on it]."

The sisters reported that ingenuity was likely to be interpreted as disobedience.

There were no supplies for cleaning. There was always a fight. We had slippery coal oil to wash the bathtubs. You'd kill yourself. So Mary Donald's brother was working at Joyce Brothers store. There was a big store near St. Hugh's. Mary Donald asked for some supplies from home. So she got a big box. In it – *Sani-Flush*, cleanser you could use for scouring, you know, brushes and things – lots of supplies for cleaning. So Mary Donald got this nice big box. She put it up in the clothes closet. There were three clothes closets in that dormitory. And she said, "Now, kids, I have all these supplies. Just take them anytime you need them but don't tell the white veils [postulants] because they'll take them, too. So the novice directress found this box of supplies. That was it. No privacy.

Another sister reported that her mother objected to the way her collars looked and took them with her after her Sunday visits to a local laundry. When the novice directress noticed how nice they looked she demanded an explanation. The sister's response was that she didn't like "the way they were done here, and neither did my mother."

That she didn't send me home that night was a miracle. I guess God wanted me in the convent. I don't know. She told me I was proud. I was to put my pride under my feet and crush it.

Life in the convent was made difficult by the absence of modern conveniences.

> In those days, you prayed that you could hear radiators knocking before the bell [for rising] rang. Because other than that, it was cold. It was just a coal furnace and the man would come down like four in the morning to stoke the furnace and start it up – so you were really cold. If he came early enough, the heat came up so you were a little warm and you were so grateful. You got a spurt of heat around noon, and then you got a big spurt of heat around six o'clock, and that lasted you until the next morning. So you were dying of heat, but in about two hours you were happy to be under the covers because it was cold.

During the economic depression of the 1930s, life was particularly hard and the nuns were often hungry. Money was scarce and they depended on the generosity of their families, the parents of their students, and other Catholics for food.

Life outside convent walls

In addition to poverty, chastity, and obedience, the nuns took a fourth vow of "instruction." Their calling was to educate girls. The handful of nuns who came from Europe to establish the monastery in the mid-1800s were asked to come by a bishop to teach girls in parish schools. Nuns who were not in their canonical year were expected to be in classrooms. The sisters who entered the convent before 1941 were placed in classrooms immediately with no preparation other than their own attendance at parochial schools. Four of them describe their experience.

> I entered the convent on Saturday and I was sent out as a substitute teacher on Monday. An absolute greenhorn, I hadn't the remotest idea of what to do. I did keep some kind of order. I don't remember how.

> * * * *

> My first assignment was to St. Helen's first and second grade – three days after I was clothed. I didn't even know how to dress myself. I was a mess! I didn't know what to do for the kids in front of me. The whole year is a blur. I survived somehow, but I remember very little of the whole experience.

> * * * *

> I entered in August and I was sent right out to teach. At Christmas time, I was sent for [and changed to another school]. This was a

German school. In those days they taught German. The priests were all German, and you had to teach the rosary to the children in German. And I [not being German at all] had to learn the Our Father and the Hail Mary and things like that. And I had 75 in the first grade there. The pastor would come in regularly to see [the children] and he used to say to them, "Now any little boy or girl that brings another little boy or girl to school – I will give them a holy picture." I thought, "Oh dear, don't get any more."

* * * *

I was a postulant. They had started me teaching when I entered. I had the first and Sister Cosmas had the second . . . Seventh and eighth was Sister Barbara. She took me in hand. She had been my teacher. One day she said to me, "Irene, are you writing your plan for your day's teaching?" I thought, "Plan? She knows that I know that arithmetic." I was kind of offended. I had never heard of a lesson plan.

The nuns reported close relationships with older nuns to whom they were "apprenticed." As one explained,

I began at St. Kirsten's as a postulant . . . Sister John Cantius was the principal . . . I really loved her. She was like a mother to me. She taught me so many things. And gave me a lot of responsibilities which probably developed me a great deal materially. She was wonderful to me.

A nun who was asked if she thought that she had been a good teacher responded,

Well, I never thought it, but people have told me that I was . . . I think it was because we had older nuns that helped us. And I especially got a lot of help at Saint Perpetua's from Sister Chrysostom who was an excellent teacher . . . She was like a real big sister to me. Because when I went there, it wasn't easy. . . . Sister Chrysostom took me under her wing and she really helped me.

While members of this cohort were placed in the classroom with very little, if any, formal training, both Church and state had begun to promulgate education for teachers (Quinoniz and Turner 1992). In order to receive college degrees and teaching credentials, most of the nuns attended Saturday classes and summer school, primarily at the local Catholic college, which was a "normal" or teachers' college set up specifically for parochial school instructors, including nuns. Most of the nuns who were interviewed earned their degrees over the course of a decade.

The sisters did more than teach at the schools. They also cooked their noon meal and did custodial work in the parish schools in which they taught.

> It was hard teaching at a school. You carried every bit of food that you ate from the motherhouse. Every Thursday night, you had to be sure to remember to bring that food basket home or it was real trouble... Once a week we'd get these staple things. It was sometimes hard, but we knew we had to do it – so we did it. Whoever was cook – we had to cook, too. We had to eat our main meal at noontime. So that was a lot, to teach and cook, especially if you had a large school.

* * * *

> There were six nuns on the faculty there. We went on the streetcar. We had to be home for supper. If you weren't, the evening was a tragedy. You'd get a... penance. And you know it was hard. We had to clean up the rooms. If you were cook, you had to see that the kitchen was in order. You had to shine the halls. They had linoleum in the center of the hall and we had brooms. So Sister Albert and I, who were the youngest, would get out and shine that hall before we'd go home.

On Saturdays the nuns prepared the Catholic churches in their parishes for Sunday services and taught religion to children who did not attend parochial schools.

The religious community also staffed a boarding school, which initially taught girls through high school but soon added a boarding school for boys through grade eight. The sisters who taught there lived there because the boarding schools were too far from the convent to make commuting feasible. Because of "the rule," special permission from the local bishop and the pope was required for nuns to reside outside the convent walls and to teach boys.

Religious age

Seniority, or the length of time someone had been in the community, was very significant with respect to who did what: "We went to Communion strictly according to age. It started with the superiors, and no one stepped out of line." Chronological age and seniority or religious age were essentially synonymous when the nuns joined the community. With few exceptions, postulants were in their late teens.

Those who were the newest members were expected to do the most onerous tasks and had little control over their daily lives. Not until they had been "in vows" for a minimum of fifteen years (three years of temporary, twelve years of permanent vows) could they be "chapter nuns" who had the right to vote on matters related to the community. Their vote was only advisory, but chapter nuns were at least privy to information about important issues.

When the decision was made to sell the monastery and the actual sale occurred, those who were not chapter nuns relied on rumors about their impending fate:

> It wasn't talk so much. I guess that we surmised and guessed from what was happening. I can remember Mother Alvernia taking me up to the house and we didn't know what was happening. We did know that something was going to happen. And things like that happened often, you know, before we were told. I knew that there was an appraisal going on.

One of the nuns described how she found out that the convent had been sold.

> And when we came home from school at noon time, we would go right into the refectory and try to get our meals as quickly as possible and get washed up and on the bus that would take us back. Mother rang the bell and she said that she would just like to announce that they had just negotiated a good deal with a buyer who was going to take over the property and we would be moving out to Mater Misericordia [the boarding school property owned by the nuns] . . . And well, some people clapped. It was then when we realized what was going to happen.

Obedience affected nuns regardless of religious age, but for chapter nuns, the obedience was not quite as blind.

Sleeping areas or cells improved with rank. The newest members slept in dormitories. More senior nuns had cells with more privacy. A "directress" no longer supervised them. By the 1930s, the monastery was supplemented by two neighboring houses that the religious community purchased to accommodate their expanding numbers. Some of the junior nuns were housed in them rather than in the monastery.

There were three dining halls in the convent, one for the newest members, one for those who were in vows but not yet chapter nuns, and one for chapter nuns. The newest nuns served the older nuns, who sat at long tables according to religious age, and cleaned their dining halls.

The longer a nun had been in the community, the more formal education she was likely to have. Education qualified nuns for positions with more authority and status, such as teaching older children, and being novice directress, principal, and college instructor.

> When I first professed, the Cathedral school was my first assignment. I was there four years. I was supposed to have the first and second

grade and I knew nothing about babies, but I think I had them two years...I don't know who taught the seventh and eighth but, anyway, she got sick and I was yanked up so I had seventh and eighth grade for a year...I got an obedience one time to teach at the Fountaine Street High School. I got my first degree in 1933 and then I was sent to the college to teach.

Also, if nuns with seniority were bound by their vows of poverty, chastity, obedience, and instruction, they had perks that those junior to them did not enjoy.

Religious age related to caregiving, too. Members of the community cared for dependent nuns. When nuns were no longer able to participate in education, younger members of their community cared for them. One nun recalled,

I was taking care of a [older] nun one time, and her towels were like tissue paper, they were so thin. I said to her, "Sister, the towels you have, you could read the paper through them"...So I took care of this nun for the whole year, and I remember asking Mother, "May I please give Sister a little gift for Christmas?" [My directress] told me to remember my vow of poverty and did I think I should be giving a gift? I mentioned about the towel situation. She told me all right, but I had to show her what I was going to give. I put the two towels together and folded them. She [the directress] thought it was very lovely, but she thought that sister might not like the pink in the towel. When she saw the two of them, she was thrilled.

Between 1912 and 1941, the religious community was highly routinized. Domestic work was arduous. How to teach was learned initially not from formal training but with assistance from nuns already on the job to whom younger nuns were "apprenticed." The nuns' days were filled with activities from the time they got up in the morning until lights out at ten o'clock. Except for a few hours each Sunday afternoon when family members were allowed to visit, they were completely separated from their former lives.

The Middle Years

In 1941, the monastery was sold. For over fifty years the grand building had housed the nuns. In those years, some modern conveniences had been added,[4] electricity for one. Additional buildings had been annexed. According to the nuns, two reasons prompted the move. One was that the neighborhood had deteriorated. The nuns no longer felt safe in their convent. An attempted abduction was one among a number of troubling incidents that the nuns recalled.

> I was with Sister Jacob the night that she was grabbed . . . She became ill during night prayers and she lived in the annex. And so she asked me if I would go over with her. It was in the summertime, right around 7:00. When she leaned over to put the key into the door, the guy grabbed a hold of her and tried to lift her over the banister. I was with her. We yelled and hollered, and scared him away. But hostility rose very much against us. All those years [before] no one had even bothered us at all.

The second reason for the move was that the Great Depression had left the convent in dire financial straits. Parishes had been unable to pay the nuns' salaries during the 1930s and the community owed substantial amounts of money to grocers who had been willing to extend credit and to banks that held mortgages on their properties. The move marked a turning point in the life of the convent. Changes in their way of life after 1941 can be traced in part to their new living arrangements. New ideas about what constituted religious life, which had been brewing in the Catholic Church during the twentieth century, were also an impetus.

Adapting to new residential arrangements

Although the convent owned other properties, the only buildings that could accommodate the nuns as a group were the two boarding schools that had been built in the previous century. This was one of the first places where nuns had been given permission to live away from the monastery. By the early 1940s, some groups of nuns were also living in parishes in "missions" near schools that were deemed far enough from the monastery to make returning each evening impractical. Living away from the monastery, however, was regarded as exceptional.

The accommodations at the boarding schools, which became day schools once the nuns moved there, were far from ideal. Everyone was housed in the dormitories and conditions were crowded. The postulants, novices, and young chapter nuns were housed in one boarding school, the older nuns in the other. The boarding schools were far away from many of the schools in which the sisters taught. Commuting to the schools from their new location was both time-consuming and costly.

The nuns who were interviewed remembered the years they lived at the boarding schools as difficult. This was due in part to subtle changes in their way of life that had occurred during the previous decade. During the Depression, survival had required considerable ingenuity. Rules about accepting gifts from home and the color of undergarments, for example, had been relaxed in the interest of survival. Their contact with parishioners on whom they depended for food and other amenities had increased. Furthermore, most of the nuns interviewed for this project were young chapter nuns by the time of the move and had begun to enjoy the benefits that went with their rank. In the new location they were housed with the postulants and novices.

With the Depression behind them, the directresses appointed to supervise the younger nuns seemed bent on restoring obedience to "the rule." One nun recalled,

> We were all very miserable. We were treated as children. Sister Madonna spied on us. She was the novice mistress. Every single night Sister Sarah would go to the phone and tell the General Superior all the things we did. She came over and called us snips and snakes and gave us a long lecture. . . . That's when I fainted. All the nuns were so happy to stop the lecture. I couldn't believe she called us those things. I don't feel guilty about that. I don't think we were. None of us were. Why she called us that, I don't know. It seemed like we were always treated as if we were infants.

The nuns were so unhappy that they eventually complained to a bishop who came to the convent to instruct the young nuns each summer. This was a clear violation of their vow of obedience, but the bishop was sympathetic.

> Not that he was being easy on those nuns. But I guess he must have told Mother Edward some of the things that were told to him. I guess she came over and, oh, she was so angry after he left. She told them they were all going to have penances. . . . I think the Lord took care of it because He sent the fire.

The building in which the younger nuns lived burned to the ground five years after the nuns had relocated, further compromising the living arrangements in their makeshift monastery. Their small rebellion, however, showed that that the strict hierarchical structure of the religious community could be challenged, which perhaps was a portent of things to come.

The issue of community living was one that had been raised numerous times in the previous fifty years. The number of Catholics and Catholic children had begun to increase dramatically due to immigration in the early part of the twentieth century. The city expanded geographically to accommodate its increased population. This was made possible, first, by public transportation and, later, by the widespread adoption of the automobile. Newly established parishes were so far from the old monastery that cloistered living became increasingly difficult. Nevertheless, every time the issue of breaking up the community into smaller residential units was officially raised, the majority of the chapter nuns voted for retention of their cloistered way of life. On several occasions, however, bishops had overruled them and ordered nuns to live in mission houses. At the time of the move to the boarding schools, then, some nuns were living in mission houses away from the convent.

After 1941, it became increasingly difficult to keep the rule of cloistered living. The old convent had been near the center of the city. The new one was not. Once the already cramped and inconvenient boarding schools were reduced to one by the fire, the situation took on crisis proportions. The crowded conditions were relieved initially by moving a large group of nuns to a newly acquired and renovated campus for one of their girls' schools, but that solution was short-lived. The bishop ordered parishes to provide mission houses for the nuns who taught in their schools. By the 1950s' baby boom when schools were so crowded that many had double shifts, mission houses had become the norm.

In the 1960s, on property away from the central city, both a motherhouse and buildings for the community's women's college were built. The motherhouse was not large enough to accommodate all of the nuns. It was intended to house only the most junior nuns, the retired nuns, and the nuns who taught at the college. Most of the nuns who were neither new nor senior lived in small groups in the parish mission houses. The general superior continued to have final say over how each group implemented "the rule." One sister described the aftermath in her mission house of a visit by a delegate of the general superior:

Her visits wrought havoc everywhere. There were only four of us there. Maybe there were five. And we'd have dinner together. And then we all did a job right then and there. Somebody would take care of the pot and pans. Somebody would clean up the kitchen table. We'd clear out the dining room table and set the table for the morning. And then it would be almost time for night prayers. But we laughed and talked and had such a good time during that time. And Sister Irene wanted to know when we had formal recreations. Well, we didn't because we were all working together and having a real good time. But we did take recreation together. We sewed together and did lots of things together, but we didn't have that formal recreation every night. So she said we had to do that ... So then three had to do the cleaning up and two had to go and recreate. Now that was ridiculous when I think of it.

The status hierarchy was maintained at each mission, with jobs assigned by religious age. The rule was observed, but the communal aspect of the convent in which the old nuns had been "formed" was seriously undermined.

The nuns noted how much living in missions had affected their community.

> I think the big change came when we all dispersed to the missions. That's the big change in our community. Because you get out into the missions, you kind of get away from your community living. Because of circumstances there. For instance, if you have meetings at night or have meetings at a certain time, you can't go to prayers at that particular time. That's quite a change of lifestyle. After you change your lifestyle, it's going to change your thinking and your attitude about things.

* * * *

> I worry about those missions. Well, there isn't any community living on the missions any more because of the work that they're doing... They all come in at a different hour at night, so the supper is going on from about six o'clock until nine o'clock, somebody's eating. That's one thing. Therefore, they're not there for morning prayer, they're not there for evening prayer. I know that little one at St. Alexander's [the principal] says, "Sister, sometimes I go to bed with such a headache. For hours I sit and try to figure out how we can manage." She said, "This one has to be at her place at this hour and this one has to be her place at that hour. And there's no provision for prayer." I said, "Why don't they say their prayers while they're traveling?" She said, "That's not the same as praying with the community." She said, "It's just a big worry, that's all."

One nun succinctly summed up her opinion of the effects of the new living arrangements: "When you have people in smaller groups, you're bound to be human some of the time."

The changes described above, which radically affected the nature of the religious community, were largely adaptive to widespread social change. The nuns interviewed for this project shared with their age peers the need to adjust to modern technologies, urbanization, increased population and diversity in the city, and changes in modes of transportation. At least some of the labor that the nuns performed when they were novices became less arduous as it was taken over by machines. Increased distance between home and work was also something that many Americans experienced during this period. The religious community benefited from the affluence of the country. The old nuns contributed directly when they became eligible for Social Security and Medicare in the early 1970s. Like the rest of the population, the religious community adapted to new social arrangements brought about by urbanization and increased use of technology.

Pressure from within

The religious community also faced pressure to change from the Catholic Church itself, which as early as the 1920s had decreed that women religious update their rules.[5] This distinction is somewhat arbitrary, of course, because the Catholic church was also adapting to new social contexts. Nevertheless, the way that the Church chose to adapt had profound effects on the religious community.

Beginning in the 1920s, the general superior had responded to the call of the Sister Formation Movement (Quinonez and Turner 1992) for better education for teachers by seeing that the nuns used Saturdays and summers to earn college and advanced degrees as well as teaching credentials. One sister recalled,

> I got my B.S.E. at Saint Anthony College. I finished down there. It took me ten years and in that time I had trained ten teachers. They'd send one per year. They were all nuns. It was at that point demanded of them to get a degree – to do their student teaching, because they couldn't get a teaching certificate without it. It was just beginning to come in then. I had some who had taught for ages, and I could just let them take over because they were so superior...I was there from '36 to '46. Then I went to the College.

In the 1950s, during the height of pressure on schools from the postwar baby boom, the general superior asked for and was granted permission by the bishop to send young nuns to college full time before they entered the classroom.

After the general call for change in the Church in the 1960s, which is usually referred to as Vatican II, changes in the community were no longer predominantly reactive but became proactive. During the 25 years prior to the interviews with the nuns, the rule of the religious community had been under constant scrutiny. Changes were made in the degree to which nuns could be involved with those in the outside world. In the past, the nuns held themselves apart from "lay people," as one nun explained,

> In those day we had no contact with the lay people. Maybe a family here and there who was very good to us. But other than that, except for school business, we never had any contact with people, except for the children in our room. We'd go to Mass and come back. We didn't talk in those days, you know. We just – maybe a few brave people ventured to talk to us. But as far as building up a friendship with the people in the parish, we just didn't. Those that were nice to us, never expected

anything of us . . . Even with the lay teachers in the school, you never got overly friendly.

Instead of family members coming to the convent to visit the nuns on Sundays, the nuns now were allowed to visit their families and friends in their homes and not only on Sundays. They were given yearly monetary "allowances" that they could use for vacations or retreats, the amount of which was gradually increased and became a monthly allotment, with fewer restrictions on spending it. In addition, what constituted "instruction" was expanded to include activities that were related to neither children nor the classroom.

The ringing of the bells at the motherhouse was even discontinued.

> Some of the nuns pleaded with her [the general superior] to have the bell rung in the morning. They said, "You will not let it happen that the bell will not ring in the morning." But you know, the nuns kept asking not to have the bell rung so she finally gave in. Little things like that meant a lot to the older nuns. And see, she had to answer to the younger ones and she had to answer to the older ones. She was really on the pendulum.

Democratization of decision making undermined the power that the senior nuns had once enjoyed when the right to vote in chapter meetings was extended to the junior chapter nuns.

In the process, first the habit and then the veil were made optional. Dressing in a uniform signals both to self and others one's place in the world (Michelman 1997). The self reflected in the looking glass is highly consistent for anyone who wears a uniform. The habit signaled exactly who they were both to the nuns and to anyone they encountered during their daily rounds. It guaranteed that one "institutional self" (Gubrium and Holstein 2001; Holstein and Gubrium 2000) prevailed regardless of social context.

The optional habit was difficult for many of the old nuns to accept. One nun described the modifications in the nuns' dress code, which began gradually and then changed precipitously.

> We questioned some of the things that I would say were accidental to our religious life, the little customs we had that really didn't make you a good religious or a bad religious. But you came out of your cell without a night veil – you just didn't do that . . . And wearing undersleeves. We just started doing little things like taking one pleat out of our habit, or whatever it was. And then we started talking about changing the headdress – way back in the sixties. And we had a fashion show, and [some of the nuns said] that all you saw was hair and bosoms and hips and legs. Like you weren't supposed to know a nun had breasts or

something. It was like you covered them, and no one knew you had them...I remember the first time we had in chapter the parade of different people coming in. Everybody was wearing it down real low, and had their hair covered...I remember Imogene saying that they looked like they just got off the boat at Ellis Island.

As the styles became more diverse, some of the sisters in the cohort under study expressed fears that the distinctiveness of their order would be lost.

I don't like the change in the habit. Now I don't expect everyone to wear the traditional habit. But I wish we wore uniforms, because we don't know the Sisters now anymore. We're just like every other community. We don't have something that really identifies us.

Finally, after more than twenty years of changes, the sisters voted to make optional the last vestige of their uniform – the veil or headdress. This had occurred shortly before the interviews and was fresh in their minds.

I don't mind those who are wearing the short habit with the veil, they're still nuns. But these people who are wearing all these different things without the veil, Sister, they aren't nuns.

* * * *

Even my nephew said, "What's wrong with your nuns? They don't dress like nuns." He's a very simple little man. He would get on the bus at Granger there. He lived out that way with the nuns from St. Jean's. He said, "Everybody used to step aside and let them on the bus first. Now," he said, "They aren't dressed like nuns, so I get on the bus first."

After fifty years or more of wearing a uniform that marked their identity in the world inside and outside the convent walls, many of these nuns found incomprehensible that the younger nuns apparently would prefer no longer to make obvious the "institutional self" of nun in all settings.

One of the nuns who was interviewed chose to abandon not only the habit but the veil as well.

I have not had anybody say anything to me, like, "Why don't you put your veil back on?" When I still had the veil on – like maybe three weeks after we changed – I wasn't one of the first to take it off – people would say to me, "I'm so glad you kept your veil." And maybe there are nuns who don't say anything to my face because I would say something back and they know that. And maybe they have turned me off or something because I don't have the veil on. But there are others who I feel have not given up the veil themselves, but accept me.

The old nuns were faced with a choice of whether to join the younger sisters or to hold to their "old fashioned" ways. Most of those who were interviewed were adamant about the importance of the habit not only to them but to the religious community.

I have hopes to live and die in the habit. I'll wear the veil and that's that. Period. I have no decision to make. I mind [the optional headdress] more than I mind any other change...but there's just no use. If I disapprove, I'm one, and a hundred have gone along with it.

* * * *

We should worry about it. It's our community and we're just going to go down farther and farther...when they go out to shop or someplace else, I don't care what they wear. But I do think around the house... I wonder what people think, you know. I don't know.

Discarding the uniform that had signaled who they were both to themselves and to the world at large was difficult for most of the nuns in the group to see as progress. How could their community survive without the overarching symbol of the habit and veil that marked its members as nuns of a specific order?

The Retirement Years

By the time the nuns retired they had experienced many changes in their community. The meaning of the vows they had taken when they were young under very authoritarian conditions had changed subtly at first and then dramatically during their lives. The changes can be seen in one nun's account of her decision to retire.

Toward the end, when I finally was weary, I said to the superior, "If you want to change me, this is my last change. The change is going to be to the motherhouse. I can't go it anymore." She said, "Why don't you come home?" I said, "Thank you, I will." I felt keenly the change that was taking place in our mission houses, especially if you lived in the inner city. I couldn't keep up with the night life. First of all, I was never accustomed to it. I would find myself home alone at St. Hugh's where you're surrounded by drugs and so on. So I thought, "I'm not going to tempt Divine Providence – get out." And that was basically why I asked to be removed from there. I loved the work that I was doing. I was working with Meals-on-Wheels. And I was working with the elderly and I really liked it. But I didn't like where I would have to be home at night alone so often. I have to admit I was afraid. The pastor was hurt that I was leaving. . . . But I said, "Father, I can't. This way of life, it's just too dangerous. Anyone could break into the convent." I think he understood after a while.

Just prior to her retirement, this sister lived in a mission house, ironically, very near the monastery where she had begun her life as a nun. She was involved not with teaching children but with helping the elderly in the parish. She felt that too many of her evenings were spent alone, unlike her early years in the monastery, where she had been surrounded each evening by nuns who shared a routine. Also significant is that she reported having some say in her decision to "go home" (although other sisters told of being ordered home).

In relating their life histories to the interviewer, the nuns, all of whom were living in the motherhouse, implicitly and sometimes explicitly compared the old ways with the new. Their harsh early years were remembered with nostalgia.

It was my eighteenth birthday and one of the postulants . . . was going to have a birthday party for me. [Our novice directress] wasn't home. I slept in the corner. My whole bed was spread out with goodies, you know. Then we hear knock, knock at the door. We were laughing and talking (you never even opened your mouth in the dormitory). And Mother Justinia stood there: "My, my, what's going on?" They said, "We're celebrating Sister Stranton's eighteenth birthday." She said, "Well, have a good time, but hurry up before Mother Coretta gets home." I'll never forget her for that. I thought she was so kind. I think there was nothing wrong with that compared to what they do now.

They described how hard they had worked during their lives and with what devotion.

I was principal six times. For twenty years, I was teaching principal. My first time was at Saint Barnabas. And you thought nothing of it. Eighth grade, you know, get them ready for high school. And that was something. You had no office help. You did your office work on Saturday and Sunday, at home, or something. And everyone was like that. You didn't expect anything else.

* * * *

A strong factor throughout the community – our nuns have just taken for granted that teaching included more than just talking . . . Some children didn't have food or their clothes would look a mess, so they would brush the kids' clothes so they wouldn't feel queer. This wasn't just during the Depression. They did a lot of caring. The vocation was seen as a classroom teaching thing, but classroom teaching included a lot of caring for the children being taught.

* * * *

Many nuns should still be teaching rather than going out to do other work. I feel that we are neglecting teaching the kids. We should have stayed in the schools. We shouldn't leave the schools just because teaching is getting harder.

Typically, the nuns believed that the harsh conditions that they experienced because of a different rule and harsh economic circumstances had made them the good nuns that they were. They also worried that less rigid expectations would make the younger nuns less committed to the religious community.

Well, I'm not too familiar with [the current nuns in] formation. We don't even see them here. The fact is they breeze in here two days a week, I heard someone say. I really don't know. I know our formation was hard – tough. And I'm grateful for it today. Because I probably wouldn't be the good nun that I am, because many of those things just come back to me. . . . I think there's something lacking. I don't hesitate to say with the present set-up of formation – not that I know much about it. I just wonder. What direction will our community take in the future, if this is what it's like now? I fear for the community.

* * * *

I don't think our novices are trained. Anytime they feel like it they go to the movies and they tell you that the next day. We went to see so-and-so. I'm not saying they shouldn't ever go, but I don't think they should go every time they want to.

* * * *

I used to spend a lot of time in the chapel, then. We didn't have television or radio. So most of our leisure time was spent in the chapel. The nuns were good that way. And one thing I liked and I miss now is the old prayers . . . We don't pray together, except for the office. That we finish in ten minutes. The nuns don't come. We see some of them reading the newspaper or watching *Divorce Court*, and nobody is at night prayers, and nobody ever says anything to them. I don't think we have the right to say anything, but the superiors should and they don't.

* * * *

First of all, you're not going to have nuns that will keep the rule if they don't keep it when they're postulants. Now, here's what I'm referring to. They have permission to take a car – I don't care if they do it – it's none of my business, but I'm just saying they go to the ice cream parlor when they want to. I don't think that's the right beginning. They should have it a little tougher than they do. They just entered, and they should get grooved into religious life. And not only I, many of us feel that way. And where do they sit at Mass? They should be in the middle or in the front of the church where they are actually seeing the Mass, not talking as they do in the back. And, Sister, we need prayer!!! And if we don't pray, we don't stay. They don't pray!

All of the sisters who were interviewed for this project lived at the motherhouse. As noted above, they shared it with the newest nuns and the college instructors. Their proximity was a continual reminder of how different their formation had been from that of the most recent nuns. Rather than being housed in a community comprising nuns of all ages, as they had been in their early years, the retired nuns were segregated from all but the newest nuns and the college instructors and administrators. Although some of them provided services for the community, most of their time was spent with one another.

One thing I liked and I miss now is recreation. We don't . . . I don't talk to anybody – really sit down and talk – even like I'm talking now. You can't give way to your feelings. In the old days, at least you could talk to the people next to you. We had a lot of fun. It wasn't directed recreation. We used to mend our stockings or sew. We'd laugh a lot. Sometimes we'd sing and that. At least you were together and you could talk to people and you got to know them. This way you don't.

* * * *

There was a very close – a closeness among the nuns. I think it was because we got together at night and had recreation together. We'd sing, or we'd talk, or we'd play cards, or do whatever we liked. We were all in the same room. When it was over, they went to say their prayers or did their school work. But we really knew each other. I can't say that now. There's a loneliness in the community. You eat your supper at night and some might get together, but it's always the same little group, to go and play cards. And you go into the TV room and maybe six or eight will be there and they're watching the TV. Nobody says anything. And then you go up to your place and go where you want and do what you want. It's nice to be able to do what you want but there's a lack of closeness. You know the name of the person, but you don't really know them.

In old age, the nuns interacted primarily with one another and felt isolated and out of place:

> You know, whether you like it or not, as you grow older, your younger nuns don't have too much in common with you. And you feel it. And you're left out there to bridge the gap... And I think you come to a point when you feel that this is not the place for you.

Conclusion

Unlike most of their age peers in the United States, who lived through the same years but not in religious communities, the nuns in this study began their lives with one foot in the 1600s and the other in the 1900s. By the end of the 1900s, their community was firmly planted in the twentieth century. They lived through a time in which much of what they had learned and taken for granted in their early lives was transformed. The nuns' formation had been cloistered, demanding, and austere. Over the course of their lives, their vows of poverty, chastity, obedience, and instruction were modified to such an extent that by the time the nuns were old, these vows and the rule, which dictated how they were to be kept, seemed almost unrecognizable to them. The religious community in which their monolithic institutional self had been formed no longer seemed supportive. For some of the old nuns, then, it was as if the proverbial rug had been pulled from under them.

As young nuns in the community, they had seen that age mattered. The older nuns were revered and had power, conditions more typical in the United States prior to the Revolutionary War (Fischer 1977). Nuns of all ages had lived together in a community in which everyone had followed the same schedule. Now retired, they found themselves segregated within their community and they interacted primarily with one another. Although they officially outranked the newest nuns, they had no authority over them.

During their lifetime, they experienced "modernization," a process which effectively reduces the status of the aged (Rosow 1974). As young nuns, they had been apprenticed to older nuns from whom they learned to teach. As time passed, education replaced the special knowledge of the seasoned teacher and younger nuns often had a better education than their seniors. Democratic ideals when the nuns had been young meant that they had had to assume the domestic responsibilities previously performed by a "servant" group of nuns. By the time the nuns were interviewed, their power as chapter nuns had been eroded by democratic principles that gave younger nuns the vote.

In addition, individuality began to outweigh communality as the higher good. The monastery was broken up into small residential mission houses. Younger nuns had more choices about what constituted instruction than the older nuns had ever enjoyed. Dress became a matter of personal preference and no longer signified the religious community to which they belonged. Money became the important medium for exchange.[6] Ironically, the retired nuns, most of whom had never had money to spend on themselves, helped fill the coffers of the convent with monthly Social Security checks. The religious community, which had been a life-term social arena when the nuns joined, became a limited-term job venue (Moore 1978) that was less communal, more differentiated. In short, the community had become modern.

Coming to terms with the changes in their community was difficult for the nuns. As the interview data indicate, a comparison was often made between their lives and those of the younger nuns whose formation seemed too undisciplined to produce lifelong commitment to vows of poverty, chastity, and obedience. The mass exodus in the 1960s and 1970s and the declining number of women who joined religious communities thereafter, support their position (Ebaugh, Lorence, and Chafetz 1996; Stark and Rinke 2000). The nuns feared for the survival of the religious community to which they had given their lives.

The decision to house the retired nuns with the postulants and novices in the motherhouse meant that the old nuns could not easily ignore changes in their community. In the old monastery, the differences between the lives of the newest and the oldest members was tempered. Middle-aged nuns, like the nun whose doctoral dissertation is the foundation for this chapter, shared enough of the experiences of the old nuns to be sympathetic to their perspective. Difference between the oldest and youngest members of the community would not have seemed so radical. Now, the reflection that the old nuns saw in the young faces – the majority of the faces – around them was not supportive of the monolithic institutional self that many years of religious life had taught them to expect, leading them to wonder about who they and their fellow sisters were in today's world.

Notes

This chapter is based on a Ph.D. dissertation in sociology written by Sister Colman Gayer (1990). I supervised her dissertation and worked closely with her throughout the project. Sadly, Sister Colman died without having made her research available to a wider audience. This chapter is dedicated to her memory. She was a delightful person with a wonderful sense of humor and I deeply regret that our friendship was cut short. Names and places have been changed to disguise the identity of the nuns and the community. Any errors and shortcomings in the manuscript are mine.

1 The fact that the interviewer knew the informants and lived with them in the motherhouse is both an advantage and a disadvantage. The older nuns were comfortable talking with her but, because she was intimately familiar with much of their world, they did not need to explain as much to her as they would have to an outsider. On the other hand, they may have been more guarded with her than they would have been with a stranger.

2 According to my *Random House Dictionary of the English Language*, a guimpe is "a part of the habit of nuns of certain orders, consisting of a wide, stiffly starched cloth that covers the neck and shoulders."

3   The official ranks were postulant, novice, junior professed, young community nuns, and chapter nuns. Postulants had entered the convent but had yet to be clothed and given a new name. This status, typically lasting less than a year, ended when a group of postulants was clothed, given a new name, and promoted to novice. Nuns were novices for two years. One of these years was a "canonical year" during which they were instructed. Junior professed nuns were those in "temporary vows." After a period of three years in this status, nuns took permanent vows. After twelve years in permanent vows the nuns became chapter nuns which entitled them to vote in meetings, although the general superior had the authority to overrule the chapter nuns. The bishop could overrule the general superior.

4   To appreciate the changes in general that occurred between 1900 and 1940, see Allen (1952). For changes in domestic labor, see Cowan (1983).

5   For a history of the impetus for change among nuns in the United States, which this chapter does not begin to cover, see Quinoniz and Turner (1992). Initial pressure came from the Sister Formation Movement that was initiated by American nuns.

6   Two studies of "Plainville," one conducted shortly before the Depression (West 1971 [1945]) and the other afterward (Gallaher 1961), provide evidence of how the increased importance of money affected social life.

References

Allen, Frederick Lewis. 1952. *The Big Change: America Transforms Itself, 1900–1950*. New York: Harper.

Cowan, Ruth Schwartz. 1983. *More Work for Mother*. New York: Basic Books.

Ebaugh, Helen Rose, Lorence, Jon and Saltzman Chafetz, Janet. 1995. "The Growth and Decline of the Population of Catholic Nuns Cross-Nationally, 1960–1990: A Case of Secularization as Social Structural Change." *Journal for the Scientific Study of Religion, 35*: 171–83.

Fischer, David Hackett. 1977. *Growing Old in America*. New York: Oxford University Press.

Gallaher, Art. 1961. *Plainville Fifteen Years Later*. New York: Columbia University Press.

Gayer, Sister Colman. 1990. *Aging and Social Change in a Religious Community: A Case Study*. Ph.D. Dissertation. Case Western Reserve University, Cleveland, Ohio.

Gubrium, Jaber F. and Holstein, James A. (eds). 2001. *Institutional Selves: Troubled Identities in a Postmodern World*. New York: Oxford University Press.

Holstein, James A. and Gubrium, Jaber F. 2000. *The Self We Live By*. New York: Oxford University Press.

Michelman, Susan O. 1997. "Changing Old Habits: Dress of Women Religious and Its Relationship to Personal and Social Identity." *Sociological Inquiry, 67*: 350–63.

Moore, Sally F. 1978. "Old Age in a Life-Term Social Arena: Some Chagga of Kilimanjaro in 1974." In Barbara G. Myerhoff and Andrei Simic (eds), *Life's Career – Aging: Cultural Variations On Growing Old*. Beverly Hills, CA: Sage, pp. 23–75.

Quinonez, Lora Ann and Turner, Mary Daniel. 1992. *The Transformation of American Catholic Sisters*. Philadelphia, PA: Temple University Press.

Rosow. Irving. 1974. *Socialization to Old Age*. Berkeley: University of California Press.

Rosow. Irving. 1978. "What is a Cohort and Why." *Human Development, 21*(2): 65–75.
Stark, Rodney and Rinke, Roger. 2000. "Catholic Religious Vocations: Decline and Revival." *Review of Religious Research, 42*: 125–45.
West, James [Withers, Carl]. 1971 [1945]. *Plainville USA*. Westport, CN: Greenwood Press.

Chapter 8

Identity Careers of Older Gay Men and Lesbians

Dana Rosenfeld

C. Wright Mills (1959) once argued that biographical narratives are not just accounts of lifelong experience, but are significantly shaped both in form and in content by the ideas and values of the historical period in which they are embedded. How people experience their later years, for example, is strongly influenced by the historical context in which they came of age. This bears especially on their sense later in life of who and what they were and have become – their *identity careers*.

Gay men and lesbians have confronted a special challenge posed by the tumultuous sexual identity politics and related political events of the late 1960s and early 1970s. Critical to the post-World War II emergence of identity politics surrounding race and ethnicity (Espiritu 1992), sex (Moghadam 1994), sexuality (Blasius 1994; Bernstein 1997; D'Emilio 1983), illness (Klawiter 1999), and disability (Anspach 1979), the 1960s and 70s provided a new, symbolically fertile context within which the selves and identities of then middle-aged gays and lesbians were constructed. Now in their later years, these individuals continue to formulate their biographies in relation to the changing identity landscape.

The ways in which identities are shaped by their historical context were strikingly impressed upon me during a recent study I conducted to explore the lives and experiences of older gay men and women (see Rosenfeld

1999). In 1995, I conducted open-ended, in-depth interviews with 50 self-identified gay men and lesbians of various class and ethnic backgrounds, who were aged 64 to 89 years. I identified subjects in the greater Los Angeles area by means of "snowball" sampling (see LeCompte and Shensul 1999: 55) and conducted interviews in subjects' homes. I tape-recorded these interviews, collecting demographic information and life histories, which included accounts of current and future concerns, friendship and family networks, religious beliefs and practices, and feelings about the organized lesbian and gay communities.

As I started analyzing the transcripts from these interviews, I immediately noted how the emergence of gay liberation in the late 1960s and 1970s – which divided subjects' lives into an era in which homosexuality was exclusively constructed as a shameful stigma and a new period in which being gay was increasingly viewed as a positive identity – affected their recollections of sexual experiences and the identity issues that flowed from them. A central theme resonated throughout the interviews: These subjects were members of a cohort who formed sexual identities at a time of tremendous change, and they were now constructing narratives of life experiences that reflected just how much their identity careers were still being shaped by these events, even later in life.

Based on these interviews, this chapter traces the various narrative paths constructed by subjects who were challenged by this historical period as they developed and embraced lesbian and gay selves. As the recollections will show, their identity careers reflect ways of aging mediated by changing understandings of what might be considered the proper interpretation and enactment of sexual desire. Following Mills, we can see how much of what individuals say about who and what they are and were, over the course of life, reverberates through their historical experience. If Mills is correct, future generations of older gay men and lesbians will recount their ways of aging as less distinctly stigmatized identity careers than did the subjects of my study.

Gay Life and Historical Change

Consider the climate for homosexuals who were coming of age or first considering their sexual identities in the early to mid-twentieth century. Throughout my subjects' youth and middle age, homosexuality was defined and treated as a medical, legal, and moral aberration. The medical establishment considered homosexuality to be a disease until 1973, when the nascent gay movement's lobbying efforts resulted in the American Psychiatric Association's vote to rescind this definition (see Marotta 1981: 324). Homosexuality was widely viewed as an unnatural existence devoid of healthy social, familial, or emotive ties. Indeed, throughout the

1950s and 1960s, medical and psychiatric constructions of homosexuality increasingly informed the popular depiction of gay men and women as isolated, immature, ashamed, and incapable of achieving either personal satisfaction or social integration. These images dominated the limited press coverage of homosexual life, and censorship of gay-positive texts and films kept homosexuals dependent upon a medical and popular literature that stigmatized them (Faderman 1991). These depictions were invoked and elaborated by the federal government during the McCarthy era (Nardi and Sanders 1994: 11), when homosexuals were constructed as security risks by the State Department and other federal agencies (D'Emilio 1983: 43–4). Federal policy toward homosexuality found a natural ally in state and local police, who had a long history of harassing gays and lesbians.

The construction of homosexuality as a pathological condition provided gay men and women with both an identity category in which to place their often-secretive feelings and a language with which to discuss and describe themselves and their position in society. This language, of course, was negative and stigmatizing. As a result, while some homosexuals embraced the stigmatized roles made available by the gay underground (Chauncey 1994), others saw their sexual desires as a condition to be suppressed, remaining single and celibate or adopting heterosexual marriage patterns. Yet others engaged in sexual, social, and emotional relations with other gay men or lesbians, understanding their homosexuality to be an aberrant condition which, while capable of being satisfied, nonetheless required them to pass as heterosexual. While the severe stigmatization of homosexuality was seen by these individuals as merited, they saw their persecution as avoidable through their own attempts at normalization. They condemned both the underground homosexual life that exploded in the post-war years (see Berube 1990) and those immersed in it as unnecessarily legitimating stereotypes of gay men and women, which they figured invited the persecution of all homosexuals. In Peter Nardi and David Sanders's (1994: 11) words, "For many in the 1950s, the debate to organize 'a highly ethical homosexual culture' centered on assimilation, either to seek respectability within the framework of the dominant ideologies or to recreate alternative socio-political structures."

Early opposition to this approach surfaced in the 1950s in the form of the Mattachine Society, organized in Los Angeles by Harry Hays and other communists. Until its takeover by more conservative members, Mattachine explicitly "pioneered in conceiving homosexuals as an oppressed minority" (D'Emilio 1983: 38) composed of individuals with a unique gay identity and a valid and distinctive culture. Rather than adapt to heterosexual society, homosexuals were encouraged to "rely on a change of consciousness, an active evaluation of their identity and relationship to society to obtain future power" (Timmons 1990: 151) and thus to agitate for an end to persecution. This persecution was seen not as avoidable punishment for the blatant expression of a stereotyped self, as it was by assimilationists, but as evidence of heterosexual bigotry.

Although this destigmatizing approach was overshadowed by the assimilationist stance and was effectively limited by the active surveillance and persecution of homosexuals, it resurfaced in the 1960s and 1970s, galvanized by the 1969 uprising by patrons of the Stonewall Tavern (a gay bar in lower Manhattan), an event now referred to as "Stonewall." This spawned "a distinctively new culture of protest" (D'Emilio 1983: 223), which

> presented in many respects a turning point in American history. . . . "Identity politics" was on the rise, giving birth to social movements such as feminism and black power. A huge cohort of young people, products of the postwar baby boom, was creating a distinctive culture that embodied antiestablishment values, fashioning itself against its parents' generation and against authority figures of all sorts. (Stein 1997: 13)

The civil rights and the New Left movements of the 1960s informed an emergent oppositional stance within the homosexual subculture, which began to formulate homosexuality as a valid identity to be openly embraced and enacted, rather than a stigmatizing condition to be hidden. Both the gay liberation and the lesbian feminist movements (Weitz 1984; Faderman 1991) of the early 1970s called for all homosexuals to condemn both the stigmatized understanding of homosexuality as well as those who continued to embrace this view, and to come "out of the closets and into the streets" (Young 1972) to live openly as gay men and lesbians. This position is the dominant ideology of lesbian and gay communities today.

(Homo)Sexual Identity Careers

My subjects were born between 1906 and 1931 and were aged 64 to 39 when gay liberation began to systematically challenge both the dominant stigmatization of homosexuality and homosexuals' adaptation to it. While most had identified as homosexual according to the stigmatized formulation of homosexuality, living relatively secret lives by passing as heterosexual in public, some had not then identified as homosexual at all, although many had had same-sex desires and relationships. The latter group encountered gay liberation and lesbian feminism at a time in their lives when they were aware of their attraction to members of their own sex, but did not yet view themselves as gay or lesbian. The emerging formulation of homosexuality provided them with a new way of understanding and enacting these feelings, and they adopted the new homosexual identity that was now available.

When recounting their identity careers, these subjects often described "always knowing" that they were different. They spoke of being attracted to members of their own sex during their early years, often in childhood. When speaking of these early desires, many echoed 77-year-old respondent Manny's (pseudonyms are used throughout) statement that "I knew something was wrong with me all my life." Recognizing and evaluating inchoate desires were, for these subjects, coterminous aspects of the same project: to understand the nature of their desires and their implications for self. They described feeling bewildered about both the meaning of these desires (and, often, their own fulfillment of them) and their implications for identity and value. Brian, aged 74, for example, "kept thinking, 'Well, that's quite different. Is it something you outgrow?' I remember having that in my mind."

Some did not act on this awareness for years, as there was little in the air at the time that encouraged them to developed related identities. Susan, aged 75, reported that when she "was in high school, I was aware of certain girls. And I found myself attracted or interested. But I didn't do anything about it. I just, I was conscious of it. It was one of those things. I lived with it." Similarly, 72-year-old Tex's belief that a man could be attracted to him was "a phase [he] was going through" prevailed well into his marriage. As he explains, he

> was attracted to men, the more I fought it, the more I dreamed about it. I thought it was a phase that I would get over, but I didn't. I never tried to put a name for it. I thought I was different. I didn't think anybody else felt like that except me.

Most, however, pursued these desires, still failing to understand their meaning for self. Many experienced their associations and relations as relatively unproblematic. While they "knew" that these were best enacted in certain contexts and not in others, pursuing same-sex relations while unaware of their severely stigmatizing "nature" allowed them to experience these connections as "natural." Jan, aged 68, noted, for example, that she

> didn't label it because I didn't know there was such a thing as a lesbian, it was just the most natural thing in the world. I don't suppose I knew what a homosexual was. If someone had asked me: "I don't have a clue." As I told you I started dating a neighbor kid, even before I got involved with this woman. And I always assumed that I would marry and you know do all this stuff because that was what people did where I grew up.

Most subjects spoke of searching for accounts of these differences in textual and cultural representations and in others' remarks. For example, Rodney, aged 81, wrote to the editor and publisher of a homoerotic "muscle" magazine for advice to "determine where I stood in life." Jeannine, aged 66, and her female lover searched the dictionary for female versions of the word "faggot." Others described pondering their interactions and characterizations to uncover the nature and consequences of their desires. Without exception, the accounts formulated same-sex desires as a pathological yet curable condition. This discourse "explained" subjects' experiences to them in stigmatizing terms, and thus supplied a much-needed identity category. The interpenetration of these messages and responses can be seen in 66-year-old Sharon's account of

> reading medical journals on how to deal with the brain because I thought I was crazy because of being gay. I thought I was insane because it was not normal. Probably by the age of ten or twelve I was getting books at the library on Havelock Ellis and Kraft-Ebbing because I would look up the term homosexual – don't ask me how I found that word – but I would look up the term homosexual and would refer to notes. And it told about all the horrible things that the insane people did, so I thought that's what gay people did.

The stigmatizing discourse of the times provoked the challenge of making the self intelligible and, at the same time, preserving its value in the face of a devalued identity. Subjects described feeling caught between a need to understand and pursue their desires on the one hand and to avoid the negative implications of a stigmatized identity on the other. Recognizing and fulfilling sexual desires served to discredit them, making them subject to ridicule and rejection.

Distancing

Many found the implications of a stigmatized identity so severe that they worked to avoid interpreting their desires in its terms, managing the tension between their desires and the consequences of enacting them by distancing themselves from one, the other, or both. "Distancing" refers to the variety of ways in which subjects modified, weakened or resisted the applicability of the term "homosexual" to themselves; these consisted of "putting it on the back burner," pursuing heterosexual relations, and cultivating a heterosexual identity.

Those who "put it on the back burner" made same-sex desire a background concern of significantly less importance to them than other interests, needs, and obligations, which, according to them, provided greater rewards. Ryan, aged 81, "would see men that I thought I liked, you know at a distance, and I would like to get better acquainted with them, but I didn't dare go any further than that, and I just let it go at that." Similarly, Marge, aged 81, recalled "staying away from it."

There was a female that everybody called "old dyke" because she was out and she had a girlfriend. She was almost like an outcast. [Also] conversation would come up with the kids that I would associate with and other people and they would speak of people like this, not only women but men, too, that were feminine. I knew I was connected with it, but I wanted to stay away from it because I did not want to be ridiculed. I didn't do anything about it. I went out with guys, you know.

For many, distancing included pursuing heterosexual relations. For example, Patricia, aged 77, "had boyfriends," Kate, aged 76, "occasionally would accept a date, usually fixed up by anxious family or anxious friends," and 81-year old Ryan saw heterosexual relations as "the lesser of two evils." According to Ryan, in his teen years, he was

semi-interested in girls. It was the lesser of two evils, let's put it that way. We would be going to parties or to dances and things like that, I enjoyed dancing in those days, and we enjoyed dinners and bake-outs.

Subjects said they had expected that the frustration of unmet needs and desires would be precluded or offset by replacing those needs with others which were more easily met and which presented no negative implications for self. After her psychoanalysis failed to "cure" her lesbianism, Kate sought to fulfill herself through her job. "I was also deeply involved in my school and my teaching, which was very satisfactory, very all-consuming. And the other stuff I put on the back burner."

For many, however, distancing techniques caused them to see themselves as without value or definition. Dan, aged 70, spoke of defining himself as "active neuter. No sex, nothing" while engaged in distancing. Deborah, aged 74, explained that "I wasn't defining myself at all," and Kate considered herself "a mess, sexually, practically without identity." This distress led some to actively pursue a heterosexual identity, which they saw as providing a fulfilling family life on the one hand and protection from the harassment and ridicule homosexuals faced on the other.

They did this in one of two ways. Some entered conventional heterosexual marriages, less as a means of "hiding" their homosexuality than as a way to achieve a heterosexual identity that provided positive rewards. A few had married, only to have their homosexual desires emerge and coalesce during their marriages. Luke, aged 69, for example, accounts for his heterosexual marriage by stating that when he "met her I was trying to get away from gay life. I was trying to get out of being gay, I was trying to get out and raise a family and everything. I don't know. I just wanted a family." Mark, aged 71, married when he realized that the man he was in love with was more interested in what I had to give. Then along came June, my ex-wife. I decided that I was going to give up being gay. I figured that [there] just wasn't any future in it for me. We went to a dance, came home, I took her underneath the porch, I had sex with her. And then four months later, she says, "I'm pregnant." So I says, "Well, better get married." We got married and I gave up Joe. I was 28, 29.

Others constructed a kind of liminal heterosexuality by embracing the medicalized formulation of homosexuality as curable through therapy, which provided a positive and rewarded role and promised a future heterosexual identity. Rather than see themselves as permanently diseased, these subjects embraced the medicalized discourse's most positive version of "pervert" – s/he who is committed to a cure. Although immanently homosexual and thus stigmatized, this constructed them at the same time as adequately oriented to the medical establishment's norms and goals and committed them to achieving a normal life. Seventy-two-year-old Leonard, for example, sought therapy after being fired from the State Department for being homosexual.

So I went to New York at that time, mainly because they had suggested that, you know, therapy in New York was the place. I was gonna get cured. I was in pretty bad shape. I went to therapy with this general idea in mind.

Embracing a new identity

Several subjects who had had same-sex desires but who did not know how to interpret them described their first sexual or erotic contacts as clarifying these desires, learning how to fulfill them on the one hand and providing insight into "what they were" on the other. Dan, aged 70, for example, reported that he "still wasn't aware of anything" when, in his mid-twenties, he

wanted to get rid of my glasses, so I went for eye exercises, and the guy giving [them] was gay. So, he started massaging my eyes and things and I was very attracted to him, and then finally he kissed me. And then I was in heaven, you know. And that's when I became aware, when he kissed me in New York.

Meeting and associating with other homosexuals either alone or in groups was key to subjects' interpreting their desires in a new light. At the very least, it showed them that they were not "the only ones in the world" and that there were venues for associating with others like themselves. Many searched for and patronized lesbian and gay bars to determine if they had anything in common with the other patrons. They spoke of feeling as though they belonged "there" ("there" being a subcultural homosexual world). Abby, aged 70, described this happening

> the first time that I went to a bar ... I was 25. I think it was Bleecker Street, and it was the Swing Rendezvous was the name of the place. It was primarily women. As soon as I walked in there, and I don't think it took me very long to realize that this is exactly where I belong. And that was my first introduction.

Subjects also explained how changing relational contexts inspired a reformulation of homosexuality and its relation to self. Many spoke of the emergence of emotional needs that could only be fulfilled through erotic or romantic relationships with same-sex partners. While they had initially limited their same-sex connections to sexual ones that did not, for them, implicate a homosexual identity, these new desires caused them to reexamine their sexual selves. While 75-year-old George, for example, "did homosexual things before," he didn't "realize" he was gay until

> that night that I told Jack. We were sitting in my car, holding hands. This is when I had this wave of emotion, and I turned and looked out the window and I said "I want to tell you something." And he said, "Don't worry about it, so am I." He was also at the same point where I was. In coming out we were discovering ourselves. I knew that I wanted him, he knew that he wanted me.

The breakup of Mark's marriage provided a new context through which to reassess his sexuality and his future. Having given up "being gay" (see above), he "found out that the straight life wasn't what it's kicked up to be" when he found his wife in bed with his brother. He then "went back to Joe, said 'let's get the hell out of Syracuse.' And Joe and I moved to California. We were lovers for three years after that."

For 66-year-old Mary, her husband's request for an "open marriage" provided the opportunity for experimenting sexually, allowing her to look "at women differently." Her first lesbian affair, "other problems in the marriage," and pressure from her female lover created a need "to make a decision."

> I started going around with a girlfriend of mine who had always played around. And all the men that we ran into, everybody was telling me how good-looking I was and what they could do for me, and I thought, "Oh no." So I don't know, somewhere along the line ... And I had always had gay and lesbian friends, and all at once I realized I was looking at women differently than I had before. So, I got myself

involved in an affair, and told my husband about it. There were some other problems in the marriage, I finally decided that I needed to make a decision. I didn't like living that way. And of course by this time the other lady had decided that I wasn't ever gonna leave my husband, and so I asked my husband to move.

As a result, she added, "I made a conscious choice to my way of thinking to become a lesbian when I was about forty-three."

For these individuals, who were still engaged in distancing practices when gay and lesbian liberation emerged, the movement provided both a very broad social context through which to form new relationships with gay men and lesbians and a new symbolic framework through which to assess their desires and actions. This granted the opportunity to reformulate oneself not from a non-homosexual to a stigmatized homosexual, but from a non-homosexual self to a liberated gay or lesbian person. Marilyn, aged 66, who encountered lesbian-feminism and the possibilities for a new identity at a meeting of the National Organization for Women in the early 1970s, referred directly to the link between changing times and changing selves.

It was a gradual process. What really kicked it off for me was reading an article by a woman in the National Organization for Women, and I said "Hey, that's me." It was just a revelation. I went to the National Organization for Women, I met other women who identified themselves as lesbian. It was the first time that I had lesbians around me, identifiable lesbians. I became involved, we had a march in West Los Angeles and had speakers for hours. It was a *fantastic* time for feminism and gays and lesbians and a lot of energy; it was a great time.

Identity and Family

The identity careers of older gay men and lesbians also implicated family life. This had profound consequences for how these individuals lived out the details of their most mundane, day-to-day existence. Close relationships, enduring bonds, and domestic commitments were strongly shaped by the norms surrounding homosexuality and family life that subjects confronted earlier in time and by the commitments demanded by subjects' identification as a particular type of homosexual.

Marriage and family life

Of the nine subjects who had had conventional marriages, three men and two women had children, and of these five, only the two women were actively involved in their grandchildren's lives at the time of the interviews. Mark, aged 71, is close to his daughter, who lives on the east coast, visiting her and her two children every year, but is "not as close as we'd like to be" with his son. Luke, aged 69, was close to his daughter before her death in 1994, and is not close to his son, who, he commented, "was in the Navy. And the way I understand, he was down here in Long Beach and never even came to see me, so." Tex, aged 72, left his wife and family in 1968, when the eldest of his five children was "eight or nine." Although he and his children "had a good relationship for a while," it ultimately "all fell apart," and he remained estranged from his children until

> the eldest girl pulled all this together a couple of years ago. Got in touch with me again. Prior to that, I hadn't spoken to 'em in about fifteen years. She said she just ran across my phone number. I don't know whether it was true or not, but it was fine with me, I wasn't arguing. . . . It was just like we had never – there were no time lags, you know? We just took off right where we spoke the last fifteen years ago. I didn't whoop or holler or anything like that. It was just so nice to speak to her, that's it.

Tex and his children are "hoping to have a family reunion in March," and he feels "no pressure anymore, because they know who I am and what I am and they've accepted that." Nonetheless, barriers remain.

> The one problem is the youngest daughter's husband will not accept me under no circumstances. 'Cause they have three boys which I've never seen, I just heard about. She called me for the first time this year. She was the most difficult to get a hold of and I didn't get a hold of her. My oldest daughter was the instigator; she talked her into calling me.

For the two female subjects with children, the familial scenario is quite different. Having raised their children in their own homes after divorce, their relations with their children and grandchildren are closer and more open than are those of the male subjects. Susan, aged 75, took her three then-teenaged daughters with her when she moved to California after her divorce in 1964 and remains close to all three, although her relationship with her middle child is strained by the latter's religious beliefs condemning homosexuality. She is also close to that daughter's son, who lives in the area, as does her youngest child, who has a son of her own. Susan spoke of encouraging her children to remain close to their father and was pleased when she and her eldest daughters persuaded her youngest daughter to attend her father's eightieth birthday party. She also was pleased that the entire family will join her to celebrate her seventy-fifth birthday: "I told everybody that all I want is my family together, this family now. I don't care what we do, but that was it. So they're all coming, they're bringing the family."

Similarly, 66-year-old Mary remains close to her three children, six grandchildren, one great-grandchild, and ex-husband, who has since remarried. With the exception of one grandson, all live in California, and she sees and/or speaks with them frequently, which, she explains, "depends upon what our schedules are." Indeed, one daughter was staying with her while doing some graduate work. Mary elaborates:

> My whole family is close. Christmas time, we all had dinner out with my ex-husband and his wife. Thanksgiving they were all here. We just have that kind of a family. Once you're in this family, divorce does not put you out of it. You only get out of this family if you choose to. That's the way it is.

For most subjects, child rearing was rare, although some are involved with others' children. Several subjects expressed regret and sadness that they hadn't had children of their own; many named their childlessness as the most significant consequence of their homosexuality. Mitch, aged 68, for example, explained that while he valued his relationship with his nieces and nephews, they did not fill the place that children would have: "I have no children. Fortunately, I'm so blessed 'cause I have my nephews and nieces. But they have their lives – I'm not their mother." Eighty-six-year-old Franz recalled that, when he identified as homosexual in his teens, he felt "bothered" that "it meant I couldn't have family and I couldn't have children." The times were not yet set for the open domestic partnerships and homosexual adoptions now accepted in many places.

Several subjects contrasted the options younger homosexuals have now with the limitations their own homosexuality imposed on them in their younger years. Kate, aged 76, explains.

> If I were, you know, 25 and a lesbian today, I could make a decision: do I want children, don't I want children? But there was no option for me in my day. I didn't have children. Which means that my genes die with me and I leave nothing behind me except a memory.

Similarly, Marge, aged 81, pointed out that she

> did not want to have children because I was gay and I felt like I couldn't take care of them. I mean it's not like it is now. People have different ideas about all this but before, let's say that they already had children before they acknowledged the fact that – men always had children even though they were homosexual or not, but a lot of females didn't

consider having children when they knew or when they had affairs or living with you know other females.

But these subjects weren't necessarily isolated from younger relatives, to whom they had strong emotional attachments that some of them likened to parenthood. Many mentioned nieces, nephews, and cousins to whom they are close, and indeed often pointed to them as those with whom they were the closest. Seventy-eight-year-old Gabrielle is "very close" to her niece and nephew, speaking with them "every day" by phone, explaining that "my niece is like my child, my nephew is like my child." Brian, aged 74, has been very close to his 50-year-old nephew "ever since he's grown up" and visits him and his family every year.

I have seven nieces and nephews, all who have married and have kids. One nephew I'm very close to back in New York. He and his wife, I go and visit them every year. I'll be going this summer. That one in particular, we're very close. He's like a son. He'd be my heir, you know, and all that. He's my favorite of the group. I'm in touch with them all, really, even though we're all scattered. He's more special, you know, than the others.

Mitch, aged 68, also names his nephew as "my favorite person alive, really the apple of my eye, and I am of his." As he explains,

I have an extraordinarily loving family, unfortunately they're all back east, but I'm Uncle Mame. I've introduced them all to theater, I've introduced them all to good reading, I've introduced them to so many things. I know I will live on because I had three sisters – I have two now – and their children have always been very close to me, and now I'm getting to know their children's children. Oh it's so neat, they're really great. But I have one particular nephew who's an absolute favorite of mine, and I've engineered his career in a lot of ways. I get all the pleasures of being a father. And see I forget how much they adore *me*. And that's really what the big high is, of course.

For many, continued contact with their families is very important, and they call and visit them often, or try to. William, aged 76, sees his cousin frequently and "is with them on major holidays, except Christmas I'm with her parents in New York," and 68-year-old Jan is "quite close" to her sisters, talking to them "usually about once a week." Jan adds that they "get together every year for a cousin reunion, in Tulsa. And I have two sisters from the other coast, and I come and people from Missouri and Texas and all over, so it's really a fun time." Two had considered leaving

Los Angeles and moving closer to their families. Seventy-four-year-old Brian spoke with his nephew

> when I got down and depressed and thought, "Oh, I should be in a town where relatives are." Run over for dinner and all that. I thought, well there'd never be any lonely moments, I suppose I felt like that, that's all.

For others, family life had negative resonances. As Dan, aged 70, explained, "I have *nobody*, really, but see I really don't like family. I have no feeling for family." Although 75-year old George has "two nephews in Modesto, one nephew in Van Nuys, and one niece who's married in Santa Ana," they "never contact each other." Mark, aged 70, is close to one brother, who is gay, but "then I got a brother who says if he ever sees me on the street, he'll kill me. That's because I'm gay." Eighty-one-year-old Ryan was close to a nephew before the latter's death from AIDS, and would "prefer to be closer" to his only sibling. But he is currently

> not [involved with family] and I wish I were. I feel very stranded. I have a lot of hurt feelings here and enormously hurt feeling here. I just feel – they know that I'm alone.

Clearly, family relations were varied. A scarce few had children and grandchildren in the area, and were close to them; a slightly larger group had children and grandchildren elsewhere in the country and were not. Most named nieces, nephews, and cousins as people to whom they were close, and spoke with and/or visited them regularly, while others were alienated from family. Engaging in heterosexual marriage before identifying as homosexual certainly made for a "more traditional" family, with children and grandchildren for some. Despite the differences, all took account of "the times" in recollecting the family resonances of their identity careers.

Coming out to family members

For those who identified as homosexual before gay liberation, close relations with family hinged on avoiding discussion of their homosexuality. Those who came out by way of gay liberation, in contrast, were committed to broaching the issue with family members at various times and places.

Members of the first group saw their homosexuality as a private matter that should not be raised as a topic by any members of the family, including themselves. They explained that doing so was unnecessary and could create tensions and even distress for their loved ones. For example, Brian, aged 74, "kept that separate from the family." Even his nephew, to whom he is extremely close, has no idea. We're so separated geographically that there's never been any reason to tell [the family], you know, or for them to think anything of it. All they know is, "Oh, he was married once and he's divorced." So it doesn't enter their mind, you see. I haven't felt that there's any reason to talk to them about it; it'd just shock them.

These subjects felt this way even though several felt that their families "already knew." As 77-year-old Manny put it, "I don't tell anybody that I'm gay, but everybody knows. But nobody says anything. It's taken for granted." Declining to discuss their sexuality was not necessarily a matter of passing as heterosexual, but was rather understood as respecting the family's perceived feelings of discomfort and shame were the topic to be raised. Patricia, aged 77, stated that she

never mentioned it. They all know that I am. My sisters know I am but we've never talked about it. I'm sure my dad and mother [knew but] we never discussed it. They knew when I went to live with Deborah, especially my mother, but never discussed it. It was just something that [they] didn't want to have to go through [or] live with. My sisters are very good friends and I talk to them but we don't discuss anything like this. We discuss everyday life. Things that are going on.

Similarly, Jan, aged 68, describes herself as "still very, very *guarded* in terms of being open with most of the people that I know," explaining that "I guess I came up in the wrong era," expressly tying her biography to history. She feels that

there are no illusions, everybody who knows me I'm sure knows that I'm a lesbian, I'm sure they do, but it's never discussed. It's not something I would particularly bring up, but I wouldn't *avoid*.

Indeed, these same subjects were upset and insulted when other members of their families disclosed their homosexuality to them. Seventy-seven-year-old Manny described a nephew's including him in the process of coming out to his family as an unwelcome intrusion into the appropriate distance he had established with his relatives. In his view, this was ultimately irrelevant to him and his position in the family.

I have a nephew that's gay, in Montreal. He's a college kid. And he came out to his mother and father when he was in college. And of course, I went home, and this is part of the family that I don't like. So the mother said, "Manny, call Josh. Manny, call Josh." I said, "Okay, I'll call Josh." So I'm leaving Montreal and I didn't call Josh. So Josh calls me, "Uncle Manny? You're leaving – I'm gay." So I said, "What do you want *me* to do?" You know?

Given the commitment of this set of subjects to keeping their homosexuality private, it is not surprising that the rare instances when they were expected to disclose their homosexuality to others were met with outrage. Sixty-nine-year-old Lillian, for one, felt that her cousin's anger at her failure to come out to him was unwarranted, and his expectation that she come out to him unreasonable. As she explained, his desire that she disclose her lesbianism to him displaced his responsibility for raising the topic onto her shoulders. Since he was the one who saw her sexuality as relevant to their relationship, it was his obligation to ask her about it. To expect her to raise the issue was to expect her to "make an announcement," to gratuitously make her sexuality evident and obtrusive.

> My cousin Louie did something I didn't like and he got very mad at me because I never told him I was gay. I said I never heard of something like that. First of all, I'm not one to wear a sign on my back, and like I told him if he were that curious to know what my lifestyle was, why didn't you ask? If you would have asked me I would have told you, but I'm not about to come to you and say, "Hey, Louie, I'm gay," you know. I just don't want to deal with that, you know what I'm saying? I mean he's 72 years old. I said, "You're a grown man, if you were that curious, why didn't you ask me? I would have told you. But I'm not about to make an announcement."

Subjects who identified as gay or lesbian by way of gay liberation, however, viewed the discussion of their homosexuality as essential to close relations with family members. Marilyn, aged 66, made this explicit when discussing her relationship to a niece, equating being close with being out (clearly, she was not close to the niece she discusses below).

> If you're asking me close, I'm not out to her. I don't tell her my personal problems. I tell her about, you know, problems with the apartment and other things. But she's not somebody I would go to with relationship problems.

This equation is even clearer when we consider Marilyn's relationship to her cousin, who is "almost like a sister to me" and to whom she did, in fact, come out.

Kate, aged 76, spoke in similar terms of her

> cousin in Chicago to whom I'm out. In an odd sort of way, I'm fond of her. She came the closest to being a sister, simply because for a while, in

Texas, we lived near each other and our mothers were not only sisters but very, very fond of each other, and we had a lot of contact as children.

In stark contrast to Manny's account above, these subjects welcomed younger gay people into their lives, offering support and guidance, even help in handling their homosexuality in the context of the family. Seventy-year-old Abby, for example, suspects that

> one of my great-nieces is going to turn around some day and say something to me, and if she does, then I will tell her flat out, and I will tell her where to go and what to [do], and steer her away from any of the pitfalls that I possibly can. And if I have to run interference for the rest of her family and mine, I will.

Similarly, Susan, aged 75, described how she looked forward to a visit from her granddaughter and her gay friend:

> My whole family's fully aware of who I am and that's what's important to me. ... My granddaughter's supposedly coming to visit here. She's bringing a couple of friends with her and it so happens, she tells me, one of her friends is gay, a young girl. She said, "I told her about you, Grandma. She'd love to talk to you." I said, "Sure, fine." So they think I'm gonna be an advisor to this young kid. Anyway, it'll be interesting to talk to her. But I think it's kind of cute, that she's gonna take her friend to visit her grandmother who's gay.

While Manny fumed when his nephew told him of his own homosexuality, 66-year-old Sharon was incensed that her brother has not come out to her, interpreting his reticence as an affront to the closeness they'd felt while growing up.

> My brother is not married. He has never said anything to me about being gay. *Ever.* Can you believe it? And he and I were just *this close*. We grew up like twins, there was a year difference. We were very close, he and I were raised very close. Yet he will not tell me he's gay.

Being Old and Gay

Clearly, there are many ways to experience being old and gay. In discussing the impact that homosexuality had on their lives and on growing older, gay men and lesbians often related to family issues in contradictory terms. Many expressed regret that they lacked the "support system" that the traditional family offers. For example, Ryan, aged 81, noted that, for homosexuals, growing older was "much more difficult. I don't think I have the support system, I don't have the family support system that I would otherwise have. I guess that's the main thing." Sixty-six-year-old Ricardo felt that "because we grow old normally separated from families" and heterosexuals "grow old *within* the families," gay aging

> is by definition a little different. You just can't define [yourself] isolated without any relationship to family or society. So in this case you have to project yourself to your family. I don't have any family, possibly because I wouldn't feel comfortable in the heterosexual world. So growing older, it makes a little difference.

At the same time, many also claimed that the absence of traditional family ties made for a better life in old age. For example, Jeannine, aged 66, while recognizing the importance of children as caregivers to older people, saw the family as a potential obstacle to happiness in old age, as the following interview exchange suggests.

> **Jeannine:** They don't have the family support that straights would. They don't have a daughter that's dutifully going to – usually – take care of Mom. Or a son who's going to be an advocate. So, in that sense, they're a little more isolated, they don't have the broad family thing. But it may be a blessing, too. 'Cause I've seen the vultures circle too, with straights.
> **DR:** You mean waiting for Grandma to die so that they can have the Porsche?
> **Jeannine:** Yeah. Or jostling to be nice to her before she dies so that they can have the Porsche.

Several subjects felt that the absence of conventional family relations freed them from constraints and concerns that took their toll on individuals' freedom, appearance, and health. These respondents linked the absence of a conventional family to what they perceived as the relative vitality and youthfulness of the gay and lesbian elderly. For 68-year-old Jan, childlessness is said to free older homosexuals from children's constant reminder of their relatively advanced age, resulting in subjective feelings of youthfulness.

> I don't think of myself as old, elderly or even aging. And I think if I were in the regular mode – a husband and kids, grandchildren – I'd have grandchildren at this point, and a constant *reminder* from all these years that have crept up and having all these generations younger than myself I would tend to feel much older I think than perhaps I do now. [Heterosexuals] usually do age faster.

Others explained that the relative vitality of older homosexuals was due to their freedom from the worries over family, from which heterosexuals suffered. Brian, aged 74, compared his gay friends to his heterosexual friends from his days in the Navy, claiming that the latter's marital and parental roles bring with them "worries" that cause "feebleness":

> Maybe gays aren't quite as feeble as straights now. Because I think that these friends I see just don't seem as old as the straight friends that are the same age. They haven't had kids and all this and that. I'm sure that [straight] people have kids, and they're with spouses. It's just maybe a little more worries or something.

Still others, such as Luke, aged 69, described the traditional family as threatening the autonomy and freedom of the elderly. According to Luke, older homosexuals are free from these impositions and hence relatively carefree in their youthfulness. He saw older heterosexuals, in contrast, as vulnerable to institutionalization by their children, which makes them "lonelier."

> Their sons and their daughters take them and make them lonelier by putting them in convalescent homes and getting rid of them. When you're gay, no one can do that to you, you have to do it to yourself. So you go on by yourself until you don't have any more strength to go on. And that's why I'm 68 and I still feel like I'm 55.

Some saw their homosexuality as irrelevant to their old age, resisting the narrative linkage of sexual nonconformity, social stigmatization, and their impact on the later years typical of many others. As William, aged 76, put it, "Some people, both gay and heterosexual, age gracefully and some don't. And I don't know that being gay has anything specifically to do with it." Mary, aged 66, felt that "getting old is just getting old, as far as I can tell." To 75-year-old Susan, "You're a person first, aren't you? Gay people get ill, gay people have the same problems that straight people do." For Kate, aged 76, the circumstances under which people age center on social support, which she felt is independent of sexuality. As she explained, the isolation of older persons depends upon

> whether they were ever married or had children, what kind of families they have. A straight woman who never married, if she has a loving niece, you know, great. If she doesn't, too damned bad. I think it's a matter of old age *per se* and the kind of friends and the kind of family you have. It's a question of you're single, you damned well better have a support system and/or some sort of family. You know most people that are my age and single do have nieces and nephews, you see. Having

been a single child I don't have that. I think that cuts across the whole society in terms of old age. That has nothing to do with the gay/lesbian part. We join the mainstream in old age.

Future Cohorts

In considering future ways of aging among gays and lesbians, we need to avoid a full reliance on the heterosexual/homosexual divide. History has shown that this divide is now not as clear as it was for the older subjects under consideration. Just as the historical era in which my subjects identified as homosexual affected their identity careers, so will the historical era in which future cohorts of lesbians and gays age affect their identities and their views of the later years. Future cohorts of homosexual elderly will have moved through life in the context of concerns and opportunities related to sexuality almost unimaginable a generation ago.

The shape of lesbian and gay families (see Weston 1991), if not legally binding, is nonetheless now part of the discourse and practice of lesbian and gay life. The emergence of same-sex partner benefits, while by no means universal, allows gay men and women to cement their relationships financially and legally, and to move to and from jobs as families, with massive implications for security in old age. This also allows gay men and women to be "out" at work, an almost mind-boggling change from the 1950s, when homosexuality was grounds for immediate dismissal from a job. Indeed, the homosexual "baby boom" of the 1980s and 1990s will undoubtedly have immense consequences for the quality of gay life in old age later in the century. The emergence of gay voting blocs and of gay lobbying will provide a new arena for the political engagement with, and enactment of, diverse homosexual identities and policies in the public sphere. These rapidly developing historical changes will undoubtedly provide new biographical opportunities for future generations of homosexual elders.

Accompanying this is the explosion of venues for the discussion and contesting of homosexual identity in the mass media, which suggests that future cohorts of older gay men and lesbians will have devoted a shorter period of their lives to identity issues surrounding their sexuality. It is doubtful that today's teenagers experiencing same-sex desires will spend as much time plowing through a discourse of difference to interpret their desires. Indeed, the now classic coming out story may become less dramatic and less painful than it has been, one which seems to have been a narrative watershed for the older subjects of the generation under consideration.

Gay liberation, lesbian-feminism, and queer politics have complicated a field of sexual discussion that had, in my subjects' earlier years, been dominated by an identity landscape almost wholly reliant upon the condemnation of homosexuality. Imagining the future impact of these changes on the identity careers of homosexuals further highlights the importance of the link between biography and history as it relates to ways of aging.

Notes

This study was supported by the UCLA Center on Aging and the National Institutes of Health, National Research Service Award MH15730.

References

Anspach, Renee R. 1979. "From Stigma to Identity Politics: Political Activism Among the Physically Disabled and Former Mental Patients." *Social Science and Medicine Medicine*, 13A: 765–73.

Bernstein, Mary. 1997. "Celebration and Suppression: The Strategic Uses of Identity by the Lesbian and Gay Movement." *American Journal of Sociology*, 103(3): 531–65.

Berube, A. 1990. *Coming Out Under Fire: The History of Gay Men and Women in World War Two.* New York: The Free Press.

Blasius, Mark. 1994. *Gay and Lesbian Politics: Sexuality and the Emergence of a New Ethic.* Philadelphia: Temple University Press.

Chauncey, George. 1994. *Gay New York: Gender, Urban Culture, and the Making of the Gay Male World, 1890–1940.* New York: Basic Books.

D'Emilio, John. 1983. *Sexual Politics, Sexual Communities: The Making of a Homosexual Minority in the United States.* Chicago: University of Chicago Press.

Espiritu, Yen Le. 1992. *Asian American Panethnicity: Bridging Institutions and Identities.* Philadelphia: Temple University Press.

Faderman, Lillian. 1991. *Odd Girls and Twilight Lovers: A History of Lesbian Life in Twentieth-Century America.* Middlesex: Plume.

Klawiter, Maren. 1999. "Racing for the Cure, Walking Women, and Toxic Touring: Mapping Cultures of Action within the Bay Area Terrain of Breast Cancer." *Social Problems*, 46(1): 104–26.

LeCompte, Margaret D. and Schensul, Jean J. 1999. *Designing and Conducting Ethnographic Research.* Volume 1 in *Ethnographer's Toolkit.* Walnut Creek: Altamira Press.

Marotta, Toby. 1981. *The Politics of Homosexuality: How Lesbians and Gay Men Have Made Themselves a Political and Social Force in Modern America.* Boston: Houghton Mifflin.

Mills, C. Wright. 1959. *The Sociological Imagination.* New York: Oxford University Press.

Moghadam, Valentine. 1994. *Identity Politics and Women: Cultural Reassertions and Feminisms in International Perspective.* Boulder, CO: Westview Press.

Nardi, Peter M. and Sanders, David. 1994. *Growing Up Before Stonewall: Life Stories of Some Gay Men.* London: Routledge.

Rosenfeld, Dana. 1999. "Identity Work Among Lesbian and Gay Elderly." *Journal of Aging Studies*, 13(2): 121– 44.

Stein, Arlene K. 1997. *Sex and Sensibility: Stories of Lesbian Generations.* Berkeley: University of California Press.

Timmons, Stuart. 1990. *The Trouble with Harry Hay: Founder of the Modern Gay Movement*. Boston: Alyson.

Weitz, R. 1984. "From Accommodation to Rebellion: the Politicization of Lesbianism." In T. Darty and S. Potter (eds), *Women-Identified Women*. Palo Alto, CA: Mayfield, pp. 233–48.

Weston, Kath. 1991. *Families We Choose: Lesbians, Gays, Kinship*. New York: Columbia University Press.

Young, A. 1972. "Out of the Closets, Into the Streets." In Karla Jay and Allen Young (eds), *Out of the Closets: Voices of Gay Liberation*. New York: Pyramid Books, pp. 6–30.

Chapter 9

Expectations and Experiences of Widowhood

Deborah Kestin van den Hoonaard

Most women become widows; it is a way of aging that is statistically expectable (Martin Matthews 1991). But statistical predictability doesn't directly translate into personal meaning. There is no comprehensive set of norms that govern what a widow should expect from others, what others might expect of her, or indeed what she should expect of herself in the circumstances. Nonetheless, widows' reports of their experience show that they do have related expectations and that these shape their views of themselves and others in widowhood.

This chapter reports the results of an in-depth interview study with widows aged over 50, whose husbands had died within the previous seven years.[1] The participants lived in New Brunswick, Canada – a largely rural, maritime province. Half of the women lived in one of New Brunswick's small cities and the other half in rural areas. In the interviews, I encouraged each of the widows to tell her story in her own way. Here, my analysis focuses on their accounts of what was expected or unexpected about widowhood.

The accounts indicate that expectations play a significant role in the way women convey the experience of being widows. Regardless of the objective attributes of widows' lives – such as the number of people who attended their husbands' funerals, how often they see their adult children, or who makes the phone calls that keep them in touch with their friends – their accounts suggest that each woman's anticipation of what should have happened and who should have done what, makes the difference in how she experiences her situation. The language of expectations is both positive and negative; it conveys a wide range of complex meanings of widowhood. Equally importantly, the language is used to delineate the emotional contours of widows' experience.

Expectations in the Early Days of Widowhood

Women's memories of the first days of widowhood are often vague, but surprises, both positive and negative, continue to have a strong impact on their stories. Many women express gratified astonishment at "the outpouring of love" they received. People demonstrated this love by going to the visitation and funeral and by sending cards or letters of condolence.

Although most women probably could not have said how many people they had expected to attend their husbands' visitations and funerals, the actual numbers often clearly exceeded their expectations.[2] Sharon, for example, marvelled at the turnout, conveying the resulting positive feelings this way:

> I looked out the door [of the funeral home] and it was clear down to the street, the people, and I thought, "Oh, this is, I cannot shake hands." But somehow something came over me, and I went through it and I enjoyed that, if you can enjoy something like that. It was such a touching feeling that so many people [came].

The image of long lines is not unusual. Another widow, Eleanor, remembers that "hundreds of people came through."

Typically, many more people attended the funeral than a widow expected. Participants in the study painted a very evocative picture of rooms overflowing with visitors. Marie reported,

> Oh, it was overflowing. It was in the funeral parlour. They had to open everywhere, all the rooms in there because it was packed, it was packed. And I was really surprised not expecting that at all.

Another widow, Eileen, put her surprise in the context of not having enough food for the reception, explaining,

> When we had a memorial mass for him, I catered for about 300 people. I thought about 300 people would come to the reception, and it was 950 people. My church seats a thousand, and there wasn't a pew to be had.

The stories suggest that it is not the actual number of people that is important, but rather that the number is larger than was expected.

For some, a particular individual's unexpected display of affection for the deceased spouse was noteworthy and heartwarming. One woman recalled that the mayor of her city had to "come three times before he got in." Others referred to colleagues, nurses who had cared for their husbands, or particular individuals whose affection for their husband was unanticipated. Sarah's comments stand out in this regard:

> One little boy, I just still can't get over it. It was a child that I'd taught in school. He used to come down here on a Sunday. He came to the funeral and he cried and he cried. He said, "He was the only father I ever knew." We didn't know this when he was alive.

The women also discovered unexpected affection for their husbands expressed through condolence cards and letters. The missives elicited a particularly powerful reaction when they came from unexpected sources or, again, in large numbers. Eileen reports:

> I got notes and letters from people that he had worked with [and others he] had helped with [things]. [Some] I didn't even know. He did all this in silence. He was quite a man.

Expectations can go both ways, of course, and there were a few women who talked about those who let them down in the early days, constructing their experience in more negative terms. Most women, for example, expected that someone in their family would stay with them right after their husbands died. Frances, whose interview was notable for showing little emotion, was moved to tears as she remembered the surprise of being left alone the first night after her husband died. Another widow, Marion, commented, "Afterwards, I felt a little resentful that no one was here. You go through all the difficult times alone."

Equally important are problems with family members who show up in unexpected ways during the first days of widowhood. Judy expressed deep shock years later that her stepchildren seemed to turn against her right after her husband died because he had left her a generous inheritance. June was embarrassed that her son did not stay long enough to communicate real caring after the funeral. This was exacerbated by the inappropriate clothes her grandchildren wore to the funeral.

> Well, it was very hard for me because I have a son [out west]. They came, but they didn't even have jackets for their [teenaged] boys. The boys didn't even have a suit on; they just had jeans and a shirt, you know, to the funeral, his father's funeral. They went back right after the

funeral. They never even drove back over here to see my daughter, so that hurt a lot with my son.[3]

Although these positive and negative experiences happened at a time when most women report being numb, the feelings around them remain strong years later. Related expectations not only shape the varied meanings of the early days, but serve to highlight the emotional aspects of their relations with others.

Expectations and Adult Children

The widows in the study expected their children to be supportive during their fathers' illnesses and, for the most part, they were. Lydia's comment is typical: "I am very fortunate, really, because my daughter came down. She was here when her father died." According to another widow, her daughter greatly exceeded expectations in this regard. The daughter went so far as to become a nurse because she anticipated that her father would need care in the future. When her father was very ill, both parents moved into their daughter's home where he could be taken care of with love by a professional nurse.

Some adult children surpassed their mothers' expectations by their actions right after their fathers' deaths. Sylvia was very touched when her son, who lives far away, immediately came to be with her.

> The real strong one was [my older son]. Our relationship's better, definitely. I admire him and I appreciate him. When I needed [him], he was right here. [He] drove up immediately.

This was especially striking, as Sylvia explained that she had been married only ten years and her husband was her children's stepfather. Interestingly, although this son exceeded his mother's expectations, he also seems to have raised the bar for his siblings, underscoring the significance of the other children's absence in the process. She commented that she was "sad" that the other children did not come to her husband's funeral and that she felt "let down."[4]

Views of widows' abilities

Expectations were also used to communicate adult children's sense of the widows' abilities. According to some of these widows, their adult children expected their mothers to be incapable of carrying on and became overprotective. These comments were linked with longstanding views of marital roles.

For example, Muriel felt that her daughter's inclination to "take over" resulted from her misunderstanding of how her mother's marriage had worked. This daughter thought that her father had "been in charge," but that perception had been incorrect. As a result, the daughter had expected her mother to be incapable of making decisions. Imitating the daughter, Muriel stated, "Oh, Mom, are you sure you can do that? Do you think you can do that? Are you sure you couldn't do that?"[5] Muriel feels that if she hadn't "displayed some strength" immediately, a pattern in which her daughter made all the decisions might have been established, leading to her becoming very dependent.

Most women reported that it was easier to train their daughters than their sons to give them the space they needed. This may reflect the unspoken expectation that the oldest male needs to be "the man of the family." As such, relationships with sons sometimes led to situations that felt to at least one widow like "role reversal." Edith, whose sons wanted to know where she was at night, remarked, "I mean, now I call them and I say, 'If you call the house and I'm not there I'm at ____.' Or 'I'm here tonight' or something like that. Goodness, I'm not a child!" Her sons' assumption that she is not competent to make her own decisions regarding her whereabouts has led to her repeatedly having to deal with pressure to let her sons make important decisions for her.

Not all women found their children's concern smothering. Polly, for example, appreciated her son's interest in her welfare. She now lives in an apartment above his detached garage and finds it a satisfactory arrangement. Regarding waking up in the middle of the night, Polly explained, "Well I got up and I put on the light and it wasn't two minutes and my phone rang and it was my daughter-in-law. 'Are you all right?' " Polly feels that she and her son have worked out a good balance between his need to know that she's safe, their mutual privacy, and independence. These two situations are objectively alike. In both cases, widows' sons want to keep close tabs on their mothers. It is each woman's expectations about what is reasonable that led to her reacting positively or negatively to similar circumstances, a point implied in each of the women's surrounding narrative.

Other women reported that their children expected their mothers to be capable. Several of these attributed this expectation to their children's having seen them as competent while their husbands were still living. Emily, for example, had been in business with her husband while Lydia had held a very responsible position in a voluntary service organization, which, Lydia felt, had shown her children that "I am able to look after myself."

Closeness and living alone

Whether or not their children are protective, most widows report that their relationships with their children are close. If anything, the relationship is said to be closer than it was when they were married, which was somewhat unexpected. One widow described the difference this way, "If it has changed, it would be closer because they've been very good about being here more because I'm alone. I see more of them; it's a closer relationship."

But simply describing relationships as closer obscures the complex and subjective nature of mothers' opinions about their relationships with their children. As with their accounts of the widowhood experience in general, the complexity is partially grounded in objectively reported actions and also markedly affected by their expectations about what their children should do with and/or for them. While the research literature shows that most women prefer to live alone rather than with their children,[6] the widows of this study were deeply gratified to be able to declare that their children offered to have them live with them. The women explained that their children felt that they should offer their mother a home. At the same time, the women believed that it was important for them to recognize that their children "have their own lives" and, therefore, to refuse to move in with them.

A central reason for not wanting to live with children was the expectation that it would damage the relationship, a point highlighted time and again in the interviews. Peg noted, for example, "I definitely think it would be disastrous to live with your children. I don't think I'd ever do that. It's been offered to me by my daughters but I said, 'No, I don't think so.'"

There is also a danger that a mother may expect too much of her children if she moves in with them or lives too close to them. Cathy's story demonstrates this problem. In response to her children's urging, she moved into the same apartment building where one of her daughters lived. Although it was only a move across town, it meant that she became isolated from her own friends. Cathy reports the problem was that she "expected too much" from her daughter in the way of emotional support and, as a result, finds herself feeling both neglected and demanding. Here, related expectations emphasize the emotional complexity of the situation.

Eileen's story reflects what she describes as more realistic expectations about living close to an adult daughter. She gave more thought to issues of independence and privacy than did Cathy, who was mostly responding to pressure from her daughters. Eileen had worried about leaving an empty house when she traveled and came up with the idea of building a wing onto her daughter's house. She waited a full year before putting her house on the market. Eileen recalled, "The more I thought about it, the more I thought, 'Gee, that's a good idea.' 'cause I could be close to my [family] and at the same time I could have my independence."

Difficult times

Remembering a time of life or an occasion that may be especially difficult can be very meaningful and emotional. Again this is colored by expectations.

Eleanor's son remembered to call on Father's Day because he knew that it would be a very emotional time, while Audrey's daughter, who lives on another continent, "sent flowers on the anniversary of [my husband's] death."

In striking contrast, two daughters minimized the importance of what would have been their parents' 50th wedding anniversary. This deeply hurt Cathy, their widowed mother.

> This was our 50th anniversary and that kind of provoked me. I was talking to [one of] the girls and I said, "This our anniversary." She said, "Yes, I know, Mom." I let it go at that. I was talking to the other girl here, so she said, "You sound kind of down today." "Well," I said, "I am a little bit. This is our anniversary day." "I know," she said, "but Dad's gone," she said, "Dad's gone." So I said, "Dad's gone, but I'm still here." It really hurt me, really hurt me.

The clash of reported expectations here is heartwrenching. Cathy's daughters expected her to get over things much faster than she did. Meanwhile, Cathy, influenced by members of a widows' support group, who had predicted that her daughters would "have you over for supper, or something for your anniversary," said that she expected her children to recognize that their acknowledgement of the date would not only be appreciated but also was expected.[7]

Then again, according to some of these widows, many of their adult children seem to intuitively understand the difficult times. Sarah's daughter, for example, is reported to know that one of the hardest times for Sarah is not being able to have tea with her husband when returning from an evening out.

> Now the kids always come in with me and say, why even if it's eleven o'clock, she says, "Oh, I think I'll have a cup of tea before I go." or something like that. I know why they're doing it. The always do that. They always come in.

At the same time, Audrey is the only research participant who found it possible to successfully explain these emotional challenges to her daughter. She reports that her daughter now knows that she finds hearing a particular hymn at church difficult and puts her arm around her mother when it is sung.

The widows' accounts indicate that when mother and children find a comfort level in their expectations of one another, they can achieve a mutually satisfying relationship. A change in living circumstances especially can upset the balance of expectations, making for difficult times. For example, June's divorced daughter had recently become involved in a serious relationship that included moving in with her new partner. Not only did this mean that June's daughter now had less time for her mother, but as June comments,

> It doesn't seem the same because he's built this house. [My daughter] had a house. I felt it was her house, and I could go in any time. But it's different now. I feel like I've got to call and make sure.

June went on to explain, "I'm glad she's happy, but I still miss her because I don't feel I can just drop in and do things with her."

Talk about expectations plentifully surrounds discussions of a widow's assessment of her relationship with her children. If she expects more emotional or instrumental support than she receives, she voices discouragement and resentment and sometimes shame. If she expects less or the same amount of support than she gets, she speaks of being satisfied, appreciative, and feeling pride. If a woman who gets less also expects less, she is not disappointed. The language of expectations resonates throughout accounts of relationships with adult children, sharpening the feelings that widows express.

Expectations and Friends

In virtually all studies that examine the impact of widowhood on friendship, researchers have found that widows say that they were dropped by their friends following their husbands' deaths (see Lopata 1973, van den Hoonaard 1994).[8] Nonetheless, although there have been attempts to understand this seemingly universal phenomenon, we still have not adequately explained it. Because friendship is an informal relationship (Matthews 1986), it carries unstated, implicit, and conflicting expectations with serious potential repercussions, including termination of the relationship. There are no "standardized" norms, and, therefore, a crisis such as a change in the marital status of one member of the friendship pair may lead to misunderstandings based on prior expectations.

The widows interviewed for the study understand that is it is their job to "keep up appearances" when they are with other people. They explain that it is essential that they not cry, be very down, or talk about their husbands all the time in front of others, especially friends. As one widow noted, crying or appearing too sad will "depress your friends, bore everybody, drive people crazy, or burden people." Friends often do not understand what the widow is going through and will get "fed up" with a widow who is always despondent. One widow, Lynn, informed me, "If I'd wept and wailed and howled in [my friends'] soup for the last six months, [my husband] would be very upset with me, very disapproving, ashamed."

Widows, themselves, can be intolerant of those who do not succeed in keeping up appearances in this regard. As Emily explained,

> I had a friend, acquaintance, and she lost her husband shortly after [me]. So I was trying to be of comfort to her and it drug me down. My daughter-in-law took me aside and she says, "Emily, you can't take that, you know you need to be around people that are uplifting."

Still, there were a few women who did feel that they could share their grief with a particular friend or a support group. This possibility required a sense of reciprocity in the expectation involved – each woman had to be willing to both hear and talk about the difficulties of widowhood in order for this to be acceptable.

Expectations of how their friends should provide support affected widows' interpretations of what has happened with friends who have disappointed them. Many expected their friends to call, invite, include, or drive them to events. Expectations in this area often centered on courtesy, not the actual extension of practical support. Thus, when Emily's friends invited her to attend an event sponsored by an organization to which they all belonged, she also had expected them to offer her a ride there even though she would have turned down the offer and taken her own car. Because she had expected the offer, she felt excluded when it wasn't offered and did not attend.

Peg, on the other hand, felt that it was *her* responsibility to keep in touch with her friends, expectations related to support in this case centering as much on herself as on others.

> You have to make the effort of keeping going with people. I network. I keep it going. I'm not going to drift into the woodwork, vanish into the wallpaper.

Peg made sure she invited people to her home and made a conscious effort to stay in touch with others, reaping their supportive friendship in the process. Because she expected it to be *her* job to keep in touch, she did not mind being the one who took responsibility for keeping the friendships going.

Concentrating on disappointments, however, leaves out the other side of the picture. Women also reported receiving unexpected support and help. Some persons previously considered to be mere acquaintances became good friends. Eileen, for example, recounted her experience with people she had previously thought of as only her husband's friends:

> [They] called me and invited me to the house for supper or lunch [and] have always called me. It's been different now. [Those I] expected to be

here all the time, to be friends with, to call you, haven't, and others that you didn't expect [to call or visit] are the ones that really come forward.

Other women talked about neighbours, particularly younger neighbours who provided instrumental support. Sylvia's neighbours were a young couple who, she notes, "did things for me in the house, checked on and washed out the refrigerator and did stuff like that."

Emotional support also came from unexpected sources and led to deepening relationships. Marie, a nurse who received unexpected support from the people she worked with, commented, "I did not think they cared that much." This support took the form of offering a cup of tea or asking how she was, simple gestures that were conveyed as all the more meaningful because Marie did not expect them. Marilyn commented that small acts from an unexpected person made a difference in how she felt, such as "the girl at the checkout at [the grocery store] brought [me] a little bunch of flowers."

Expectations in this area also related to social awareness. Lydia told me that she was surprised that there were so many "people around to do things with, [that] are looking for friendship." The awareness of others available for friendship prompted the widows to expect them to reciprocate overtures to become friends. Some reported renewing friendships with women who already were widows. As Edith remarked, losing her husband, "made me more aware of other people. You get in a rut when you're married and it doesn't make you care really about other people." She pointed out that she was disappointed with her married friends, but could see that she had acted the same way as they did before her husband died.

Expectations and "Other Men"

When it comes to other men especially, the widows' stories reflect feelings of uncertainty. As married women, study participants were comfortable interacting with men. As newly single women, however, they are not sure how men will react to them or how to interpret the men's actions. Several widows described situations that include misread intentions on the part of both other men and themselves.

Although few of these women expressed a keen interest in either marrying or becoming romantically involved, some did mention a desire for male company. Sylvia and June, reflecting both a desire for companionship and the discomfort many women feel when they are alone in public, wanted someone to go out with. June, a ballroom dancer, put it this way:

Just to go out for dinner and dancing for a few hours. And then you just go home and you've had a lovely evening and look at my husband's picture up there on the wall. I think it's a nice night's adventure.

Audrey missed conversations with men. She commented that she actually preferred talking with men to talking with women. Although Audrey thought she could be friends with a man, she also thought it likely that a man would misunderstand her interest. He might think "you're looking for a husband, and that's not necessarily it; it's nice just to have a friend."

The common belief that cross-gender friendship implies romance, courtship, and sexual intimacy is reflected in the uncertainty of expectations and apprehensions about probable misunderstandings (Adams 1985). Several women reported that the potential for men's misreading any friendliness on their part is one of the reasons that they continue to wear their wedding rings. The wearing of rings is not only a symbol of loyalty to their husbands, but also protects them from unwanted attention from other men. Several women noted that they would like male companionship for the physical contact, but, for the most part, they were not looking for sexual intimacy. The expectation that men might be interested in casual sex led to both creativity in finding safe avenues for contact and to the avoidance of any romantic relationship.

Contemporary mores regarding sex – principles and practices that have changed drastically over the past half century – presented a challenge even for the few women who were interested in possibly having a sexual relationship in the future. Going out with a man for the first time could be "traumatizing." When these women were growing up, intimate relationships were, for the most part, confined to marriage, and they did not want to "crawl into bed with somebody" (Emily) because "there has to be a relationship." As Eleanor pointedly remarked, "And I don't believe into jumping into bed with every man that comes along."

Women do not expect men to share this attitude. In at least some cases, this concern was said to be justified. Edith, for example, had gone out to dinner with someone thinking they were going to "go out and just talk." The man she was with wanted her to "go around with him, go away with him and all that – you wouldn't imagine that at our age, but he did." Many women, like Edith, assume that men and women have different attitudes in this area, and the anxiety surrounding possible misunderstandings serves as a barrier to any relationship with men at all.

A safer means to physical contact, one less fraught with the threat of embarrassing or difficult situations, was hugging. Martha and Sharon both relied on specific men at their church for "safe hugs." The security of the Sunday service setting was enhanced by the fact that these hugs took place in front of the men's wives and were so obviously harmless that nobody could possibly misread the intent. One of them noted, "Like Tom and I, we'd never think anything of it, we'd start hugging each other up [at church], but [his wife] is such a sweetheart." June had found a safe environ-ment in formal ballroom dancing. The partner you dance with knows that "you don't date anybody or anything." Her dancing provided a protected place where she could "dance with someone and I think I'm dancing with my husband." June, Sharon, and Martha all had found environments where they knew the men involved shared their expectation of no courtship or romance.

Some other men were exceptional. Marion found that men expected her, as a widow, to be "interested" in them and, oddly enough, felt that they could be threatened by this. As one widow explained,

> If you bake bread or give them something, they get all nervous. And I just think it's nice to do things for people. I have to be very careful not to overwhelm them, I guess.

Two stories illustrate the difficulty widows may have in interpreting other men's intentions. Audrey recounted the story of a phone call she received from a man who had seen her at the cemetery. He had been visiting his wife's grave at the same time Audrey was visiting her husband's grave. The man was interested in getting together. Audrey's reaction was to avoid him, even while she initially felt sorry for him. Marilyn also received attention from a man who had seen her at the cemetery. When he approached her and started chatting, she had the same reaction as Audrey: "I felt sorry for him." But it turned out that the man had seen some younger men in the area who were drinking, and he was simply warning Marilyn: "I immedi-ately jumped to the conclusion he was going to come there and meet me the next night. And I thought, 'Isn't it a riot that you jump to these conclu-sions?'" Both women felt uncertain and vulnerable because they did not know what to expect. They and all the other women in the study were meeting and interacting with other men on a new basis. Some avoided men because they found it too difficult to anticipate men's new reactions to them as single women. The rules of intergender relations had changed, and the women evidently did not know the new ones.

Widows' Expectations of Themselves

Most of the women I studied had low expectations of their own abilities to manage as widows and were surprised when they discovered they could manage on their own satisfactorily. When I asked participants if there was anything about being widows that surprised them, several expressed the unexpected in this regard. The most common responses revolved around newly found emotional strength and the unexpected ability to do new things. Sharon, for example, had expected to "go to pieces" when she became a widow. She remarked that she had done "real well." Others used stronger terms. They had seen the loss of their husbands as the end of their world. They had not been able to "envision going on alone." Even surviving amazed Marion, and Sarah thought she would be a "basket case." The unexpected combined with the new discoveries, punctuated these accounts of emotional triumph.

Some women discovered that they really enjoyed making decisions while others found out that their "personalit[ies] came out more." Part of this was learning to say no. Martha, for example, reported that she had stood up to a neighbor who wanted to buy a piece of property adjacent to her own. The neighbor had caused her some problems in the past, so she told him in no uncertain terms that she did not want to sell him the property. Martha was surprised at her own assertiveness and found that her expectations of herself were lower than the reality: "I thought I was a baby, [but] I wasn't afraid to give my opinion."

Discovering new competence

The ability to learn to do new things also was unexpected. The way Muriel tells the story of learning to program her VCR underscores the low assessment these women had of their capacity to develop skills for which they had previously depended on their husbands. As Muriel explained, "The electricity had gone out and the clock was blinking, 12:00, 12:00. I never adjusted that thing and I didn't even know how to open the little box there." Because Muriel assumed that she would not be able to set the clock, she let the light blink on and off for a week. At that point, she said, "I put a book up so I wouldn't see it." Muriel finally realized that she would either have to fix the clock or unplug the VCR. She used the instruction book and went step-by-step until it was done. For Muriel, this was not only a large accomplishment but also exceeded her expectations of her own abilities. She felt quite satisfied with herself as a result.

Many other experiences convinced these widows they could handle jobs they had not thought they could. Peg found that she was good with a hammer and nails, while Audrey found she could do simple repairs. Lydia showed me the black-and-blue thumb she had acquired from her first and successful attempt at hammering. She observed, "It's the first thing, but it's surprising."

A few women learned to drive for the first time, and this was a major accomplishment (see Berger 1986). Muriel felt that she needed to learn how to drive:

> I didn't drive at all, so I went out to Young Drivers with all these teenagers [and] I learned how to drive the car. It feels good, too, you know, nothing really spectacular.

Learning to buy and take care of an automobile presented special challenges. The women were concerned that unscrupulous sales people or
servicemen would try to take advantage of them because they were older
women and not expected to know anything about cars. For some, this fear
was grounded in reality. Two women told stories of salesmen not taking
their interest in buying a car seriously, while Polly told a distressing story of
buying a used car.

Soon after she bought the car, Polly recounts, a dashboard panel light
came on that read "check gauges." She took it to the dealer, who simply
offered to take the car back if she didn't want it. But she was in a bind
because, "Geez, you know, I really want this car; I really like this car." Her
son trivialized the problem, remarking, "Why are you worrying about that
light? I can't imagine why you would let a little thing like that bother you."
Still, Polly's feeling was that a light comes on for a reason, but then was
surprised that both her son and the dealer suggested it would cost her up to
$2,000 to fix it. When I interviewed her, Polly was still driving around with
the "check-the-gauges light" intermittently coming on and off. It had
continued to bother her that something might actually be wrong. But,
later, other than the loose wire that she was told might be causing the
problem, Polly reported that the dealer told her, "Look, I'm not convinced
that that's doing anything other than telling you to check your gauges,"
adding, on her own behalf, "and I'm not prepared to pay 12 or 1500 dollars
for the repair of something that isn't broken."

Living alone

The discovery that they can live alone is especially significant to widows of
this generation, as few had lived alone at any time in their lives. In this
particular group of 28 women, only seven had ever lived alone before.
Living alone was a brand new experience for most of the women, and
they did not know what to expect. For some of them, the ability to live
alone was the most surprising aspect of being a widow. Doris, for example,
did not like living alone, but her capacity to be by herself was a pleasant
surprise. Martha noted that she had feared that she might have to "give [my
house] up and go live in an apartment or something." Sharon's biggest fear
had been coming home to an empty house. But she recounted an experience of feeling that her husband said to her one day as she was unlocking
her door, "Mom, you're going to be all right," which led her to overcome
her fears. She was no longer afraid to be alone in the house.

Much of the women's discussion of living alone centered on safety issues.
The issue of feeling secure was usually the first thing the women addressed.
Eileen commented that she "heard more noises and more wood creaking or
the windows or whatever." But there were exceptions. While both Marilyn
and Audrey thought my question about living alone was really about being

afraid, they reported that they weren't personally frightened. Marilyn had not married until she was 46 and had, therefore, lived alone for a number of years prior to her marriage. When I commented on this, she replied,

> Yeah, like I have never been afraid to stay alone, and I admit I have no patience with those who are. If I'm nervous, it's nervous of something real. But I don't think about people breaking in.

Audrey responded to my question of whether or not she had lived alone before this way:

> I'm not afraid to be alone. I feel very comfortable out here [in a suburban neighborhood]. I've got wonderful neighbors here. I mean I think I'm safer and less at risk of my house being broken into and everything out here than I am in town.

Lydia said she was not afraid to live alone, but she did take new precautions, "As long as things are secure and I've got blocks of wood in the doors and things, it doesn't bother me." She also had a boarder and a dog, both of which increased her sense of security.

The expectation that living alone would be difficult and that the widows would have to overcome their feelings of vulnerability made it difficult to resist the temptation to have people stay with them for too long after their husbands died. Martha, for example, had let her daughters spend four nights with her right after her husband died. After that, she told them, "'I've got to face it. If I'm going to live in my own home, I've got to face up to it. I will stay here.' So I did from then on." Doris forced herself not to stay with friends "in town" because, as she explained,

> I'm not old enough to have someone with me forever, and I'm not old enough to go somewhere else for the rest of my life, so I have to stay here. So I did, but it was not easy.

The expectation that if they did not bite the bullet and force themselves to stay alone, they might put it off forever, is reinforced by Eleanor's cautionary tale:

> Because a couple my age [in their 50s] live up [here]. Her father died, and every night her mother goes to her house, and now she's so old, she stays there all the time. But at the time, every morning at twenty to eight, she went down the road with her Save-Easy bag [a local supermarket], with her nightgown in it. And I said, "I will not be coming home with my bag with my nightgown in it every morning. I've got to do this. I've got to learn to deal with it. I've got to learn to be alone."

For the most part, these women expected living alone to be a bigger challenge than it was. But, surprisingly, as with most single, older women (Doyle et al. 1994), they not only preferred to live alone rather than with family, they also discovered that there were aspects of living alone that were enjoyable. They did not have to come home to cook dinner for anybody, they could stay up all night reading or vacuuming if they could not sleep, or they could listen to the music they liked, as Marion said she discovered.

Conclusion

It is tempting to look at these materials regarding widows' expectations and conclude that their lives would be much easier if they simply had more realistic expectations or, even better, if they had lower expectations. In fact, Jay Mancini and Rosemary Bleiszner (1989) did find that older parents' high expectations are inversely related to their morale. If, on the one hand, your expectations are high when you are old and especially if you are a widow, you are likely to be disappointed. If, on the other hand, your expectations are low, you will probably be pleasantly surprised and, consequently, satisfied. Leah Cohen (1984: 131), for example, has described this generation of women's way of aging as having low expectations and "accept[ing] hardship and suffering as an inevitable fact of life," while Lucille Bearon (1989) has written that "no great expectations" provide the underpinning of older women's life satisfaction.

Older women and widows, in particular, occupy a lower status than younger and/or married women (Lopata 1976; Matthews 1979). In addition, older widows work hard to conform to the "strongly felt imperative" (Aronson 1990: 68) not to burden their children or friends with their problems. Widows consistently insist that their children "have their own lives," while the widows must "keep up appearances" in front of both their children and their friends.

Still, the lack of clear norms makes it challenging for widows and their friends to negotiate the obligations in their relationship successfully. Widows' lower status upsets the equilibrium that characterizes friendship, and all of a sudden it is up to them to take the responsibility for maintaining the friendship both by conforming to emotional expectations and taking the initiative to keep in touch. Few women respond, as Peg did, by unquestioningly assuming this responsibility, partly because they are unaware of the necessity and partly because single women of this generation do not feel comfortable instigating social contact with couples. In a social context that valued older, single women, they might have the opportunity to more explicitly communicate their expectations to friends and children who would find them legitimate. As we have seen, social change regarding sexual mores as well as uncertainty regarding intentions makes it difficult for widows to engage in social relationships with other men. The resulting way of aging for many older widows is to live in a world of women where all find it easier to read intentions and agree on acceptable behavior.

When we look at women's expectations regarding themselves and their abilities, the picture is much brighter. The mastery of chores that they had previously thought were beyond their capabilities, as well as the ability not to only live alone but to enjoy some aspects of it, have led, for many widows, to an enhanced level of confidence in themselves and the discovery of their capacity to be assertive and to make important decisions.

Although widowhood is a statistically expectable way of aging for women, its lived characteristics are, in many ways, unexpected. Most women overcome the disappointments of unfulfilled expectations on the part of friends and, less often, children. Contrary to current, widespread stereotypes (Arber and Ginn 1991) that depict older women as passive and ineffectual, these widows' way of aging manifest creativity, resilience, and growth. Their stories especially, of what they expected and what they discovered, go a long way toward explicating the meaning and emotional contours of their situations. The language of expectations, in particular, serves to construct the significance of the events recounted. Regardless of whether expectations are accurate or not based on some objective criterion, the language makes meaning in the narrative context of the experiences under consideration.

Notes

1   The study was funded by a Community Researcher Award of the Seniors' Independence Research Program of Health Canada (NHRDP award no. 6604–111–603).

2   Although most women preferred large turnouts, the reaction is not universal. One woman had expected only close family to be involved. She was visibly upset that many others came and referred to it as a "horror show."

3   This particular woman already had trouble with her son stemming from his embarrassment about his father's Alzheimer's disease. Nonetheless, as she reported, she had still hoped for more from her son during and after the funeral.

4   The case of stepchildren and stepparents is complex. See van den Hoonaard (2001) for an in-depth discussion of this topic.

5   A younger widow, in a pilot interview for the study, remarked that when her husband died people began to question all her decisions. It was one of the more challenging aspects of widowhood for her.

6   See Doyle et al. (1994) for an in-depth look at why many older women agree that living alone is preferable.

7   It is not that unusual for children to have difficulty dealing with how long their mothers grieve for their fathers. For example, some years ago, a widow brought her daughter to my class just so that the daughter could hear me say that it is normal for widows to grieve for what may seem like a very long time.

8   In fact, when I was a guest on a CBC phone-in show in Montreal, just about every woman who called wanted to talk about disappointments regarding friendships.

References

Adams, Rebecca G. 1985. "People Would Talk: Normative Barriers to Cross-Sex Friendship for Elderly Women." *The Gerontologist*, 25(6): 605–11.

Arber, Sara and Ginn, Jay. 1991. *Gender and Later Life: A Sociological Analysis of Resources and Constraints*. London: Sage.

Aronson, Jane. 1990. "Women's Perspectives on Informal Care of the Elderly: Public Ideology and Personal Experience of Giving and Receiving Care." *Ageing and Society*, 10: 61–84.

Bearon, Lucille B. 1989 "No Great Expectations: The Underpinnings of Life Satisfaction for Older Women." *The Gerontologist*, 29(6): 772–8.

Berger, Michael L. 1986. "Women Drivers: The Emergence of Folklore and Stereotypic Opinions Concerning Feminine Automotive Behavior." *Women's Studies International Forum*, 9(3): 257–63.

Cohen, Leah. 1984. *Small Expectations: Society's Betrayal of Older Women*. Toronto: McClelland and Stewart.

Doyle, Veronica with B. Backman, E. Cassiday, B. Cumby, B. Ferneyhouch, J. Florczyk, W. Gladman, P. Hall, P. Joyce, A. MacLean, M. Miller, P. Rafferty, R. Riley, D. Ritchie, J. Smith, D. Trohan, V. Ward. 1994. *It's My Turn Now: the Choice of Older Women to Live Alone*. Gerontology Research Centre, Simon Fraser University at Harbour Centre.

Lopata, Helena Z. 1973. *Widowhood in an American City*. Cambridge, MA: Schenkman.

Lopata, Helena Z. 1976. "Widows as a Minority Group." In Bill D. Bell (ed.), *Contemporary Social Gerontology*. Springfield, IL: Charles C. Thomas, pp. 348–355.

Lopata, Helena Z. 1996. *Current Widowhood: Myths and Realities*. Thousand Oaks, CA: Sage.

Mancini, Jay A. and Blieszner, Rosemary. 1989 "Aging Parents and Adult Children: Research themes in intergenerational relations." *Journal of Marriage and the Family*, 51(May): 275–90.

Martin Matthews, Anne. 1991. *Widowhood in Later Life*. Toronto: Butterworths.

Matthews, Sarah H. 1979. *The Social World of Old Women: Management of Self Identity*. Newbury Park, CA: Sage.

Matthews, Sarah H. 1986. *Friendships through the Life Course: Oral Biographies in Old Age*. Beverly Hills: Sage.

van den Hoonaard, Deborah Kestin. 1994. "Paradise Lost: Widowhood in a Florida Retirement Community." *Journal of Aging Studies*, 8(2): 121–32.

van den Hoonaard, Deborah Kestin. 2001. *The Widowed Self: The Older Woman's Journey Through Widowhood*. Waterloo, ON: Wilfrid Laurier University Press.

Epilogue

Chapter 10

Positive Aging

Mary Gergen and Kenneth J. Gergen

As the aging population expands, concern among scholars, policy planners, and ordinary people tends to focus on the decline and degeneration that seem inevitable with aging. A powerful theoretical framework stresses the importance of disengagement as the major outcome of the aging process (Cummings and Henry 1961). Almost no attention is paid to the years of potential growth and development that lie ahead for most people over 65. The negative focus is nicely illustrated in recent issues of the *Journal of Gerontology*, which featured the following topics: Alzheimer's disease, diabetes, hospitalized injuries, dementia, chronic rheumatology, chronic stress, balance impairment, antidepressants, depression, hypertension, muscle impairment, cerebrovascular disease, functional decline, and ulcers. Only a single article in the journal focused on the positive possibilities of aging. Such phrases as "over the hill," "out to pasture," and "the geriatric set" carry the negative image into everyday conversation.

In this chapter, we ask whether this vision is the best or the only way in which aging can be conceived? We think not! Taking an oppositional stand, we attend to the great benefits that aging can afford. We discuss how people are able to experience aging as an adventurous and fulfilling time, despite physical deterioration or other handicaps. We focus on the vast majority of elders who are not living below the poverty line (90 percent of older Americans live above it.), those who typically have some form of higher education and are able to enjoy a large variety of cultural resources. This focus is appropriate given that by the year 2010 the vast majority of those over sixty will have had some college education and will be in better condition both economically and physically than in any preceding generation in history.

Thus, this chapter is about the not-too-distant futures of most readers. Our message is a hopeful one – that the last third of life need not be filled with despair at the loss of one's youth, but can be beautiful in its own right. We also stress that living positively is not just something for the rich, the strong, and the healthy, but is within the grasp of anyone, even those who might appear from some perspectives to be handicapped or ill (Seligman and Czikszentmihalyi 2000). Elsewhere we discuss various forms of systematic research relevant to positive aging (Gergen and Gergen 2000; in press). In the present chapter, we focus on individual cases that illustrate the many potentials for positive aging.

The Social Construction of Age

Before illustrating forms of positive aging, it will be helpful to understand more fully the conceptual context from which this work springs. Specifically, our work grows from a social constructionist standpoint. A key assumption of this perspective is that the ways in which we describe and explain the world are not demanded by the nature of the world itself. Rather, it is through the active negotiation and collaboration of people that such understandings are constructed. In effect, people in their social groups create their realities (K. Gergen 1999; M. Gergen 2001). Thus, there is no "one correct way" of describing the world, in science or elsewhere. Many constructions are possible, each with a utility for particular groups of people. In this sense, we are not bound by existing ways of describing and explaining the world; the creation of new possibilities depends on the character of our present dialogue. And, as we generate new ways of understanding, so do we open the door to new patterns of action.

With regard to the concept of aging, constructionist theses are particularly catalytic. They unsettle the widespread tendency within the social and biological sciences to search for the *naturalized life course*, that is, to chart the innate development and decline of human capacities, tendencies, interests, desires, and so on over the life span (see Holstein and Gubrium 2000a). This tendency is strong in gerontological science, with its proclivity to chart various forms of physical and mental decline, as mentioned in the introduction above. With its strong emphasis on culturally and historically situated knowledge, social constructionism serves as a challenge to these efforts (Gubrium and Holstein 2000; Holstein and Gubrium 2000b). There is nothing about changes in the human body that require a concept of *aging* or of *decline*. There is no process of aging *in itself*; the discourse of aging is born of interpersonal relationships within a given culture at a given time (Hazan 1994). Dancers in "gentlemen's clubs," Olympic gymnasts, and professional football players all become "old" at a rather young chronological age; most people classified as "old" within the culture at large feel quite young (Ronai 1992). The strong tendency to devalue the older person in Western culture can be contrasted with many traditional cultures in which the eldest are viewed as the wisest and treated with honor and respect.

In this same sense, we must also view the scientific literature of later-life decline as culturally constructed. That is, the extensive research demonstrating deterioration of physical and psychological functioning during the latter span of life is not a simple reflection of what is there. Rather, whether a given configuration constitutes "decline" – or, indeed, is worth mentioning at all – derives from a particular domain of values (such as productivity and individualism), along with various assumptions, vocabularies, measuring instruments, and the like (Gergen and Gergen in press). In effect, to find someone biologically or cognitively impaired constitutes what James Holstein and Jaber Gubrium (2000a) call a *collaborative accomplishment*. It is an accomplishment of particular professional groups, working with particular assumptions and values, within a complicit culture. And so it is that we must continuously reflect on the way in which the sciences construct the life course, and most particularly accounts that treat decline as a natural fact of growing older. In this sense, the narrative creates the life (Gergen and Gergen 1986; Sarbin 1986). When the story treats a phenomenon as "natural," it is often difficult to counteract (Tiefer 1995). The imagination is blunted, and the status quo remains firm.

When we avoid essentializing tendencies of naturalism, we become conscious of the possibilities of cultural transformation. If we emphasize the constructed nature of theories of aging, we become alerted to the potentials of reconstructing the course of aging in more positive ways (Hazan 1994). The American construction of aging has yielded enormous suffering, and it could be otherwise (cf. Campioni 1997; Gergen 1996). We may begin to explore other, more uplifting, ways of understanding the latter years of life, and indeed launch discussions from which new visions emerge. We may seek out or initiate research that lends itself to an optimistic view of possibilities. We are invited to share stories and other resources that help us to realize these positive potentials in our own lives.

Varieties of Positive Aging

With this constructionist orientation in place, let us consider the various pathways by which older people today are creating lives that are full of meaning, joy, and satisfaction. Front porches are becoming obsolete and so are "old folks" in their rocking chairs. With advances in wealth, health supports, political power and sheer numbers have come major shifts in life patterns of the elderly. Myriad opportunities have opened in numerous directions, and the new breed of the elderly are actively exploring them as indeed we write. There is no way we can capture the richness of these new developments in this concluding chapter. However, we do feel that several prominent life themes have become evident in recent decades, themes that are central to the positive aging process. Here, we identify three major life themes, the first centered on *the self*, the second on *interpersonal relationships*, and the third on *contributions to community*. Delineations among these themes are seldom clear, and many people will engage in all of these realms at one time or another. However, we do find that lives of the new elderly are often centered around one of these themes as opposed to the others.

The life theme centered on the self is one that is dedicated to self-enhancement in physical, psychological, and social ways. This focus might be called the "sybaritic life style." This lifestyle is dedicated to the pursuit of personal pleasure. The potentials for creating or maintaining a beautiful body, for expanding knowledge or self-awareness, for learning new skills or improving those already acquired, and for finding new ways to enhance one's sensual pleasures are the motivators for everyday life. One of the major avenues for the satisfaction of personal goals has been to create and maintain a level of personal attractiveness never before available to older people. With the use of plastic surgery, a medical specialty that has exploded in its popularity in recent years among men as well as among women, no one needs to be ugly. Face-lifts are now the operation of choice in many social groups, and as one very attractive professional woman in her fifties explained, "Among my friends, it is not IF you will get a face-lift, but WHEN." Actor Robert Redford in a recent interview had to defend his decision not to get plastic surgery by claiming that his wrinkles were the markings of his soul. Few other celebrities follow this philosophy, and the notion that one should look as good as one can physically is a demand that is prevalent in the aging population to the extent that it can be afforded. Bright, gleaming white teeth are now the standard for public personalities, and dentists specializing in cosmetic work are in high demand. Beauty does not stop with the head, however; a shapely, athletic body is also in vogue. Body work, itself, is a major new pastime for older people, as well as a new consumer offering for the purveyors of well-being. Spas, beauty ranches, gyms, yoga classes, and workout rooms in hotels, workplaces, and resorts all cater to the demands of the elder population. Lotions, vitamins, dietary supplements, and potions of all kinds are in demand to strengthen, enliven, and relax the body. Personal trainers and Eastern mystics, charged with enhancing spiritual tranquility and physical fitness, have gained popularity as well.

Self-development also includes educational programs, sports training schools, therapy and self-development workshops of all kinds. Pleasure seeking, through cruises, adventure holidays, singles clubs, parties and get-togethers all serve the self-seeker in the older years as well. Because older people now control vast economic resources, and account for approximately one-half of all discretionary spending, they have become a market that attracts a variety of purveyors of pleasure (Onks 2002). In these activities, older people represent a vision of retirement that attracts younger people who look forward to their turn in this stage of life.

The emphasis on interpersonal relationships can also be a common theme in the lives of older people. The important elements in the lives of these people usually revolve around maintaining and expanding the network of social relationships. Most frequently the network is an outwardly spiraling circle from intimate relationships with spouse and children to extended family members and then outward to neighbors, friends, and more distant acquaintances; for some, as in our example below, there may be many networks that are in motion all the time. For some, the creation and maintenance of networks of associates may be produced by continuing to be actively employed in the workforce. In recent years, more and more so-called retired people have reentered the workforce through part-time jobs. Although financial incentives have been created through changes in social security laws, people return to work for social as well as economic reasons. Having a place to be, to be recognized for your activities, and to have a social life among colleagues is highly valued by most people, and a job can be a means to continue to receive these benefits.

For many older people, the emphasis on the relationship itself is satisfied through family connections. The joy of life is in celebrating family occasions, of recognizing mutual advantages, and of sticking together in the hard times. Notions of solidarity and togetherness are the highest priorities, more meaningful than individual success and pleasure. Among those that value this lifestyle, there is less emphasis on having a big bank account. With family ties or close friendships, the rituals of togetherness may be very simple and inexpensive. Often differences in monetary wealth lead to pooling resources, such that one family member may have a boat, another a swimming pool, a third tickets to sporting events, and the "cousins" all share their advantages with one another. When one falls on hard times, the others help to stabilize the ones in difficulty, as Colleen Johnson and Barbara Barer's chapter in this volume illustrated. Accomplishments of individual members of the group shed a positive light on the rest; older people are included in the swirl of family and friendship connections, even their troubles, without the segregation that might be more typical of those involved in the sybaritic lifestyle.

The communally based lifestyle expands the involvement beyond the family/friendship networks, and may even be competitive with them.

People at younger ages who get involved in political activities in their local communities, in civic clubs, such as Rotary, the Lions Club, Chambers of Commerce, in their religious organizations, in educational institutions, or in charitable organizations, for example, often continue their commitments far into old age. Because they are reaching the end of their occupational lives, they are more available to serve these organizations in a voluntary capacity. More older people are engaged in voluntary activities in the U.S. today than any other age group. Thus, the elected officials and the board members of major community organizations are frequently the most senior in age. Through their vast experience, their long histories of involvement, and their availability, they become the leaders of their communities.

Often the demands of their offices or the extent of the communal need is so vast that the obligations of the voluntary commitment take on the proportions of a full-time job. For these people, there is often a sense of self-efficacy, pride, and fulfillment in these activities, but there is also the danger of feeling burned out when the problems of community life are too immense for the numbers that are addressing them, and of feeling unappreciated for work that is unpaid. The balance between feeling fulfilled and stressed is one that the communally oriented person of any age must constantly experience. For most older people, if the commitment is not overwhelming, communal service represents a golden opportunity to make a difference in the world. This sense of being useful and productive is satisfying at any age, but especially when other employment opportunities have ended.

The following sections amplify these themes and furnish brief illustrations of positive patterns of aging.

Personal Development: The Infinite Extension of the Self

Traditional cultural wisdom separates the life span into three parts: development, maturity, and decline. By common standards, the developmental phase is accelerated during the first six years of life, and gradually tapers until near closure by the late teens. With voting privileges and a driver's license, the individual *should* enter maturity! Yet, while not wishing a return to childhood, seekers of positive aging have largely abandoned the traditional view of developmental closure. For them, the end of employment and child rearing obligations offers freedom to continue their developmental process. As many feel, the obligations occupying them during the "middle years" often froze or impeded a process of development that should otherwise be open-ended. The old-fashioned meaning of the term "maturity" – associated with a conservative, toiling and unimaginative lifestyle – is no longer acceptable. Outfitted with both resources and time, there seem to be no limits to personal growth and fulfillment for the older person today.

This "return to personal development" is also supported by the individualist values central to the Western tradition since the 1600s. In this tradition, it is the individual (as opposed to the family or community) who serves as the fundamental atom of society. Strong value is placed on individual knowledge, morality, motivation, and responsibility. When these are well developed, it is believed, human relations will thrive, and society will function effectively. At the same time, the emphasis on the individual is linked to a Darwinian view of the survival of the fittest and a hedonistic vision of individual pleasure and pain. In the former instance, improving one's individual strengths and resources is to further one's survival, and in the latter the search for individual pleasure is viewed as a "natural" or biologically based proclivity. We mention these various threads of the individualist tradition because we find the life theme of personal development can take several different forms, depending on which aspect of the individualist tradition is emphasized. Let us consider, then, the way in which three different forms of personal development are played out: cultivating self-knowledge, building an empire, and pursuing pleasure.

Audrey Lermond: Cultivating the self

One vision of development long prominent within the upper classes (and particularly among women) is that of personal cultivation. In this case the dominant metaphor is that of the flower; the individual can be viewed as an emerging flower that requires cultivation in order to reach fruition. Cultivation requires continuous nurturing of the organism as a whole. Thus, the cultivated individual should not only possess wisdom, but sophistication and appreciation of art, literature, music, dance, the world's many languages and cultures, and more. The later years of Audrey Lermond nicely illustrate the continuing cultivation of the self.

Here we trace the last twenty-seven years in Audrey's life, in which she constantly expanded her knowledge, her talents and her skills from late maturity until her death at age 87. After five years of widowhood, Audrey was married for the second time at age 60 to a man who was 70, and they lived together until his death twenty years later. For many decades, Audrey had been intensively involved in various clubs and organizations that were primarily sponsored by the university where both her husbands had worked. One of the clubs was for wives of professors (going back to the days when educated women were married to professors, rather than serving as professors themselves). The Three Arts Club, as it was called, had a rotating series of lectures given by the members, and one of the lectures that Audrey prepared was on the life and work of Mary Cassatt, the American impressionist painter. Audrey spent almost a year preparing for her presentation, which subsequently earned her kudos from the group. Another group she joined in her late 60s was dedicated to playing recorder music. She bought her first recorder at that time, and spent the next decade playing Renaissance music with a small ensemble. Audrey also attended church services regularly on Sundays, and participated in Bible study groups and women's circles up until her death.

For many years Audrey had heard about plans for a retirement village in an area near the university where she had once lived with her family. While her second husband was not eager to leave his vegetable gardens in the countryside, she insisted they sign up so they would be eligible to move when the facility opened. When he died shortly thereafter at age 90, Audrey was happy to know that she would be able to move into the livelier context offered by the retirement village. Another reason for leaving was that her house had been broken into once when she was out, and she had been robbed of some of her most valued pieces of jewelry, including her wedding ring from her first marriage. Now that she was alone, she no longer felt secure in the house. Driving was also becoming an increasing challenge, especially late at night, and she felt isolated and lonely without intellectual and social stimulation.

In the retirement village, Audrey chose a one-bedroom apartment, with a study, a dining/living space, kitchen, bath, and a tiny balcony, which overlooked the woods surrounding the buildings. She furnished it with antiques that had belonged to her mother, as well as more modern pieces she had acquired during her marriages. Her books filled her study shelves, her small art collection adorned the walls, and her elegant and copious wardrobe, including a mink jacket for which she had splurged on her 75th birthday, hung in the ample closet. Her crafts and collections created a homey and elegant atmosphere, and she would often entertain her bridge group in her apartment, continuing a tradition that she had upheld for 30 years with the same members.

Residents in the village were required to eat one meal a day in the formal dining room and had available to them a vast array of services, programs, classes, library and computer facilities, and other activities both on and off the grounds. The selection of available activities bedazzled Audrey, and in the seven years she lived in this apartment she participated in many of them. Among the highlights were joining a dance group that eventually performed in a ballet with children from a local school. She regaled her friends with stories of what it was like to dance on a stage with little boys who were not always so attentive to the music or the choreography.

Perhaps the greatest pleasure she found in the last two years of her life was yoga class. She was fond of the teacher and felt the exercise was very beneficial to her heart and lungs, as well as for her flexibility and stamina. She had twice suffered bouts of lung cancer in her earlier years, and it had impaired her ability to breathe easily when exerting herself. Living in this community also stimulated her interest in travel. She had done little traveling before the age of 60. In her elder years, however, she not only visited her four adult children, now spread across the country, but traveled as well to the Holy Lands, Greece, Italy, France, and England. Her last trip, taken as a member of an Elderhostel group, was to Russia, a year before she died. Her trips not only were opportunities for her to expand her knowledge of the world, but they also stimulated months of prior research so that she would be prepared to take advantage of all her experiences. None of her family could match her thirst for knowledge, one that time could never quench.

Audrey Lermond never let go of the developmental vision. The image of "aging as decline" played little role in her life. Rather, she continued to believe that stored within the traditions of the world were untold riches, and that the opportunity to grow through these treasures terminated only with death. And, with this belief in the forefront, indeed Audrey's life remained enchanted until its end.

Sandy Lewis: Power at play

The infinite extension of the self takes many forms. Particularly within the competitive tradition of masculinity, one's self-esteem may depend on accumulation of wealth. In this sense, the availability of unencumbered time provided by retirement functions much like an untethering. The male springs free to play the Darwinian survival game more fully, and the stakes are frequently those of power, prestige, and property. This theme is most apparent in the lifestyle adopted by Sandy Lewis.

Sandy Lewis, like many sons of self-made men, has spent his life comparing himself to his father. For him, one of the most significant achievements in life is to measure up to a father's success. Even better, according to Sandy's philosophy, is to do better than one's dad. At the same time, Sandy developed other interests and values; he came to believe strongly in a solid family life, and had the distinct pleasure of marrying a woman with whom he could share his ambitions. Together they parented two sons to carry on the family traditions. As a youth, Sandy was never very interested in intellectual activities, and college for him was a place for playing sports, having a good time, and making connections. From the time he entered high school, what interested him most was how to make a great deal of money. He settled on a strategy of learning as much about the business world as he possibly could and by making himself indispensable to the boss whenever possible.

After he left college, Sandy devoted himself to empire building. His long hours of work, hands-on dealings, charming social style, and creative and risky decisions ultimately paid off. With the help of his very involved and intelligent wife, he created a plan by which he could amass a considerable fortune and be able to leave the daily grind by age 55. Having had his children as a young man, they were on their own, making their fortunes, and he and his wife were able to travel extensively, buy a dream home in Arizona, and take up golf.

Although the day-to-day management of business operations was over for Sandy, the itch to be making deals never lets up. Retirement has become a time for enhancing his opportunities to engage in entrepreneurial activities. In Arizona, he has met a new group of men who have also taken early retirement, but are still active and engaged in business, via the phone, the Internet, and in face-to-face meetings. Mornings do not go by but that Sandy is on the telephone with his broker, his partners in various business deals, his accountant, or his lawyer. The pace of his business life only slackens when he is out playing golf, tending to his gardens, or having dinner with his wife. Even on the golf course, talk of money, tax laws, capital gains, and the price of commodities is ever present. Every hole is a chance to gamble, and the adrenaline is always pumped by interactions with other men. At times, Sandy is overwhelmed by the wealth of various business partners and friends in his new world, and he feels humble and a bit low on the food chain among the people he calls the "high rollers." But, his happy family life, his pride in his sons, his religious faith, and patriotic virtue keep him feeling balanced and secure.

For Sandy Lewis, then, retirement was not a loss of power. It was indeed the opportunity for the free expansion of entrepreneurial interests. Is there an end in sight, a point when Sandy will be content to settle down? We expect not, primarily because the joy for Sandy is not in sedentary activities, but in "playing the game."

Julie and Carl Brown: The pursuit of pleasure

The hedonistic view of the self – a being primarily devoted to maximizing pleasure and minimizing pain – has played a prominent role in the individualist tradition. Yet, in the workday world of "mature adulthood," one's job is typically seen as antagonistic to one's natural urges for pleasure, leading to the common distinction between "work" and "play." The result is that for many retirement from the world of work opens the door to "natural," hedonistic being. The primary aim of life becomes that of maximizing pleasure. The lifestyle of Julie and Carl Brown demonstrates this ideology in action.

Carl met Julie when she was going through nurse's training and he was a cadet at West Point. Each of them had exceeded the expectations of their families, who had dreams for their children of a college education that they themselves never had. The path that stretched between the first days of their marriage to retirement was often tedious, frightening, and long. In their first years of marriage, they lived meagerly on an army base in Germany. During the Vietnam war, Julie lived with her in-laws and their tiny baby while Carl served in a helicopter rescue squad in Vietnam. For many years, Carl devoted himself to working for a large stockbroker firm. Later he was transferred to Wall Street, and for five tension-filled days each week he wrestled with the bulls and the bears. Frequently, the evenings were occupied as well with entertaining wealthy customers. On weekends he returned home to his wife and children for repair of mind, body, and spirit.

Carl promised himself that as soon as he could arrange it, he was going to retire from the rat race and make a new life. The motto of this new life was to be "enjoy every minute to the fullest." When the stock market flew up the register, Carl abandoned New York. The nest was empty, and he and Julie decided to move to a resort area in Colorado. There they found an elegant community, designed around skiing, golf, and party time. Carl was 57 and Julie was 55. Handsome, outgoing, happy-go-lucky, healthy, athletic, and open to every indulgence, they were welcomed into the community with open arms. They treated themselves to golf lessons at a luxurious resort, bought skis for all snow conditions, purchased a satellite dish for maximum film and musical enjoyment, and explored the finest restaurants in the area. They played tennis indoors and out, and Julie's charming and cheery personality, along with her wicked forehand shots, won over even the most competitive players.

Travel became an important part of their lifestyle. In the summer, they might spend some days on Martha's Vineyard with old Boston friends, and a weekend on Long Island with acquaintances from New York. Sybaritic friends in Florida host them on the Gulf side, where they jog, play tennis, and drink Margeritas on the deck. (Julie never leaves home without her own thermos of Margeritas.) Carl and Julie are now members of the "Go Fifty" club, a group that requires members to be at least fifty years old. The monthly meetings usually involve hiking, picnics, outings, and travels. Often the meetings end up with a dinner at some cozy gourmet hideaway in the mountains. Carl is the informal group DJ; he always brings his own box of CDs to any gathering, and he controls the tunes. He creates the mood with labels such as "Bump and Grind," "Sexy and Slow," or "Rock'm Sock'm." Julie's expressive dancing matches the moods he creates. Since moving West, they have also been introduced to spas, massages, and other herbal treatments that are fashionable with this set. Their new home has a Jacuzzi, which is populated on the weekends by houseguests and visitors. Piling into the tub, in tribute to Mother Nature, they pop the champagne and toast the beauty of the moonlit mountains.

The pleasure-seeking style of aging evidenced by Carl and Julie is found primarily in the resort areas of the country. Further, such pursuits seem to thrive on the availability of others. However, this does not mean that wealth is essential to the pursuit of pleasure. Many pleasures are far less expensive than those enjoyed by Carl and Julie. Activities such as fishing, cooking, camping, movies, and just "hanging out with friends," are major sources of pleasure for many.

The Return to Relationship

A prevailing vision of individual development in the West is that of emerging independence. That is, while activities with family and friends are important in the early years, the ultimate hallmark of maturity is personal autonomy. In this sense, emotional dependencies are a detriment to the fully functioning adult. Feminist scholars (see, for example, Chodorow 1978) point out that it is the male child who is placed under the most severe pressures to become independent. And, indeed, there is a long-standing distinction in the sociology of the family between what are called the *instrumental* and *socio-emotional* roles.

The instrumental role is filled by the individual who can work in independence of the family to earn wages (traditionally the male), while the socio-emotional role falls to the individual who nurtures and sustains emotional dependencies within the family (the stereotypic female). As recent decades of feminist theory have discredited the division of roles (in which the woman is seen as non-instrumental) and two-career families have become the norm, instrumentality has become a dominant theme for the middle years of life of both women and men (Hochschild 1989). With retirement, however, the structure of life is redefined. For many, the domain of relationships looms as the long-neglected or uncompleted challenge. One is free again to return to the joys of emotional interdependence. The life of Lauren and Tom illustrate the way in which relationship becomes the dominant theme for many in the later years.

Lauren and Tom: Life as the art of loving

In the 1970s, Lauren expressed the deep yearning that Betty Friedan (1963) called the "problem without a name." For Lauren, it was the desire to establish herself as a professional artist. After much soul-searching, she separated from her husband and left the suburbs, her comfortable home, and her two children to pursue her career in the city. Her husband, who had some understanding of the depths of his wife's despair at living the closeted, suburban life, took care of the children for many years and helped financially to support her quest for "self actualization." Over time, the couple divorced and the stipend was terminated. In their high school years, Lauren's children came to live with her in her small loft apartment, in which she carved spaces adequate for tiny bedrooms for her daughter, son, and herself. She continued to struggle daily to make ends meet and to develop her artistic career.

From the time she was thirty until she was in her mid-fifties, Lauren lived a life that was full of creative ingenuity and self-sufficiency. Yet, despite some occasional art shows and sales, she could not support herself as an artist. Her aesthetic theme, mostly the female nude expressed in large oil canvases, was too daring for most local collectors, and they did not sell. Finally, Lauren was on the verge of abandoning her dream of becoming a full-time artist when an angel stopped at her doorstep. A wealthy collector fell in love with her and her work, and declared his willingness to promote her at all costs. She had opportunities to work and to show unlike any she had had before. Over time, however, the gild on the lily of their romance chipped away, and they separated acrimoniously. All she retained were her paintings, and the expensive clothes and gifts he had given her. She seemed destined to live alone, unable to sustain a relationship and struggling to make ends meet.

Soon after her sixtieth birthday, she met Tom, a man who was quite the opposite of her former husband, her previous lover, and herself. He was a retired accountant, widowed, with a large family of children and grand-children to whom he was devoted. His major hobby was collecting ships in bottles, and he did this with a passion. As much as she was creative, sensitive, moody and intellectual, he was solid, stable, and sensible. While she was the charismatic butterfly at the center of attention, he was the quiet one, at the periphery of the crowd. None of her friends gave this new beau much of a chance among the artistic crowd in which Lauren was known.

Yet, over time, the significance of the relationship became increasingly clear. Tom was there to appreciate her work, to help her hang her shows, to fix her a cup of tea when she had worked herself to the bone. He planned and took care of things when she was overwhelmed. He offered a shoulder to cry on. He went with her to every concert, art opening, theatre produc-tion or poetry reading she could arrange, and he tried to be interested. He looked at her adoringly across the crowded room. After all the years of struggle and loneliness, at age 64 she finally found herself deeply in love; she cried for joy when Tom proposed. During the wedding ceremony, which they created for themselves, she said she felt truly cherished for the first time in her life. They held a reception in their beautiful new artist's loft, where their extended families and friends toasted the new bride and groom. Since that time they have created a life that is centered in each other. They face the seventh decade of their lives as a beginning, not an ending.

Lauren and Tom find that their elderly years do not signal the end of romance and intimacy, but indeed a unique opportunity for exploration. As each will admit, in terms of loving relationships, "they never had it so good." Their route through aging is precarious; when one's major nourish-ment is drawn from an intimate relationship, the loss of the other can be devastating. However, judging from discussions with Lauren and Tom, life is now richly robust, and if tragedy comes there will be other resources available, including treasured memories of the times they have shared.

T. G. Larson: Master networker

For many people in the later years, the sphere of relationships is continuously diminishing. Theories of disengagement suggest that this is the normal pattern of life for people as they retire. The word "disengagement" itself suggests a withdrawal from active life. At the same time, other theorists argue that social involvement is the key to a satisfying old age (Bengtson and Schaie 1999). Much research seems to support the view that being active is important to a long and healthy life (Gergen and Gergen in press). In effect, there is much to be said for actively avoiding forces of disengagement. As people die or move away, steps should be taken to sustain a circle of active relationships. Such steps are much easier to take than heretofore, not only because of the increased wealth and health of the elderly population, but as well because of advances in computer communication and air travel. We bring attention here to an individual who thrives on human connection. In sustaining active communication across the land, he finds stimulation and joy, and a continuous source of creative inspiration.

Now in his late seventies, T. G. Larson is a master networker. He is well prepared for his role, as he spent his adult life in the communications industry. His most creative endeavors were the origination of two prominent national magazines. Through his capacities to communicate across a wide spectrum, he located investors, enlisted collaborators, hired innovative staff members, and scoured the country in search of interesting writers. So successful was one of the magazines that it spawned a publishing company and an educational film initiative. After creating a magazine and its associated businesses, T. G. would move on to new ventures. The thrill for him was in bringing forth from the well-spring of human connection new and worthy institutions. Self-interest seemed but a peripheral concern for T. G., and, because of the trust he established, many people were pleased to join with him.

In his early seventies, T. G. became particularly interested in the connection between health and spirituality, and developed dialogue with professors of divinity schools, active clergy from diverse denominations, media gurus, public opinion leaders, scientists, publications experts, philosophers, and psychologists in what became a synergistic matrix of creation. His hopes in the energy of positive human connection finally bore fruit. A new magazine was created with many of the dialogic participants serving on the board. T. G. himself did not take on the editorship of the magazine. The potentials of human connection seemed infinite. So, with further conversations in motion, he helped to create a massive Web resource, where issues in spirituality and human well-being could be deliberated. It is doubtful that this endeavor will serve as the culmination of T. G.'s efforts. For those who know him, one can anticipate phone calls, e-mail messages or a fax from T. G. at any time of day or night – perhaps brief, but containing an idea he thinks might be of interest or urging a connection with another friend who is "on your wave length." T. G. derives enormous satisfaction in life from breeding the conditions where trusted people of good will are able to make something happen, something of value to the world more generally.

As the world context changes, so do the prevailing forms of aging. In many respects T. G. Larson represents a cutting-edge style of life among the elderly. It is a lifestyle given birth by the explosion in communication technology. The availability of computers, cell phones, faxes, and air transportation means that the relational matrix can endlessly expand. In this sense T. G. may be in the vanguard of a life form of major magnitude.

Communal Contribution: Transcending the Self

Thus far, we have placed a strong emphasis on the individualist tradition, and the way in which it plays out in various themes of positive aging. We have seen how this tradition fosters a variety of later life patterns centered around self-development. We have also explored how many people find later life an opportunity to shuck the individualist demands for autonomy in favor of bonding relationships. There is a third, highly important outgrowth of the individualist tradition that may be viewed as ethical in character. To elaborate, we have seen how the individualist tradition concentrates on developing, empowering, and rewarding the self, creating a condition in which others are secondary or unimportant. If "I look out for Number One," then others are relegated to lesser positions of significance. Religious leaders, ethicists, and social thinkers have long decried this condition, and have, as a result, placed a primary emphasis on dedication, devotion, and sacrifice to others. To put it succinctly, if it were not for the strength of the individualist tradition, the religious admonition to "love thy neighbor as thyself" would be unnecessary. We must be reminded in myriad ways to give to others, and when we do we can enjoy a deep sense of worth. In fact, society grants its highest awards to those who sacrifice their lives for the greater communal good.

Many people find that because of the demands of work and family that dominate adult life, they do very little to help others outside their immediate family circles. There may often be an abiding sense of guilt that one's life is so self-centered. With retirement, the door is again open to reconstitute life. And for many, there is great joy to be derived from now dedicating time and energy to making a better world for all. Here we furnish a glimpse into two elderly lives in which the theme of communal contribution came to play a major role.

Gerry Ramon: One is never too old to count

Gerry Ramon is a widow who retired from teaching at age 65. She describes herself as a Luddite, one who is resistant to technological "advances," including computers. She does not own a television, a clothes dryer, or a microwave. She gets her exercise hanging out her clothes to dry, and she picks vegetables and fruits from her own gardens. Her one important concession to the late twenty-first century is an answering machine her son installed when he was looking for a job. She is quite adamant about her preferences for simplicity, and she sees it as a part of her Quaker heritage and style of life. Her religious community of Friends, which has been a part of her life since she was a girl, sustains her in unseen ways. Part of her vigor and sense of direction seems to originate in the sense of the spirit within her that is fulfilled through her service to the community.

Fulfillment through community service ultimately became life-saving for Gerry. Her husband died at retirement, and grief at this loss persisted for another ten years. Relief from the process of grieving only began as Gerry became involved in community affairs. One of her most noteworthy endeavors, and one from which she derives the greatest reward, involves work with prisoners. As a member of the Prison Society, Gerry became an official visitor of prisons. Her duties include talking to inmates about their lives and the prison conditions. She helps the inmates with their medical problems, gives them advice about various complaints, locates legal support for them, and often writes letters to prison or governmental officials about the treatment of prisoners. On occasion, Gerry has testified at parole hearings and state hearings on the treatment of prisoners. She also attends conferences related to prison reform and mentors others who wish to continue her work. When she is not doing prison work, she is also involved in volunteering at a homeless shelter. She serves food, organizes the kitchen, and brings in spare blankets, clothes, and other items useful to the poor.

Recently, Gerry was asked by her local school to substitute teach. A key teacher was ill, and the school was desperate. Gerry agreed and found the work very rewarding. She enjoyed the camaraderie and action provided by the staff and the students, even though it was a substantial addition to her already full days. She has had to cut back on some of her volunteer work to make time for grading homework and other preparations at school. She is a stickler for excellent grammar and usage, and adheres to some rather old-fashioned ideas of how students should perform.

Gerry is also an active alumnus of her college, and belongs to a book club sponsored by the school. Part of her pleasure in this membership is that professors from the English department occasionally give lectures to the group. She loves to discuss the books and to create some intellectual ferment at these gatherings. Sometimes she worries that she expresses herself too forcefully and that this habit may annoy some of the other members. She is quite opinionated and knows a great deal of literary history. She is extending her willingness to help others to those in the group who have no transportation, and she has become actively involved in helping them "sort out" their lives in a variety of ways.

In the college years, one of the most frequently voiced aims in life is "to help other people." Yet, seldom is adult life devoted to such ends. In Gerry Ramon's case, the elderly years offered the long-sought opportunity to put her life to use for the greater good. Scholars have recently sounded an alarm regarding the decline of civic participation in the United States (see, for example, Putnam 1995). In the coming expansion of the population over age 60, we may hope to find a reversal of this trend. The elderly population may be the needed glue to hold communities in place.

Lyle Gifford: Creating for the community

There are many ways of serving the broader community of humankind, and one of them is to add to the storehouse of cultural riches. Contrary to the widespread belief that creativity diminishes with age, and that most great cultural achievements are completed by people in their early adulthood, many of the greatest cultural achievements in the Western world have been generated by individuals working into their nineties (Simonton 2000). As many attest, it is engagement in this creative work that is the wellspring of their continued zest for life.

Lyle Gifford was well prepared for an old age devoted to creative activity. His life was always devoted to music – as a cathedral chorister, organ scholar, cathedral organist, and as a college professor. Born in Gloucester, England, he is still actively involved with music at age 90. Lyle's first attempt at retirement occurred at age 65. However, for the next fifteen years he continued to teach college part-time and served as an organist and choir director at a nearby church. At age, 80 he elected to retire completely from academic life, and took up residence in a retirement community in the Southwest.

Lyle has scarcely retired. He spends many hours a day with his music, primarily composing. Lyle has also discovered the advantages of using the computer for composing – printing, playing, and editing his music. His output increased vastly since he acquired the first useful computer program in 1986. In addition to composing, Lyle is also in demand to conduct performances of his works and he continues playing the organ. In his late 80s, he conducted a large performance of a piece he had written for chorus and saxophone quartet. Later, he accompanied his daughter in a recital in Clare Hall, Cambridge University, England; she sang ten of his songs.

Perhaps a crowning achievement was to attend a performance in a British cathedral of a festival anthem he was commissioned to compose for the occasion. In his "spare" time, Lyle plays the organ for a community-based orchestra, and conducts chorus and symphony for a state orchestra.

Lyle is convinced that his musical creativity plays an important role in his current well-being. "To get out of bed eager to get back to the computer to continue work on a composition, and then to experience the pleasure when it all works out (especially now that one can hear the results immediately via the synthesizer and stereo without having to wait for a group of players to perform it as formerly was the case) is heady stuff indeed." This means there is little time left for physical exercise. He does eat dinner regularly with a small group of residents who have formed a family-like relationship; with no plans to remarry, he still enjoys the warm friendship of women in the group. As he admits, however, his greatest source of support and inspiration comes from the love of his extended family, who make an essential contribution to his happy state of mind.

It would be a mistake to suppose that Lyle Gifford's form of aging is highly common. There are all too few who have the training, creative imagination, and confidence to create works of such significance. At the same time, many initiatives are now emerging devoted to nourishing the creative spirit in communities of the elderly – in painting, drama, musical performance, life history writing, and more. As reasoned in this case, the value of such work does not lie in the size of the audience, nor does bringing joy to others require a lifetime of training. The pleasure derived from creating for the community is available to all.

Resources and Positive Aging

Many gerontologists and other scholars have been enthusiastic about the possibilities of creating narratives of positive aging. This is not so surprising given that a very stable research finding asserts that happiness is positively correlated with age (Argyle 1999). Yet others remain skeptical of such aims, and claim that positive aging is out of reach for most Americans. They believe that in order to have a happy and thriving old age, one must have two critical resources – wealth and health.

We reject this notion; happiness and tranquility can neither be bought by wealth nor sealed by health at any age. As many sociologists before us have noted, the relationship between happiness and accumulated wealth is very weak (Myers 1993). While wealthier people tend to be satisfied with their lives, so are poorer people. Wealth does not in itself create happiness, although it is true that extreme poverty can be detrimental to feelings of well-being (Argyle 1999). Whether good health is essential to positive aging is also questionable.

First, the meaning of "good health" is negotiable. If people are prone to the common cold, losing their hearing, or suffering arthritis, are they in good or poor health? These are matters of conflicting opinion. Of special importance, people who live in communities of the elderly develop their own standards of what counts as "poor health," and these standards differ considerably from those shared by young adults. Second, whether people use their bodily condition to judge their well-being is also variable (Frederick and Lowerstein 1999). Many who are blind, deaf, or crippled, for example, don't evaluate their well-being in terms of these "less than perfect" bodies. They are simply irrelevant to what counts most. In contrast, many younger people who are overweight, possess a small chin or have a large nose, may be miserable. Bodily condition itself is not as important as how it is constructed.

From a constructionist perspective, what is required for a positive aging experience is primarily a repertoire of resources for creating positive meanings. If the social order is pressuring one to give up on life and one's desires as one ages, it is imperative that one not only possess resources to resist this pull but to create meaningful alternatives. Higher education may make an important contribution to such resources. Educational experience may be less important in "stamping in knowledge" than in opening avenues of interest and value.

There are many resources other than education that can be significant, including, for example, good parental role models, family members and friends who are "young at heart" despite age and infirmity, models of positive aging in public life and entertainment spheres, a community that invites a certain level of activity and participation, or a deeply developed interest in the surrounding world. To conclude our profiles, we describe Sam Watson, a local gardener/handyman, who has not had higher education, who has lived alone for many years, but who has a great love and knowledge of nature born of long years in the out of doors.

Sam Watson: Retired handyman and gardener

Sam Watson worked on the buildings and grounds crew of a local college for most of his adult life. He came to the college sometime after World War II. Sam had been wounded while serving in the Pacific – a severe leg injury – and had chronically poor vision. Nevertheless, he worked on the college grounds until he retired at age 70. At the college, Sam acquired a deep knowledge of plant life, soil, drainage systems, and the means of creating beauty in nature. Over time, he became an expert in transforming the campus into a garden of Eden. Financial support from the local factory to the college helped to expand on the possibilities for plantings and gardens, and Sam was right there, making sure each plant had a good home in which to flourish. Sam had barely a high school education, so when the college upgraded their horticultural office, they hired professionals. However, it didn't take long for the smarter ones to learn that Sam spoke to the trees and bushes, and coaxed even the most difficult plants to bloom. He became well known in the community for his skills as a gardener.

Sam's pension was sufficient to live on, but physical retirement was far from his mind. Sam thus started his "second career" by offering his services to a variety of homeowners he had met when working at the college. Word of mouth quickly spread and soon he found himself working for friends of friends. As his commitments mounted, so did the demands for his services. Soon, Sam found that he could select the properties that were interesting to him or that offered new opportunities to see nature flourish. The money was of secondary importance.

Sam had been married and had one son. His wife had died when she was in her forties, and he had never found the right woman to remarry. His son had gone away to college, and while they had a comfortable relationship, they were not often together, except on holidays, when Sam would go into the city to visit his son. Later, when his son married and had a child, Sam became interested in visiting for Sunday dinners. Sam enjoyed being a grandfather, and when his grandson was 6 years old, Sam began taking him out to learn about the countryside. Sam showed him the secrets he knew about plants and animals, and the relationship with the little boy was the closest and most pleasing human contact Sam had.

Sam's other loyal companion was a black dog, a mix of Labrador and Golden Retriever, who went everywhere with Sam in his truck. There was a deep, loving bond between the two, and Big Ben gave Sam a sense of company that served him well. They lived in a small cottage on the edge of the county park. Sam kept the house in top condition, surrounding it with plants and bushes, both native and exotic, which attracted nearby garden clubs for tours. He enjoyed taking the visitors around, explaining how his gardens grew. Often, one or two would invite him for tea, to show off their gardens in return, and perhaps to attract the eye of this gentle man. This attraction to Sam was not so surprising. The years of working out-doors and his natural proclivities had helped to shape Sam into a "Gary Cooper" looking man – tall, slim, with a tanned and deeply etched face, and a ready smile that highlighted his healthy white teeth. He always seemed rather unaware of his looks and his interest in socializing never lasted very long; soon he yearned to get back to his dog, his garden, and his work.

As Sam's late-life trajectory demonstrates, wealth, physical condition, and higher education are not essential to positive engagement. Sam's life experiences have provided him with substantial resources – a love of nature and a know-how for creating beauty. These provide a solid basis for a meaningful and fulfilling older age.

Conclusion

Each of these stories has described people who have found a way of aging that is full of vigor, interest, and challenges of all varieties. They exemplify what we wish to call "positive aging." These people are not focused on the inevitability of their deaths and potential declines. They are not taking to heart the acclamation of one of our young colleagues, who said to us, "Face it, everyone over the age of 60 is a patient." The themes that pervade these particular lives are all related to the dominant traditions of Western culture. These traditions encourage the individual who leaves the world of work to move in one of several directions.

In this chapter, we have emphasized movements toward self-fulfillment, emotional interdependence, and communal contribution. If we were to extend our review, we would also emphasize the spiritual, meditative, and contemplative traditions from which many draw nurturance as they grow older. It is also important to realize that participation in any of these trajectories may carry with it a unique pleasure. It is a pleasure that grows from an intensified consciousness of the preciousness of life, of time, and other human beings.

Sensing that one is reaching an ending creates new conditions of thoughtfulness, reflection, memory, and desire that are inaccessible to those oblivious to the passage of time. This new sensitivity can add an enriching dimension to the meaning of one's life. The people we have described are not without their trials and tribulations, nor without their fears and frailties, but they also illustrate the point of the familiar saying, "Living well is the best revenge."

References

Argyle, Michael. 1999. "Causes and Correlates of Happiness." In D. Kahnewman, E. Diener, and N. Schwarz (eds.), *Well-Being: The Foundations of Hedonic Psychology*. New York: Russell Sage, pp. 353–73.

Bengtson, Vern L. and Schaie, K. Warner, eds. 1999. *Handbook of Theories of Aging*. New York: Springer.

Campioni, Mia 1997. "Revolting Women, Women in Revolt." In P. Komersaroff, P. Rothfield, and J. Daly (eds.), *Reinterpreting Menopause*. New York: Routledge, pp. 22–41.

Chodorow, Nancy. 1978. *The Reproduction of Mothering and the Sociology of Gender*. Berkeley: University of California Press.

Cummings, Elaine, and Henry, William. 1961. *Growing Old*. New York: Basic Books.

Frederick, Shane, and Loewenstein, George. 1999. "Hedonic Adaptation." In D. Kahnewman, E. Diener, and N. Schwarz (eds.), *Well-Being: The Foundations of Hedonic Psychology*. New York: Russell Sage, pp. 302–29.

Friedan, B. 1963. *The Feminine Mystique*. New York: Norton.

Gergen, Kenneth J. 1996. "Beyond Life Narratives in the Therapeutic Encounter." In J. E. Birren, et al. (eds.), *Aging and Biography*. New York: Springer, pp. 205–223.

Gergen, Kenneth J. 1999. *An Invitation to Social Construction*. Thousand Oaks, CA, London: Sage.

Gergen, Kenneth J. 2000[1991]. *The Saturated Self*. New York: Basic Books.

Gergen, K. J. and Gergen, M. (1986). "Narrative form and the construction of psychological science." In T. R. Sarbin (ed.), *Narrative psychology: The storied nature of human conduct*. New York: Praeger, pp. 22–44.

Gergen, Kenneth J. and Gergen, Mary M. 1988. "Narrative and the Self as Relationship." In L. Berkowitz (ed.), *Advances in Experimental Social Psychology*. San Diego: Academic Press, pp. 17–56.

Gergen, Kenneth J. and Gergen, Mary M. 2000. "The New Aging: Self Construction and Social Values." In K. W. Schaie (ed.), *Social Structures and Aging*. New York: Springer, pp. 281–306.

Gergen, Mary M. 2001. *Feminist Reconstructions in Psychology: Narrative, Gender and Performance*. Thousand Oaks, CA: Sage.

Gergen, Mary M. and Gergen, Kenneth J. In press. "Positive Ageing: New Images for a New Age." *Ageing International*.

Gubrium, Jaber F. and Holstein, James A. 2000. "Analyzing Interpretive Practice. In Norman K. Denzin and Yvonna Lincoln (eds.), *Handbook of Qualitative Research*, 2nd edn. Thousand Oaks, CA: Sage, pp. 487–508.

Hazan, Haim. 1994. *Old Age: Constructions and Deconstructions*. Cambridge: Cambridge University Press.

Hochschild, Arlie. 1989. *The Second Shift*. New York: Viking.

Holstein, James A and Gubrium, Jaber F. 2000a. *Constructing the Life Course*, 2nd edn. Lanham, MD: Alta Mira.

Holstein, James A., and Gubrium, Jaber F. 2000b. *The Self We Live By: Narrative Identity in a Postmodern World*. New York: Oxford University Press.

Kahneman, Daniel, Diener, Ed, and Schwarz, Norbert (eds). 1999. *Well-Being: The Foundations of Hedonic Psychology*. New York: Russell Sage.

Myers, David. 1993. *The Pursuit of Happiness*. New York: Avon.

Onks, Gary. 2002. "Sold on Seniors: How You Can Reach and Sell the $20 Trillion Senior Marketplace." *New York Times*, Feb. 3: BU 11.

Putnam, Robert. 1995. "Bowling Alone: America's Declining Social Capital." *Journal of Democracy*, 6: 65–78.

Ronai, Carol Rambo. 1992. "Managing Aging in Young Adulthood: The 'Aging' Table Dancer." *Journal of Aging Studies*, 6: 307–17.

Sarbin, Theodore R. 1986. *Narrative Psychology: The Storied Nature of Human Conduct*. New York: Praeger.

Seligman, Martin E. P. and Czikszentmihalyi, Mihaly (eds). 2000. Special issue on happiness, excellence, and optimal human functioning. *American Psychologist*, 55 (#1).

Simonton, Dean K. 2000. "Creativity: Cognitive, Personal, Developmental, and Social Aspects." *American Psychologist*, 55: 151–158.

Tiefer, Leonore. 1995. *Sex is Not a Natural Act, and Other Essays*. Boulder, CO: Westview Press.

Index